FROM THE TRE

# MASTERING THE ART OF PREPARING WITNESSES

## EDITED BY JAMES M. MILLER

**ABA GPSOLO**
Solo, Small Firm and General Practice Division
YOUR SUCCESS, OUR MISSION™

Cover design by Cory Ottenwess/ABA Publishing.

The materials contained herein represent the views of each chapter author in his or her individual capacity and should not be construed as the views of the author's firms, employers, or clients, or of the editors or other chapter authors, or of the American Bar Association or the Solo, Small Firm and General Practice Division, unless adopted pursuant to the bylaws of the Association.

Nothing contained in this book is to be considered as the rendering of legal advice for specific cases, and readers are responsible for obtaining such advice from their own legal counsel. This book is intended for educational and informational purposes only.

Printed in the United States of America

21 20 19 18 17    5 4 3 2 1

**Library of Congress Cataloging-in-Publication Data**

Names: Miller, Jim (James M.), editor.
Title: From the trenches 2 : mastering the art of preparing witnesses / edited by Jim Miller.
Other titles: Mastering the art of preparing witnesses
Description: First edition. | Chicago : American Bar Association, [2017] | Includes index.
Identifiers: LCCN 2017052709| ISBN 9781634259279 (print) | ISBN 9781634259286 (epub)
Subjects: LCSH: Witnesses—United States. | Examination of witnesses—United States.
Classification: LCC KF8950 .F76 2017 | DDC 347.73/66—dc23
LC record available at https://lccn.loc.gov/2017052709

Discounts are available for books ordered in bulk. Special consideration is given to state bars, CLE programs, and other bar-related organizations. Inquire at ABA Publishing, American Bar Association, 321 North Clark Street, Chicago, Illinois 60610-4714.

www.ShopABA.org

# TABLE OF CONTENTS

## PART III   EXPERT WITNESSES

## PART IV    CRIMINAL AND SPECIAL PROCEEDINGS

# PREFACE

The witness is the star of any trial. All other evidence—exhibits, demonstrative evidence, the *facts*—come to life through the witness. In every successful trial there is at least one witness who told a story, held the jury's attention, withstood cross-examination, and helped win a verdict. In every loss there is usually a witness who crashes and burns. How do you explain the difference?

Preparation.

For all but the experienced expert witness, testifying is an alien experience and the courtroom is a strange and forbidding place. The witness needs help, and it's the lawyer's job to provide it.

The authors of this book have prepared, examined, and cross-examined thousands of witnesses over the course of their successful careers as trial lawyers. They have seen firsthand what works and what does not—on the witness stand and in pre-trial preparation and practice sessions. Their hard-won lessons, lessons learned in the trenches of trial practice, are contained here.

This is the second in a series of books published by the ABA under the title *From the Trenches*. The first volume was edited by my good friend, John Worden, a trial lawyer at Schiff Hardin in San Francisco. We are grateful to John for starting this series and for putting together the first volume, which runs the gamut of trial practice and contains a wealth of practical advice and trial secrets from some of the nation's top trial lawyers. This second volume, *Mastering the Art of Witness Preparation*, contains 12 chapters covering all aspects of witness preparation. Whether you are a first-time, second-chair associate or a veteran first-chair partner preparing for your 100th jury trial, this book provides guidance, thoughtful insights, and unique perspectives on preparing your witness to testify.

# DEDICATION

All of the authors in this book were originally brought together through The Network of Trial Law Firms, an association of independent law firms with substantial trial practices. This network was created over 25 years ago by a former Fortune 100 general counsel, Ellis Mirsky, who then ran the network as its executive director until his retirement at the end of 2016. All of us are grateful to Ellis for his mentoring, sage advice, and friendship. We dedicate this book to him.

# ABOUT THE AUTHORS

## Chapter 1: Michael L. O'Donnell and LaMar F. Jost; Wheeler Trigg O'Donnell LLP, Denver

A founder and chair of Denver-based Wheeler Trigg O'Donnell LLP, **Michael L. O'Donnell**'s national litigation practice focuses on complex civil litigation involving product liability, professional liability, tort, class action, commercial, and bet-the-company matters. Mike has appeared as lead counsel in 40 states and serves as national counsel for a number of Fortune 500 companies, including General Electric, Advanced Bionics, Boston Scientific, Skyjack, and Michelin. An elected Fellow of the International Academy of Trial Lawyers, American College of Trial Lawyers, and American Board of Trial Advocates, Mike was selected as the number one lawyer in Colorado for 2013, 2014, 2015, 2016, and in 2017 by Colorado Super Lawyers.

**LaMar F. Jost** is a trial lawyer and partner with the Denver law firm Wheeler Trigg O'Donnell LLP, where he has devoted the first decade of his career to successfully trying cases in federal and state courts across the country. Because of his extensive trial work in practice areas ranging from medical malpractice to environmental and commercial law, LaMar has been selected as a "Rising Star" by Colorado Super Lawyers for seven years running and named to the top "Forty under 40" of all business professionals in Colorado. Prior to joining Wheeler Trigg O'Donnell, LaMar had the honor of clerking for the Honorable Clarence Brimmer in the District of Wyoming and for the Honorable Bobby Baldock at the Tenth Circuit Court of Appeals.

## Chapter 2: James M. Miller; Akerman LLP, Miami

**James M. Miller**, a partner at Akerman's Miami office, has been trying civil cases before juries since 1976. He has tried or arbitrated a wide variety of civil cases ranging from antitrust to zoning with intellectual property, trade secrets, products liability, general commercial, and catastrophic torts in between. Jim graduated from the University of Chicago Law School and received his BA, magna cum laude, from the University of Miami. He is currently listed in Best Lawyers of America for Commercial Litigation and by Who's Who International: Litigation. He is a former chair of The Network of Trial Law Firms.

## Chapter 3: W. Scott O'Connell; Nixon Peabody, Boston & Manchester

**W. Scott O'Connell** is the chair of Nixon Peabody's Litigation Department and a member of the firm's Management Committee. He is a trial attorney who has appeared as lead counsel in 20 states. He focuses on class action and aggregate litigation, corporate control contests, and unfair and deceptive trade practices claims. He is currently representing financial services, healthcare, manufacturing, and energy companies in high exposure disputes with associated significant reputational harm in parallel civil, criminal, and regulatory proceedings. He is a former chair of The Network of Trial Law Firms. He earned his JD from the Cornell Law School where he was an editor of the *Cornell Law Review* and the chancellor of the Moot Court Board. He received his BA from St. Lawrence University.

## Chapter 4: Honorable David T. Schultz; United States District Court, Minneapolis

**David T. Schultz** was sworn in as United States Magistrate Judge for the District of Minnesota on February 7, 2017. Prior to his appointment, David was a partner at Maslon LLP for 11 years, where he focused his practice on high stakes litigation in the areas of product liability, healthcare, commercial disputes, civil and criminal fraud, and intellectual property. As a litigator, he tried cases to verdict in state and federal courts throughout the country and developed an active appellate practice, having argued more than 50 cases before several federal circuits as well as the Minnesota Supreme Court and Court of Appeals. While in private practice, Judge Schultz regularly devoted hundreds of hours to pro bono representation every year and served on the board of Innocence Project of Minnesota (IPMN). As a result of his tireless work to help free the wrongfully convicted and reform the criminal justice system, he was recognized with the IPMN's 2016 Never Forgotten Award. He was also selected as a *Minnesota Lawyer* 2016 Attorney of the Year. David graduated from Stanford Law School in 1985 and received his bachelor's degree, *magna cum laude*, from Carleton College.

## Chapter 5: Jessalyn H. Zeigler and Charles G. Jarboe; Bass, Berry & Sims PLC, Nashville

**Jessalyn H. Zeigler** is a partner with Bass, Berry & Sims PLC, located in the firm's Nashville, Tennessee, office. With more than 23 years of experience representing clients in products, environmental, health, and safety litigation matters, Jessie Zeigler's counsel has saved clients millions in losses. Jessie defends product manufacturers across various industries, including consumer products, food, automotive, pharmaceutical, chemical, and general manufacturing. She also represents clients in claims related to deceptive business practices under state Consumer Protection Acts and the both federal and state False Claims Acts. Whether she is representing a Fortune 500 company or a large municipality, Jessie has returned successful results for all of the cases she has handled for clients throughout the country.

    **Charles G. Jarboe** is a senior litigation associate in the Nashville, Tennessee, office of Bass, Berry & Sims, where he focuses on complex business litigation, with a particular focus on representing public and private companies, as well as individuals, in the healthcare, technology, communications, and financial services industries. He has experience at all stages of the litigation process, including jury and bench trials, and has successfully represented clients in state and federal courts throughout the United States. His practice also includes counseling clients in their contract and business negotiations to help them avoid costly future disputes.

## Chapter 6: Sawnie A. McEntire; Parsons McEntire McCleary & Clark, PLLC, Dallas

**Sawnie A. McEntire** is a shareholder and director in the law firm of Parsons McEntire McCleary & Clark PLLC, a law firm with offices in Dallas and Houston, Texas. He has been practicing trial law for over 36 years, and has substantial jury trial experience in both state and federal courts in Texas and throughout the country. He has been involved in several hundred depositions. He is a frequent speaker and author. He specializes in products liability litigation and complex commercial tort litigation.

## Chapter 7: Jean L. Bertrand; Schiff Hardin, San Francisco

**Jean L. Bertrand** practices primarily in the areas of real estate, toxic torts, and commercial litigation. She has substantial trial experience and has argued several cases on appeal. Jean also has extensive experience in the administration of complex litigation.

## Chapter 8: John Jerry Glas and Raymond C. Lewis; Deutsch Kerrigan, LLP, New Orleans

**John Jerry Glas** is the vice-chair of Civil Litigation at the law firm of Deutsch Kerrigan, LLP in New Orleans, Louisiana. He has tried more than 70 jury trials to verdict and has been enrolled pro hac vice in 11 states. Mr. Glas has taught trial practice as an adjunct professor at Loyola University New Orleans College of Law, and recently authored the chapter entitled "Feeding Lions During Closing Argument" in Volume 1 of the ABA's *From the Trenches* series.

**Raymond C. Lewis** is a partner at the law firm of Deutsch Kerrigan, LLP in New Orleans, Louisiana. Raymond is a civil litigator with experience in trial and appellate practice. Before joining the firm, Raymond served as law clerk for Louisiana state-court judges and attended law school at Louisiana State University, where he was a member of the *Louisiana Law Review*. He litigates commercial lawsuits, products liability lawsuits, and contractual and insurance coverage disputes.

## Chapter 9: Daniel J. Stephenson; K&L Gates, Los Angeles and Raleigh

**Daniel J. Stephenson** is a complex commercial trial lawyer with K&L Gates. Dan splits his time between Los Angeles and Raleigh, the two cities where his grandchildren live. Dan has been trying cases across the country for 35 years. He specializes in class actions, multi-district litigation, intellectual property, and cases involving computer technology, aviation, and pharmaceuticals. He is a graduate of the University of Michigan (JD) and the University of California, Los Angeles (BSME). Dan is a world champion masters swimmer and the author of a published novel, *The Underwater Window.*

## Chapter 10: Jackson R. Sharman, III; Lightfoot, Franklin & White, Birmingham

As the leader of Lightfoot's white-collar defense and corporate investigations practice, **Jackson R. Sharman III** tries federal criminal cases and represents clients in Congressional inquiries, corporate internal investigations, kickback and bribery cases, grand jury investigations, criminal environmental offenses, public-corruption prosecutions, enforcement of the Foreign Corrupt Practices Act, healthcare criminal matters, and investigations by military officials. Jack blogs on white-collar matters at "White Collar Wire" (www.jacksharman.com) and publishes the firm's Twitter feed about white-collar crime and enforcement matters at @WhiteCollarWire. Jack is a graduate of Washington & Lee University and Harvard Law School.

## Chapter 11: John R. Mitchell; Thompson Hine LLP, Cleveland

**John R. Mitchell** is a first-chair trial attorney with a national white-collar criminal defense practice. He has extensive first-chair trial experience defending individuals facing significant criminal exposure from alleged violations of federal and state law. His criminal practice consists of traditional white-collar criminal matters, internal corporate investigations, environmental crimes, grand jury investigations, and related administrative proceedings. With a comprehensive understanding of federal and state criminal laws, he also counsels public and privately held corporations and individuals facing governmental scrutiny. Many of his greatest successes are also the least publicized, especially those that resolved highly sensitive matters without criminal charges or adverse publicity.

## Chapter 12: Lewis S. Wiener; Eversheds Sutherland (US) LLP, Washington, DC; Ronald W. Zdrojeski and Meghana D. Shah; Eversheds Sutherland (US), New York

**Lewis S. Wiener**, an experienced trial and appellate attorney with three decades of trial and counseling experience, represents a broad array of clients in state, federal, and appellate court litigation throughout the United States. Lew co-chairs the firm's global Financial Services Disputes and Investigations (FSDI) practice and serves as a member of the firm's Executive Committee. His extensive litigation and trial experience as a former prosecutor and senior trial attorney with the U.S. Department of Justice includes serving as class action defense counsel, conducting large internal investigations, handling complex litigation matters, and representing entities in litigation brought by and against the federal government. Lew also represents clients in eminent domain/inverse condemnation, environmental, and land-use litigation before state and federal trial and appellate courts.

With nearly three decades of trial experience, **Ronald W. Zdrojeski** is co-head of the Eversheds Sutherland (US) and global Litigation groups. His practice focuses on counseling and defending businesses in complex commercial litigation, including market manipulation, fraud, and other white-collar matters. Ron has litigated in 48 of the country's 50 states, defending Fortune 500 companies, insurers, and corporate officers in criminal and civil investigations, including class action, toxic tort, trade secret, intellectual property, environmental, and maritime litigation.

**Meghana D. Shah** is a partner in Eversheds Sutherland's New York City office with over ten years of experience representing a broad range of clients in an array of complex commercial matters. Her industry experience spans multiple areas, including representing clients in the environmental, toxic tort, food and beverage, insurance and financial services, and energy arenas. She also represents clients in connection with domestic and international investigations involving multiple jurisdictions and federal, state, and foreign regulatory bodies.

# PART I

# Introduction and Ethics

## CHAPTER 1

# Witness Preparation Primer

## Inviting a Witness to Provide Truthful *and* Favorable Testimony

### *Michael L. O'Donnell*

### *LaMar F. Jost*

The scope of a lawyer's representation includes "the ethical preparation of witnesses[.]"[1] "Witness preparation is any communication between a lawyer and a prospective witness—client or non-client, friendly or hostile—that is intended to improve the substance of presentation and testimony to be offered at a trial or other hearing."[2] The failure to prepare a witness to testify at a deposition, trial, or other proceeding is, at best, "strategic lunacy" and, at worst, "negligence."[3]

Like many tasks a lawyer performs,[4] witness preparation is more art than science.[5] No rule of procedure specifically governs permissible witness preparation methods, and social science has yet to identify a "proven" method of effective witness preparation. The twin aims of this chapter are therefore to (1) provide guidance on the permissible scope of witness preparation and (2) suggest a general

---

1. Michael H. Berger, *The Ethical Preparation of Witnesses*, COLO. LAW. 51 (May 2013); *see also* MODEL RULES OF PROF'L CONDUCT R. 1.1, 1.3 (2016) (requiring a lawyer to provide competent representation and diligent representation, respectively).
2. John S. Applegate, *Witness Preparation*, 68 TEX. L. REV. 277, 278 (1989).
3. *Id.* at 287–88.
4. *See, e.g.*, Michael O'Donnell & LaMar Jost, *Deconstructing the Key Liability Expert: Strategy and Secrets for Successful Cross-Examination, in* FROM THE TRENCHES: STRATEGIES AND TIPS FROM 21 OF THE NATION'S TOP TRIAL LAWYERS 227 & n.1 (John S. Worden ed., 2015) (describing the "art" of cross-examination).
5. Stan Perry & Teshia N. Judkins, *Ethical Witness Preparation: Stepping Back from the Line for the Lecture*, HOUS. LAW. 34 (July/August 2010) ("Proper witness preparation is truly a fine art.").

methodology, based upon the current state of the literature, that can be used to prepare any witness to testify at a deposition, trial, or other proceeding. The chapters that follow address the nuances of various testimonial situations (deposition, direct examination, cross-examination) and types of witnesses (corporate representatives, fact witnesses, expert witnesses).

# THE PERMISSIBLE SCOPE OF WITNESS PREPARATION

In the United States, a lawyer has the right to "interview a witness for the purpose of preparing the witness to testify."[6] No jurisdiction, however, has codified a statute or procedural rule that governs the permissible scope of witness preparation. In the Restatement of the Law Governing Lawyers, the American Law Institute defines the permissible scope of witness preparation as follows: "In preparing a witness to testify, a lawyer may invite the witness to provide truthful testimony favorable to the lawyer's client."[7] If the invitation is accepted, the lawyer and witness may appropriately discuss the following:

1.  The role of the witness and effective courtroom demeanor;
2.  The witness's recollection and probable testimony;
3.  Other testimony or evidence that will be presented;
4.  The witness's recollection or recounting of events in light of other witnesses' testimony;
5.  The law applicable to the events in issue;
6.  The factual context into which the witness's observations or opinions will fit;
7.  Documents or other physical evidence that may be introduced at the proceeding; and
8.  The probable lines of hostile cross-examination that the witness should be prepared to meet.[8]

During this preparation, "[a] lawyer may suggest choice of words that might be employed to make the witness's meaning clear."[9]

Criminal law and ethical rules[10] prohibit certain conduct during witness preparation sessions.[11] A lawyer cannot improperly influence a witness's testimony.[12]

---

6. RESTATEMENT (THIRD) OF THE LAW GOVERNING LAWYERS § 116(1) (2000).
7. *Id.* § 116 cmt. b.
8. *Id.*
9. *Id.*
10. *See infra*, Chapter 2.
11. Berger, *supra* note 1, at 51–52.
12. Gerders v. United States, 425 U.S. 80, 90 n.3 (1975); Ed Finkel, *The Perils of Witness Prep*, 104 ILL. BAR J. (May 2016) at 2.

Improper methods of influencing testimony include witness tampering,[13] suborning perjury,[14] and assisting the witness to "testify falsely as to a material fact[.]"[15] Ethical rules likewise prohibit a lawyer from knowingly offering or permitting false testimony as to any material or immaterial fact and, more broadly, engaging in conduct that involves dishonesty, fraud, deceit, or misrepresentation.[16]

Thus, in American jurisprudence, the scope of witness preparation is exceedingly broad.[17] Liberal witness preparation "is allowed because it makes our adversary system work better than it would if the rule were otherwise."[18] The system functions more effectively when lawyers are given broad leeway to prepare witnesses within their ethical obligations because the lawyers are responsible for "finding out what the facts are, straining out what is not relevant, organizing what is relevant, and presenting the relevant material to the court in a coherent and convincing manner."[19] The section that follows suggests a general methodology designed to assist a lawyer in performing this duty.

## WITNESS PREPARATION METHODOLOGY

Witness preparation is an intensive, multistep process.[20] Although no magic formula exists for preparing a witness to testify, experience and science-based research on witness behavior provide a framework for witness preparation sessions.[21] To effectively prepare a witness to testify, a lawyer should follow a three-step process: (1) prepare to meet with the witness; (2) meet with the witness a first time to alleviate his or her anxiety about testifying and to discuss the substance of the case while introducing techniques for testifying truthfully; and (3) meet with the witness a second time to reinforce the information supplied during the first session, discuss the procedure related to the specific type of proceeding (e.g., deposition, trial, grand jury), and practice testifying through a mock examination. Further preparation sessions may be necessary depending upon the witness's importance and the complexity of the case. Throughout this process the lawyer must adapt to the exigencies and constraints (budget and otherwise) of the case while remaining empathetic to the witness's situation.

---

13. *See, e.g.,* 18 U.S.C. § 1512.
14. *See, e.g., id.* § 1622.
15. RESTATEMENT (THIRD) OF THE LAW GOVERNING LAWYERS § 116 cmt. b.
16. MODEL RULES OF PROF'L CONDUCT R. 3.3(a)(2), 3.4, 8.4(c) (2016); *see also* Finkel, *supra* note 12, at 2–3.
17. Richard C. Wydick, *The Ethics of Witness Coaching,* 17 CARDOZO L. REV. 1, 5–8 (1995) (discussing the differences between American and English witness preparation practice).
18. *Id.* at 12.
19. *Id.* at 12–13.
20. DANIEL I. SMALL, PREPARING WITNESSES 49 (4th ed. 2014).
21. *See, e.g.,* Robert J. Cramer, et al., *Using Self-Efficacy for Witness Preparation,* 23 AM. SOC. OF TRIAL CONSULTANTS (Sept. 2011); Robert J. Cramer, et al., *Witness Self-Efficacy: Development and Validation of the Construct,* 28 BEHAV. SCI. LAW (Nov.–Dec. 2010) 784–800.

The end goal of this methodology is to instill a confidence in the witness that will permit him or her to listen to the questions posed at the proceeding and then credibly provide truthful and favorable answers.[22] Though simple in theory, this goal may be difficult to achieve at times because each witness, case, and adverse examining lawyer is different. A proper witness preparation practice is thus essential to ensuring consistently reliable and favorable testimony.

## Lawyer Preparation

Witness preparation begins outside the witness's presence. The lawyer must first analyze both where the witness fits into the case and the adverse lawyer's reason for seeking the witness's testimony. In some instances—such as with a party to the lawsuit—the witness's role and the necessity of his or her testimony are obvious. In other situations, such as in complex commercial or medical cases, the witness's role and the value of his or her testimony are not always apparent and, therefore, must be carefully evaluated.

Next, the lawyer should prepare an electronic or paper binder for the witness preparation session. At a minimum, the witness binder should include the witness's prior testimony, if any (affidavit, deposition, trial testimony, etc.); any public information obtained from social media on the witness (Facebook, LinkedIn, etc.); any literature or other publications (including blogs) the witness has authored; all case-related documents that reference the witness's name in any fashion (with the name highlighted to avoid having to search for it during the preparation session); and the key documents in the case. During the preparation session, the lawyer and witness should always review any documents referencing or directly authored by the witness. The scope of review of the other documents, such as the key case documents, will depend on the witness's status (client, fact witness, expert witness) and his or her level of involvement in the case. For example, a lawyer will not likely need to review complex case materials with a non-critical fact witness who has no knowledge or expertise in those areas.

The attorney-client privilege protects communications and documents shown to a client in a witness preparation session from disclosure in discovery.[23] The work-product doctrine protects an attorney's interviews, statements, memoranda, correspondence, briefs, and mental impressions, among other things, from disclosure in discovery.[24] Communications with a non-client fact witness, however, ordinarily are *not* protected from disclosure in discovery.[25] The discoverability of communications

---

22. *See, e.g.*, Sidney Kanazawa & Sabina Helton, *Preparing Witnesses for Deposition*, FOR THE DEFENSE 26 (July 2006).

23. Upjohn Co. v. United States, 449 U.S. 383, 394–95 (1981).

24. Hickman v. Taylor, 329 U.S. 495, 511 (1947); FED. R. CIV. P. 26(b)(3).

25. Janeen Kerper, *Preparing a Witness for Deposition*, 24 LITIGATION 11, 13 (1998). The determination of whether the attorney-client privilege covers a communication with a witness is made on a case-by-case basis. The issue of whether a court will recognize the attorney-client privilege for a communication with a particular witness "will turn on the witnesses' subjective intentions or expectations at the time of the communications, and the objective reasonableness of those expectations." Paul R. Rice et al., *Attorney-Client Privilege in the United States—Second Edition*, AM. BANKR. INST. J. 30 § 4:52 (2001).

with expert witnesses depends upon law in the jurisdiction where the case is pending.[26] Most courts have held that the work-product doctrine protects documents the lawyer selected and reviewed with a witness during a preparation session from disclosure in discovery.[27] An exception exists, however, if the witness used the document to refresh his or her recollection before or while testifying.[28]

Federal Rule of Evidence 612 provides that an adverse party is entitled to inspect and cross-examine a witness on a document used to refresh his or her recollection before or while testifying.[29] The rule requires that the adverse party meet three requirements before he or she is entitled to the document: (1) the witness must use the document to refresh his or her memory; (2) the witness must use the document for purposes of testifying; and (3) the court must determine that production of the document is necessary in the interests of justice.[30]

Rule 612 applies in depositions and at trial.[31] Lawyers frequently ask witnesses what documents they reviewed to prepare for a deposition. Rule 612's foundational requirements—particularly the requirement that the court determine if production of the document is requisite—will, in most cases, support a work-product objection and instruction to the witness not to answer the question. The work-product protection is waived if the witness is permitted to answer.[32] Thus, a lawyer defending a deposition must understand the recollection-refreshed rule prior to the deposition.[33] The issue should be discussed with the witness in the preparation session to ensure the work-product protection is not waived.[34]

In summary, the lawyer should outline the factual and legal issues pertinent to the witness and understand the privileged nature, if any, of the preparation session prior to meeting the witness. The lawyer's planning and organization will give him or her credibility and control during the preparation session. It also will begin the process of instilling trust and confidence in the witness.[35]

---

26. *See* FED. R. CIV. P. 26(b)(4) advisory committee's note (2010) (explaining that the work-product protection under Rule 26(b)(4) protects most communications and documents reviewed with a testifying expert from disclosure in federal cases); Gwen Stern et al., *Fishing Season Is Over: After* Barrick *and Amended Pennsylvania Rule of Civil Procedure 4003.5, Pennsylvania Reached the Right Decision Regarding Work Product Protections between Attorneys and Experts*, 7 DREXEL L. REV. 329, 340–54 (2015) (describing expert discovery rules in various jurisdictions throughout the country).

27. Sporck v. Peil, 759 F.2d 312, 316 (3d Cir. 1985); Gould Inc. v. Mitsui Mining & Smelting Co., 825 F.2d 676, 680 (2d Cir. 1987); Stone Container Corp. v. Arkwright Mut. Ins. Co., No. 93-C-6626, 1995 WL 88902 (N.D. Ill. Feb. 28, 1995); United States v. Dist. Council, No. 90-Civ.-5722, 1992 WL 208284 (S.D.N.Y. Aug. 18, 1992).

28. FED. R. EVID. 612.

29. *Id.* at 612(a).

30. *Id.* at 612(a), (b); *Sporck*, 759 F.2d at 317.

31. FED. R. CIV. P. 30(c)(1).

32. *See, e.g., In re* Qwest Commc'ns Int'l Inc., 450 F.3d 1179, 1186 (10th Cir. 2006) (explaining that "production of work-product material during discovery waives a work-product objection"); Horace Mann Ins. Co. v. Nationwide Mut. Ins. Co., 238 F.R.D. 536, 538 (D. Conn. 2006) (same).

33. DAVID MALONE, PETER HOFFMAN & ANTHONY BOCCHINO, THE EFFECTIVE DEPOSITION: TECHNIQUES AND STRATEGIES THAT WORK 197 (3d ed. 2006).

34. *Id.*

35. SMALL, *supra* note 20, at 25–30.

## The First Preparation Session: Anxiety and Substance

Generally, the first preparation session should address the witness's anxieties or concerns, the substantive issues in the case (including the witness's role, if any, in the dispute), and any witness-specific documents. These issues should be addressed and reinforced during any subsequent preparation sessions.

The primary factor affecting a witness's performance when testifying is confidence.[36] The first task in preparing a witness to testify, therefore, is to reduce the witness's anxiety.[37] Anxiety breeds stress (and vice versa).[38] Both are present in nearly every witness, although they may masquerade as anger, hostility, overconfidence, or competitiveness.[39] The witness's anxieties must be fully expressed, acknowledged, and validated before they can be reduced.[40] Anxiety *must* be reduced because it distracts the witness from listening and learning during the preparation sessions.[41] For this reason, the witness's concerns should be addressed at the outset of the preparation session.[42] This critical step is often overlooked.

Situational phobias—such as fear of an unknown process (litigation) or proceeding (trial)—cause anxiety.[43] A lawyer should therefore eliminate unknowns by providing an elementary overview of the entire litigation process to the witness—chances are, aspects of a case that may seem commonplace to a lawyer (e.g., what is a deposition, what is discovery) may be completely foreign to a lay witness.[44] The witness should understand how the lawsuit started, why and how he or she became a witness, and how his or her testimony fits into the case.[45] The lawyer should explain, in plain terms, the reason the witness must testify. For example, with the deposition of a managerial employee of a corporate defendant, the defense lawyer should explain that the deposition is the only chance the plaintiff's lawyer has to ask the employee questions (a positive follow-up is helpful, explaining that certain rules prevent the opposing lawyer from calling him or her at home or ever contacting him or her personally). The witness should understand that the lawyer cannot prevent the proceeding from going forward, no matter how scared, hesitant, or unqualified the witness may feel. The lawyer can, however, offer reassurance to the witness that he or she is not alone and can identify other witnesses or potential witnesses in the case. The lawyer should also make clear that the witness's job is not

---

36. MALONE ET AL., *supra* note 33, at 177.
37. *Id.* at 178.
38. Lisa M. Shin & Israel Liberzon, *The Neurocircuitry of Fear, Stress, and Anxiety Disorders*, 135 NEUROPSYCHO-PHARMACOLOGY REV. 169, 173–74 (2010).
39. Kerper, *supra* note 25, at 14.
40. *Id.*
41. MALONE ET AL., *supra* note 33, at 178.
42. *Id.*
43. Randi E. McCabe, *Specific Phobia in Adults: Epidemiology, Clinical Manifestations, Course and Diagnosis*, UPTO-DATE (2016).
44. SMALL, *supra* note 20, at 52–53.
45. David M. Malone, *Talking Green, Showing Red—Why Most Deposition Preparation Fails, and What to Do About It*, 24 LITIGATION 27, 27–28 (1998).

to "win the case"; rather, the witness's job is simply to provide truthful testimony. It is a lawyer's job to win the case.

The lawyer should ask the witness about his or her concerns. Most witnesses have similar concerns, such as the following:

- How long will this take?
- Am I in trouble?
- Is my testimony important?
- Am I good person?
- Can I do this?
- Can I tell my side of the story?
- Can the other lawyer ask me anything?
- Is the other lawyer mean or belligerent?
- What if I don't want to answer a question?
- What if I don't remember?
- What is your plan?
- Who will be there?
- Are you a better (smarter, meaner) attorney than the other side?
- Am I getting paid?
- How do I get off work, arrange childcare, etc.?
- Will my boss know what we discuss?
- What happens if there is a mistake?[46]

These concerns and any others should be thoughtfully and fully addressed at the outset of the preparation session. Such an introductory session allows the lawyer to establish a bond with the witness, building the witness's confidence and trust in the lawyer.

The "key" to witness preparation is "reducing the witness's anxieties, letting her focus on the specific task at hand, and telling her that the specific task is simple, narrow, and well within her ability to accomplish."[47] For one example of many, nurses are notoriously nervous witnesses when a lawsuit involves some aspect of their treatment of a patient-plaintiff. The nurse-witnesses' nerves are substantially alleviated when they understand their only job is to testify about their recollection of their involvement with the patient—and not to defend the care in its entirety or explain the patient's adverse outcome. The specific task for a nurse-witness in that situation is to read the patient's medical record/chart (in some cases only the parts of the chart the witness personally authored) and testify only about the patient care he or she provided if the witness remembers the patient.

After the witness generally understands the litigation process and his or her concerns have been addressed, the lawyer should explain the factual background of

---

46. Kerper, *supra* note 25, at 14.
47. Malone, *supra* note 45, at 27–28.

the case, the issues in the case, and each side's position or theme in the case, and then review the witness-specific documents.[48] Framing the case and the importance of thematic preparation of the witness are addressed in later chapters.[49] Naturally, the preparation of a witness on the substance of the case will depend on the witness's role in the case and complexity of the issues involved.

The objective is to help the witness develop a grasp of the case given his or her specific role (client/party, critical fact witness, tangential fact witness, expert witness) in the case.[50] For example, "a lawyer in a products liability case should certainly make some effort to explain the various theories of negligence, warranty, and strict liability that may be involved."[51] It is proper—indeed, vital—for a lawyer in a witness preparation session to explain the facts of the case, explain how the applicable law applies to both the facts and the witness's testimony, and address the potential questions that will be posed on the witness's particular factual situation.[52] Similarly, the lawyer should review the witness's prior testimony with him or her, if such testimony exists, prior to testifying.[53] Rules of procedure generally afford a witness the right to review his or her prior testimony before testifying in a subsequent proceeding.[54] It is also advisable to review the testimony of other key witnesses in the case, if permitted.[55] Importantly, under the "rule of exclusion," lay or fact witnesses ordinarily are *not* permitted to review or discuss the testimony of other witnesses before they testify at trial."[56]

In summary, the first witness preparation sessions should serve as the witness's introduction to the lawyer, to the litigation process generally, to the specific proceeding, and to the facts/documents of the case as they relate to the witness. Such preparation has the effect of reducing the witness's anxiety by letting him or her know what to expect.[57] The lawyer, of course, should use the first preparation session to begin introducing concepts about testifying in the proceeding, as discussed next, in an interactive conversational process with the witness.

## The Second Preparation Session: Procedure and Testimonial "Tools"

The second preparation session should address any new anxieties the witness developed since the first session, reiterate and reinforce the factual and legal issues in the case that pertain to the witness, include a review of any new testimony that

48. SMALL, *supra* note 20, at 52–53.
49. *See infra*, Chapters 8 and 9.
50. MALONE ET AL., *supra* note 33, at 194.
51. Applegate, *supra* note 2, at 300.
52. *Id.* at 301.
53. TEXAS TRIAL HANDBOOK § 8:4 (3d ed. & Supp. 2015).
54. Applegate, *supra* note 2, at 305 & n.136.
55. TEXAS TRIAL HANDBOOK § 8:4.
56. *See, e.g.*, FED. R. EVID. 615.
57. Applegate, *supra* note 2, at 301.

has been provided since the first preparation session, and explain the procedure of the testimonial proceeding. The lawyer should then provide the witness with techniques or tools he or she can use to testify truthfully. It is this latter aspect of witness preparation where many lawyers superfluously spend the majority, if not all, of their preparation time.

## Explanation of the Testimonial Proceeding

Before testifying, the witness should understand the procedural rules governing the specific testimonial proceeding. The lawyer should explain the following:

1. The nature of the proceeding (e.g., a deposition is testimony given outside the courtroom but the witness is sworn to tell the truth just as if he or she were sitting in front of the judge or jury);
2. The purpose of the proceeding (e.g., the purpose of a deposition is to discover facts, preserve testimony, and prevent surprise);
3. The rules governing the proceeding (time limits, breaks, etc.),[58] including the scope of permissible questioning and how to handle privilege objections/instructions not to answer;[59]
4. Objections, and what to do after an objection (e.g., the witness will likely still have to answer the objected-to question at a *deposition*, but at *trial* the witness should not answer the question unless the judge overrules the objection);[60]
5. The location of the proceeding (conference room, courthouse, etc.);[61]
6. That a court reporter transcribes the questions and answers;
7. The process for correcting or changing the sworn testimony during and after the proceeding;
8. Who can or may be in attendance at the proceeding; and
9. Who will be asking questions, and the order of the examination.

---

58. *See, e.g.*, Fed. R. Civ. P. 30(d)(1) (imposing a seven-hour limit on depositions).
59. At the same time, the witness should be informed that the adverse lawyer may ask the witness if he or she intends to follow the instruction not to answer and, if posed, the witness should affirmatively state that he or she will follow the instruction. Malone et al., *supra* note 33, at 194.
60. Some commentators suggest that the witness should learn the objections, listen to them at deposition, understand whether the question is improper, and address the objection in his or her answer. *See, e.g.*, Kanazawa & Helton, *supra* note 22, at 27. This approach likely asks too much of most witnesses. For example, at deposition, asking a witness to analyze why the question "calls for speculation" or "lacks foundation" requires learning the objections and being able to understand them during the proceeding. This, again, creates anxiety in the witness and distracts his or her attention from the question and answer. A middle-ground approach that works well is to simply inform the witness to be on heightened alert or simply to be more careful when answering if an objection is lodged.
61. If the witness is unusually anxious, showing him or her the actual conference or courtroom where the proceeding will take place, as well as orienting him or her to where he or she will sit in relation to the lawyers, court reporter, judge, and/or jury may lessen the anxiety. *See* Texas Trial Handbook § 8:10.

With regard to point number six, the lawyer should explain that testimony is *not* a verbal conversation; rather, it is "a dialectic means of creating written statement."[62] The witness should have the mindset that he or she is dictating a written answer. The witness should pause for a few seconds prior to answering, formulate an answer, and then dictate the answer.[63]

Providing the witness with knowledge of the procedural aspects of the proceeding alleviates anxiety, prevents surprise, and avoids distractions during the proceeding. The witness should understand that the defending lawyer in the deposition (or the judge at trial) will ensure the adverse lawyer complies with the procedural rules. The witness needs not concern his or herself with the rules of procedure or testimonial protocol.

## Testimonial Techniques and Tools

A witness's only job at a testimonial proceeding is to provide credible, truthful testimony,[64] and the lawyer's responsibility is to arm the witness with techniques or tools to perform this job. The witness must understand that he or she will likely have to use one or all of these tools to testify effectively. Lists of such testimonial techniques or tools—sometimes referred to as "rules" or "commandments"—are legion.[65] The key to effective witness preparation is teaching these techniques to the witness in a way he or she will actually understand, remember, and use during the proceeding.

Aside from truthfulness, the most important tool with which a lawyer can arm a witness is a "home base": a thematic, true statement that permits the witness to answer even the most difficult questions in a favorable manner.[66] This provides the witness with a touchstone that allows him or her to "process and respond to each question in a clear and definitive manner."[67] The witness can come back to his or her home base again and again during the proceeding.[68] The home base statement should be selected with care for each witness, taking into consideration: (1) the primary testimonial goal of the adverse/questioning lawyer, and (2) the overarching theme of the preparing lawyer's case. For example, a nurse in a medical malpractice case, when asked tough questions regarding his or her actions or inactions in treating a patient, may use his or her "clinical judgment" as a home base—something like: "Pain medication typically causes increased heart rate, so I used my *clinical judgment* in deciding not to immediately call the doctor when the patient's heart rate increased following administration of the medication."

---

62. Kanazawa & Helton, *supra* note 22, at 27.
63. *Id.* at 27–28; *see also* MALONE ET AL., *supra* note 33, at 195.
64. Malone, *supra* note 45, at 27–28.
65. Applegate, *supra* note 2, at 298 & n.95 (collecting lists); *see also* Andrew T. Gardner, *The Ten Commandments of Witness Prep*, THE PRACTICAL LITIGATOR 7 (Sept. 1999).
66. R. Craig Smith & Theodore O. Prosise, *Your Witness—Prepare Before Stepping into the Sun*, http://tsongas .com/wp-content/uploads/2011/07/Your-Witness-0704.pdf.
67. *Id.*
68. *Id.*

Other techniques and tools the lawyer should teach the witness include:

1. **Be Truthful.** A witness should provide truthful testimony even if it is awkward, embarrassing, offensive, or hurtful, because the other option is lying. Lying under oath is a crime, wrong, confusing, and hard.[69]

2. **Provide the Shortest, Most Truthful Answer.** The lawyer must teach the witness that, unlike in normal conversation, telling the whole story in response to a question will not end the deposition.[70] On the contrary, "[e]very word they add, every adjective, adverb or extra noun or verb, creates a[n] [issue] that the opposing attorney will feel compelled to explore."[71] The shortest, most truthful answers in any testimonial proceeding are often: yes; no; I don't know; and I don't remember.[72] The lawyer should impress upon the witness that such answers are acceptable—indeed, preferred. Teach the witness about the time-honored instruction to not volunteer information.[73] The witness need not "worry about what the questioner really wants to know, or where he is going. If he wants more information, he will ask for it."[74]

3. **Be a Good Listener.** Any testimonial proceeding is fundamentally about listening, not talking. Listening "is where the process begins, and it is the foundation for everything else."[75] A witness must learn how to listen "with narrow intensity" and "precision" because the answer to each question will be written and used for the rest of the case.[76]

4. **Seek Understanding.** The witness must understand the question before effectively answering it. Lawyers—particularly unprepared lawyers—ask notoriously confusing questions. The witness is the one who knows the situation—not the lawyer—and should be comfortable telling the lawyer to "please rephrase or ask a different question because I do not understand." Understanding includes refusing to guess at the intent of the question.

5. **Be Thoughtful.** The witness must take a moment to process the question, think about the answer, and thoughtfully respond. As discussed earlier, the witness must understand he or she is *writing* his or her answer for experts and others to read in the future. Being thoughtful includes controlling the pace of the question-answer proceeding, taking time to answer questions, and not being in a hurry to end the proceeding or feeling pressured to answer too quickly.

---

69. SMALL, *supra* note 20, at 5–8, 81–88.
70. Malone, *supra* note 45, at 29–30.
71. *Id.* at 30.
72. The lawyer must explain the difference between "I don't know" and "I don't remember" as answers in a testimonial proceeding because the distinction is critical. *See* MALONE ET AL., *supra* note 33, at 187–88.
73. SMALL, *supra* note 20, at 119–23.
74. MALONE ET AL., *supra* note 33, at 186–87.
75. SMALL, *supra* note 20, at 59.
76. *Id.* at 59–61.

6. **Be a Conditionalist, Not an Absolutist.** Saying something "always" or "never" occurs is rarely true and, therefore, should be avoided. The witness should practice answering questions conditionally. For example, the witness can say: "As I sit here today, I do not remember that occurring" or "in my experience, I have not seen that occur." Using conditional statements insulates the witness from impeachment whereas speaking in absolutes sets him or her up for impeachment.[77]

7. **Be Content.** After providing an answer, be content and silent. Witnesses, as humans, have a tendency to fill silence. At a testimonial proceeding, silence is golden. The witness should "give good, responsive answers—and then be quiet."[78]

8. **Be Humble.** The witness should know, understand, and be ready to correct any mistake made during the proceeding. A mistake should be corrected as soon as the witness realizes he or she made the mistake. It is far better to correct a mistake at the deposition rather than through the errata process.[79]

9. **Be a Reader.** The witness should be instructed to read every exhibit and document placed in front of them at any proceeding.[80] The witness should not worry about time or feel rushed. The witness must understand the context of the particular phrase, sentence, or paragraph about which they are being questioned in order to provide a truthful response. The witness should not attempt to explain what the document means unless he or she personally wrote the document *and* the document is unclear.

10. **Be "Relentlessly" Polite, Positive, and Consistent.** "This is not etiquette advice. It's a survival technique."[81] The witness must be confident in his or her testimony. Being positive and polite makes the testimony credible.[82] The lawyer and witness must prepare to *never* let the questioner interrupt, and have a plan about how to politely finish all answers.[83] The witness should also know and understand that the adverse lawyer will ask important questions more than once, and likely more than two times during a proceeding. The witness must maintain consistency in his or her repetitive answers, politely incorporating previous testimony or re-answering the question in the same manner.

The preceding techniques and tools can be extremely useful to the witness *if* conveyed in an applicable manner. Mind-numbing 20-page witness preparation

---

77. Kanazawa & Helton, *supra* note 22, at 28.
78. Smith & Prosise, *supra* note 66.
79. *Id.*
80. SMALL, *supra* note 20, at 129.
81. *Id.* at 89–94.
82. Kanazawa & Helton, *supra* note 22, at 26.
83. SMALL, *supra* note 20, at 90.

forms create rather than alleviate anxiety.[84] A lawyer cannot simply tell a person verbally how to be an effective witness and expect success[85] because humans only retain approximately 20 percent of the information conveyed to them verbally.[86] Regurgitating long-used lists of "dos" and "don'ts" to a witness will almost never be effective. Instead, the lawyer must substantively teach the witness through real-world examples and role-play practice.[87]

The key to teaching a witness how to use these tools is interaction between lawyer and witness.[88] "[R]eal learning" happens through "back-and-forth exchange" between lawyer and witness.[89] As David Malone described, to make the techniques and tools for effective testimony truly resonate with the witness, use the following approach:

1.  INTERACT: the witness will internalize and remember what is said during a give-and-take preparation session;
2.  CONFIRM: constantly check with the witness to make sure he or she understands and does not have any questions;
3.  REPEAT: give key instructions more than once, phrasing the information differently but making the same point each time (which is more effective than simply saying the same thing twice);
4.  ILLUSTRATE: illustrate every important instruction with an example or two (or three or four), which will make the instruction more understandable; and
5.  REINFORCE: have the witness practice using his or her techniques and tools through a mock deposition and constantly remind the witness of the various tools during the process.[90]

The heart of witness preparation is to afford the witness an opportunity to actually practice testifying.[91] It is impossible to know or practice every question that will be asked during a deposition. Nonetheless, it is critical to "identify the key areas on which the witness is reasonably certain to be examined and to have the witness practice answering questions on those topics. But remember, this is not just a time

---

84. Kanazawa & Helton, *supra* note 22, at 25; Kerper, *supra* note 25, at 12–13; MALONE ET AL., *supra* note 33, at 177–78, 184. Too often, "witness preparation consists of the lawyer giving the witness a long, uninterrupted lecture which may go on for up to an hour and contains a set of so-called 'rules' for the witness to follow during the deposition." *Id.* at 194. The lawyer reads the list of rules to the witness because, even after years and scores of preparation sessions, he does not have the list memorized. But the lawyer expects the witness to hear, absorb, comprehend, and remember all the rules. The lawyer is then surprised when the witness testifies poorly. *Id.* at 184.
85. SMALL, *supra* note 20, at 45–46.
86. Joyce Tsongas & Shelly Spiecker, *A Key Component in the Successful Defense of Employment Cases: Witness Preparation*, OR. ASS'N DEF. COUNSEL 14, 17 (Winter 2000).
87. SMALL, *supra* note 20, at 45–46.
88. *Id.*
89. *Id.* at 46.
90. MALONE ET AL., *supra* note 33, at 184–85.
91. *Id.* at 197.

for practicing answering, but also a time to refine and improve the answers given by assisting the witness with word choice, chronology, and accuracy."[92]

At the close of the final preparation session, the lawyer should discuss the following with the witness:

- what to wear;
- what to bring to the proceeding;
- what to review before the proceeding;
- what *not* to review before the proceeding;
- whom to talk to before the proceeding;
- whom *not* to talk to before the proceeding; and
- when and where to meet the lawyer for the proceeding.[93]

By leaving nothing unanswered, the witness will feel reasonably comfortable and confident heading into the proceeding.

## A Single Preparation Session: Assuring and Teaching

Sometimes, the exigencies of a case permit only a single preparation session with the witness. Each of the tips and tools discussed previously can be employed in a single session, albeit in an abbreviated manner. As with a two-meeting methodology, the goals should be to provide the witness with a level of comfort about testifying, discuss the substance of the case, introduce techniques for testifying truthfully, and practice those techniques. The objective, as stated earlier, is to instill confidence in the witness, permitting him or her to provide truthful and helpful answers in a credible manner. When the lawyer has limited time with the witness, emphasizing the witness's "home base" may become even more important, as will taking time to practice the tools just described.

# CONCLUSION

Witness preparation is an integral part of the American judicial system.[94] "Preparation is helping the witness say what she actually wants to say, by providing word choices or assisting with organization or refreshing recollection."[95] For such preparation to be effective, the lawyer must be empathetic to the witness's situation and reduce anxiety while simultaneously teaching the witness about procedural matters and the substance of the case. This learning must occur through a dynamic and interactive multistep process. If the lawyer does his or her job correctly, the witness will credibly provide truthful testimony that is favorable to the lawyer's case.

---

92. *Id.*
93. *Id.* at 205–07.
94. Applegate, *supra* note 2, at 352.
95. Malone, *supra* note 45, at 30.

## CHAPTER 2

# Between Twilight and Dawn

## The Ethics of Witness Preparation

### *James M. Miller*

What most trial lawyers know about the ethics of witness preparation can be summed up in three words: Do not coach. How did coaching get a bad name? In all other aspects of life, coaching is a good thing. Whether it is a tennis coach or a life coach, we all need someone to teach us the basics, tell us the rules, and get us prepared for the game. And so it is with the preparation of witnesses.

Like the other authors represented in this book, I am not a law professor or legal scholar; I am a trial lawyer. Although legal ethics on witness preparation involve many rules, cases, and ethics opinions, my approach here is practical, with the goal of helping the trial lawyer navigate ethical concerns in a positive way. My problem with the prohibition on coaching is that it sends the wrong message. Of course we do not suborn perjury, but we must still advocate for our client when preparing the witness. There are rules on that, too.

To that end, this chapter discusses the rules that require witness preparation, the permissible methods of witness preparation, and things that are ethically forbidden.

## TELL THE TRUTH

Before anyone gets the wrong idea, we always strive to tell the truth, and that is the alpha and omega of our witness preparation session. I like to begin and end each witness preparation session with a discussion on the paramount importance of telling the truth. Particularly with a third-party witness, I will immediately follow that by telling her that it is ethical and common for lawyers to meet with witnesses to discuss their upcoming testimony but that she needs to be prepared to be asked on cross-examination if we had met. Then I point out that when counsel asks her, "What did Mr. Miller tell you," she can truthfully answer, "He told me to tell the truth." Sometimes that is enough to end that line of questioning.

There should be nothing automatic or perfunctory in the truth-telling discussion. It must be sincere. The witness will be looking to you for clues and will be able to tell the difference between a lawyer with a genuine commitment to the truth and a lawyer who is just going through the motions.

But truth is more than only the beginning and the end of witness preparation. Truth is everything. As the title to this chapter suggests, the line that separates proper witness preparation from that which is improper is often seen as blurred.[1] Truth is what provides focus, and, as will be explained in this chapter, a commitment to the truth allows the trial lawyer more latitude to advocate for her client when preparing a witness.

## COMPETENT AND ZEALOUS ADVOCACY *REQUIRES* WITNESS PREPARATION

Although the American Bar Association's Model Rules of Professional Conduct (ABA Model Rules) do not directly address a lawyer's obligations to her client on witness preparation, the general rules on the client–lawyer relationship provide some guidance.[2]

Rule 1.1 provides: "A lawyer shall provide competent representation to a client. Competent representation requires the legal knowledge, skill, thoroughness and preparation reasonably necessary for the representation."

Comment 5 to Rule 1.1 in part states: "Competent handling of a particular matter includes inquiry into and analysis of the factual and legal elements of the problem, and use of methods and procedures meeting the standards of competent practitioners. It also includes adequate preparation."

*"A lawyer who did not prepare his or her witness for testimony, having had an opportunity to do so, would not be doing his or her professional job properly"* (emphasis added).

---

1. The title is borrowed from Fordham University law professor James A. Cohen, quoted in Adam Liptak, *Crossing a Fine Line on Witness Coaching*, N.Y. Times, March 16, 2006 ("[L]ike the difference between dusk and twilight.").

2. The ABA Model Rules have been adopted in some form by every state except California, and they are used as the standard reference in this chapter. When California does not have an ethical rule governing a specific issue, courts may look to the ABA for guidance, although they may not consider ABA Rules and Opinions as binding authority. *See, e.g.,* U.S. v. Sierra Pacific Industries (E.D. Cal. 2010) 2010 WL 4778051, at *7. The rules of ethics, reported decisions, and ethics opinions of state bar associations should be consulted for each jurisdiction.

This was the opinion of the District of Columbia Bar Association in its Ethics Opinion No. 79 on the topic of witness preparation issued in 1979 (Opinion 79). Despite the passage of time, Opinion 79 remains a definitive and persuasive opinion on a lawyer's ethical obligations.

Rule 1.3 of ABA Model Rules provides: "A lawyer shall act with reasonable diligence and promptness in representing a client."

Comment 1 to Rule 1.3 in part states: "A lawyer must also act with commitment and dedication to the interests of the client *and with zeal in advocacy* upon the client's behalf" (emphasis added). The word "zealous," like "coaching," has developed a bad name, to the point where there is little distinction between "zealous" and "overzealous." This negative connotation is to the detriment of effective advocacy and exalts the lawyer's duty to the judicial system over the duty owed to her client. Under our adversary system these duties do not compete but must coexist.

What does zealous advocacy require of a lawyer in preparing a witness to testify? Zealous advocacy requires the advocate to do everything within her power and resources to prepare the witness to testify truthfully in a way that benefits her client. The best way to provide content to the requirement of zealous advocacy in witness preparation is to examine those methods that have been found to be permissible under the law and formal ethics opinions.

# PERMISSIBLE METHODS OF WITNESS PREPARATION

Section 116 of The Restatement (Third) of the Law Governing Lawyers provides remarkably clear guidance on what a lawyer can do in preparing a witness. Comment b to subsection 1, which states "a lawyer may interview a witness for the purpose of preparing the witness to testify," identifies nine methods a lawyer may use in preparing a witness "to provide truthful testimony." The Restatement's nine methods implicitly recognize that truthful testimony is not the same as effective and helpful testimony. Whereas the former is an absolute requirement, the latter is the product of good advocacy by the lawyer in witness preparation.

Each of the Restatement's nine permissible methods of witness preparation is quoted and discussed in the following text.[3]

## 1. "[A lawyer may] discuss[ ] the role of the witness and effective courtroom demeanor."

The typical lay witness needs help. Whether he asks it or not, the question in his mind is, "What do you want from me?" The answer is, "Truthful testimony. Let me

---

3. The nine methods are discussed in the order in which they appear in the Restatement comment. This is not necessarily the order in which the trial lawyer may want to proceed under the circumstances of a particular witness preparation session or as a matter of style and opinion.

explain." It is ethically proper for the lawyer to help the witness understand the context and purpose of his testimony. Without an understanding of his role, the witness will be confused and may feel the need to do more than is necessary or beneficial to the lawyer's client. Understanding his role will help to put the witness at ease, and a witness at ease is a more effective and credible witness.

However, there is a danger here that the witness may feel that he is unable to "play the role" assigned to him by the lawyer without stretching the facts or engaging in guesswork. The lawyer's job is to make sure that the witness is comfortable enough that she is able to provide truthful testimony within the role described. As will be discussed in connection with the other permissible methods of witness preparation, it is incumbent on the lawyer to constantly interject to ensure that the witness is able to testify truthfully to the facts and in the manner discussed.

It is also permissible for the lawyer to help the witness with his question, "How do I act?" Thus, the lawyer may give direction on how to dress, how to answer questions, where to look when he is testifying, etc. This point becomes especially critical if the witness's testimony is being videotaped.

### 2. "[A lawyer may] discuss[ ] the witness's recollection and probable testimony."

Assistance with the witness's recollection regarding the issue in question is witness preparation at its most basic and requires little discussion. An overly cautious lawyer may regard this as setting the limits on witness preparation. The point of this chapter is that it need not—and should not—begin and end here. But getting the witness to recount what he can recall in his own words is an important part of the interview in order to evaluate the witness and to inform her of the testimonial methods available.

### 3. "[A lawyer may] reveal[ ] to the witness other testimony or evidence that will be presented and ask[ ] the witness to reconsider the witness's recollection or recounting of events in that light."

Note that there are two aspects to this method: (1) telling the witness what other witnesses or evidence are likely to reveal, and (2) asking the witness to "reconsider" his previously expressed recollection of events in light of potentially contradictory evidence. It is likely that there are lawyers who regard either aspect of the method to comprise improper witness "coaching." Indeed, in *Crutchfield v. Wainwright*,[4] the court defined improper witness coaching as "directing a witness's testimony in such a way as to have it conform with, conflict with, or supplement the testimony of other witnesses." The court's definition of improper coaching, broad as it

---

4. Crutchfield v. Wainwright, 803 F.2d 1103, 1110 (11th Cir. 1986).

is, is consistent with the Restatement.[5] The key word in the court's definition is "directing." When the lawyer *directs* the witness in what to say, whether the engineered testimony "conform[s] with, conflict[s] with, or supplement[s] the testimony of other witnesses," the effect is to substitute the lawyer's testimony for that of the witness, and it is improper. The Restatement teaches that revealing other testimony or evidence and asking the witness to reconsider is improper only if used to try to direct some desired testimony without regard for the truth.

This method implicitly recognizes that witness recollection cannot be taken at face value and must be tested. Knowing what others are likely to say may help trigger a better recollection, or the witness may be able to provide an explanation that reconciles the evidence, or he may be able to show that another witness is wrong. Simply accepting potentially contradictory testimony from different witnesses is not ethically required; it is just bad lawyering. This is not to say that all witness testimony must be reconciled through the witness preparation process. Sometimes the evidence cannot be reconciled. That is why we have juries and trial lawyers. Perhaps the discrepancy is immaterial, or perhaps one witness should not be called. Again, legal ethics do not prevent good advocacy in witness preparation but require it.

There is an important exception to the propriety of this method. If the court invokes "The Rule," that is, the rule on exclusion, or sequestration, of witnesses,[6] the lawyer may not inform the witness of the testimony of others by having him sit in the courtroom to listen to live testimony or supply the witness with daily transcripts of proceedings. Providing such access after the court has excluded witnesses violates not only the court order and a likely contempt of court citation, it also violates Model Rules 3.4(c) (knowingly violating a court rule) and 8.4(d) (conduct prejudicial to the administration of justice). However, it is important to note that the standard sequestration order does necessarily prevent the lawyer from discussing previous testimony with witnesses who have not yet testified. *See, United States v. Rhynes*, 218 F.3d 310, 317 (4th Cir. 2000) (explaining Rule 615 order does not preclude a lawyer from discussing prior testimony with witnesses yet to testify and rejecting argument that the "purpose and spirit" of Rule 615 and the "truth-seeking" process would be compromised by lawyer disclosing prior testimony); *accord, United States v. Sepulveda*, 15 F.3d 1161, 1176 (1st Cir. 1993).[7] However, the trial court has considerable discretion to expand a sequestration order to bar witnesses from

---

5. The court's definition is dictum. The holding of the case is that a defendant must show that the trial court's order prohibiting certain conferences actually prevented the defendant from conferring with counsel. *Id.* at 1110.

6. *E.g.*, Fed. R. Evid. 615.

7. The *Rhynes* case is particularly instructive. There, the lawyer advised a witness who had not yet testified about the trial testimony of another witness, and the majority opinion in this en banc decision put much weight on the fact that a lawyer is bound by ethical rules. ("Consequently, lawyers' ethical obligations to the court distinguish them from trial witnesses.") 218 F.3d, at 318. However, the strong dissenting opinions show that judges may react very differently to an "indirect" violation of a standard sequestration order.

conferring with each other "before, during, and after their testimony."[8] The lawyer should exercise great care in requesting the precise terms of a sequestration order and in complying with one. The cases show that simply "invoking the rule" may not be enough.

## 4.   "[A lawyer may] discuss[ ] the applicability of law to the events in issue."

Many years ago, before *My Cousin Vinnie*, the famous director, Otto Preminger, made the film, *Anatomy of a Murder*. It starred Jimmy Stewart as a criminal defense lawyer, George C. Scott as the prosecutor, and Ben Gazarra as an Army lieutenant accused of murder. The accused, Lt. Banion, had admittedly shot and killed a man he suspected of raping his wife earlier on the evening of the shooting. During a jailhouse visit, Jimmy Stewart explains to his client that there are four ways to defend a murder charge, but only one ("legal excuse") has not been ruled out. He then asks his client if he has a legal excuse. Quick on the uptake, Lt. Banion says he must have been crazy, and then asks the lawyer, "Am I getting warmer?" Jimmy Stewart concludes the interview with the comment, "See if you can remember just how crazy you were." They ultimately arrive at a defense of temporary insanity.

In the book on which the movie was based, *Anatomy of a Murder* by Robert Traver (1958), the author describes this scene as the "Lecture," an "ancient technique" used by lawyers to lead a witness to some desired testimony while carefully treading the ethical line. Did Jimmy Stewart cross the line? Where is the line? Is it, as the title of this chapter suggests, somewhere "between twilight and dawn," that is, nearly imperceptible? Though Lt. Banion's response may seem contrived and opportunistic, can his defense lawyer make a determination as to his client's state of mind at the time of the shooting (or his state of mind during this interview), or, aided by the testimony of an expert witness, does he owe his client the benefit of the doubt on an insanity defense in a murder trial?

Because Lt. Banion never testified, it might be argued that his defense lawyer did not cross the line. However, he is examined by a psychiatrist who does testify that Lt. Banion was temporarily insane at the time of the shooting. The witness does not have to testify for the lawyer to violate ethical rules. In *Matter of Foley*,[9] a Massachusetts lawyer was suspended for three years for helping his client (an undercover agent) fabricate a defense to a gun-carrying case when the defense had been communicated to the prosecutor even though the defense was ultimately abandoned and the client never testified.

The Restatement does not require that the lawyer first get "all the facts" from the witness before discussing applicable law. There is no timing element. Even if the lawyer first fully debriefs the witness, a discussion of the law—like a discussion

---

8. *Id.* For an example of a broad sequestration order see Minebea Co., Ltd. v. Papst, 374 F. Supp. 2d 231 (D.D.C. 2005).

9. Matter of Foley, 439 Mass. 324 (2003).

of the witness's role, the likely testimony of another witness, or a review of documents—may trigger a recollection.

At least one reported decision has approved the practice of discussing applicable law in witness preparation. In *State v. McCormick*,[10] the trial judge disallowed the testimony of a witness because the judge believed he had been coached. In reversing the conviction for first-degree burglary, the North Carolina Supreme Court ruled:

> There is absolutely no evidence in this case that defense counsel procured the witness to give perjured testimony. Defense counsel had a witness who would testify that Bethea had a reputation in her community for being an untruthful woman. It is not improper for an attorney to prepare his witness for trial, to explain the applicable law in any given situation and to go over before trial the attorney's questions and the witness' answers so that the witness will be ready for his appearance in court, will be more at ease because he knows what to expect, and will give his testimony in the most effective manner that he can. Such preparation is the mark of a good trial lawyer, See, e.g., A. Morrill, Trial Diplomacy, Ch. 3, Part 8 (1973), and is to be commended because it promotes a more efficient administration of justice and saves court time.[11]

The court went on to discuss that if improper witness coaching is suspected the remedy is cross-examination of the witness concerning his preparation and discussions with counsel.[12]

### 5. "[A lawyer may] review[ ] the factual context into which the witness's observations or opinions will fit."

This one is straightforward. A lawyer can tell the witness about facts concerning the case that go beyond the witness's "role," ostensibly to provide context and to help trigger recollection.

### 6. "[A lawyer may] review[ ] documents or other physical evidence that may be introduced."

Reviewing documents, especially those authored or received by the witness, those for which the witness may be needed to provide a foundation, and those on which he may be cross-examined, is basic witness preparation. An ethical obligation to perform this task exists, particularly in document intensive commercial cases.

---

10. State v. McCormick, 298 N.C. 788 (1979).

11. *Id.* at 791.

12. *Id.* at 792.

## 7. "[A lawyer may] discuss[ ] probable lines of hostile cross-examination that the witness should be prepared to meet."

This is another standard—yet acutely critical—element of effective witness preparation. In light of the third method discussed earlier ("[a lawyer may] reveal[] to the witness other testimony or evidence that will be presented. . ."), it would be permissible to report to the witness lines of questioning and even exact questions used by opposing counsel in prior depositions. Further, it would be permissible to report the answers given by other witnesses who have been questioned by opposing counsel in prior depositions.

## 8. "Witness preparation may include rehearsal of testimony."

Again, rehearsing the witness's testimony is standard fare and necessary to evaluate the witness and his ability to stand up "under fire" and to give the witness confidence. It is worth noting that giving the witness practice in answering questions would seem to be classic coaching, albeit coaching with a small *c*.

The rehearsal of testimony was considered and found acceptable in Opinion 79:

> It matters not at all that the preparation of such testimony takes the form of "practice" examination or cross-examination. What does matter is that whatever the mode of witness preparation chosen, the lawyer does not engage in suppressing, distorting or falsifying the testimony that the witness will give.

## 9. "A lawyer may suggest choice words that might be employed to make the witness's meaning clear."

Now we come to a method of witness preparation that will strike some lawyers as classic Coaching with a capital C. Is this not "putting words in his mouth?" Here we should parse the words used in drafting this comment to the Restatement. The words that a lawyer may "suggest" are those that may "make the *witness's meaning* clear." (Emphasis supplied.) The idea is to help the witness to express himself more clearly and to better communicate his actual meaning. To this end the lawyer may only "suggest" wording. In the end, it is the witness who decides if the wording suggested does a better job of expressing what the witness is trying to communicate.

This was the first question addressed by the D.C. Bar Association in Opinion 79. Its answer to this question is worth quoting here for its substance and eloquence:

> [T]he fact that the particular words in which testimony, whether written or oral, is cast originated with a lawyer rather than the witness whose testimony it is has no significance so long as the substance of that testimony is not, so far as the lawyer knows or ought to know, false or misleading. If the particular words suggested by the lawyer, even though not literally false, are calculated to convey

a misleading impression, this would be equally impermissible from the ethical point of view. Herein, indeed, lies the principal hazard (leaving aside outright subornation of perjury) in a lawyer's suggesting particular forms of language to a witness to instead of leaving the witness to articulate his or her thought wholly without prompting: there may be differences in nuance among variant phrasings of the same substantive point, which are so significant as to make one version misleading while another is not. Yet it is obvious that by the same token, choice of words may also improve the clarity and precision of a statement even subtle changes of shading may as readily improve testimony as impair it. The fact that a lawyer suggests particular language to a witness means only that the lawyer may be affecting the testimony as respects its clarity and accuracy; and not necessarily that the effect is to debase rather than improve the testimony in these respects. It is not, we think, a matter of undue difficulty for a reasonably competent and conscientious lawyer to discern the line of impermissibility, where truth shades into untruth, and to refrain from crossing it.

We note that in the particular circumstances giving rise to this inquiry, there is some built-in assurance against hazards of this kind, to be found in the fact that the testimony will be subject to cross-examination—which, of course, may properly probe the extent of the lawyer's participation in the actual drafting of the direct testimony, including whether language used by the witness originated with the lawyer rather than the witness, what other language was considered but rejected, the nuances involved, and so forth. The risk of distortion, whether intentional or unintentional, is obviously greater where (as will often be the case with affidavits or written answers to interrogatories) the testimony is not going to be subject to cross-examination. Nonetheless, even in that context there should be no undue difficulty for a lawyer in avoiding such distortion.

This is entirely consistent with the Restatement. It is appropriate for a lawyer to suggest wording that aids in the "clarity and accuracy" of the witness's meaning, but it is unethical to mislead. In *Ibarra v. Baker*,[13] two attorneys were sanctioned for improper witness coaching of police officers in a police misconduct case. The appellate court affirmed the sanctions based on evidence that the lawyers, through an expert witness, had introduced two defense terms that the officers had not previously used—"retaliation" and "high crime area." In so holding the court noted:

---

13. Ibarra v. Baker, 338 F. App'x 457, 465–66 (5th Cir. 2009).

An attorney enjoys extensive leeway in preparing a witness to testify truthfully, but the attorney crosses a line when she influences
the witness to alter testimony in a false or misleading way.[14]

There is another method of witness preparation that was found to be acceptable
in Opinion 79 that I will add here as method number ten:[15]

## 10. A lawyer may suggest the inclusion in a witness's testimony of information not initially obtained from the witness.

Note that this is different from asking the witness to reconsider what he has told
you in light of other testimony or evidence. This is suggesting something that has
not come up in the witness's recounting of his relevant knowledge. It may be a fact
or topic that the lawyer would expect the witness to have knowledge of because of
his relationship to the case. The witness may have forgotten or does not grasp the
possible relevance of the fact. Again, every witness needs help recollecting, as long
as the lawyer does not simply tell him what to say.

This is what Opinion 79 says about suggesting information not initially provided by the witness:

> [I]t appears to us that the governing consideration for ethical pur-
> poses is whether the substance of the testimony is something the
> witness can truthfully and properly testify to. If he or she is willing
> and (as respects his or her state of knowledge) able honestly so
> to testify, the fact that the inclusion of a particular point of sub-
> stance was initially suggested by the lawyer rather than the witness
> seems to us wholly without significance. There are two principal
> hazards here. One hazard is the possibility of undue suggestion:
> that is, the risk that the witness may thoughtlessly adopt testimony
> offered by the lawyer simply because it is so offered, without con-
> sidering whether it is testimony that he or she may appropriately
> give under oath. The other hazard is the possibility of a sugges-
> tion or implication in the witness's resulting testimony that the
> witness is testifying on a particular matter of his own knowledge
> when this is not in fact the case. For reasons explained above, these
> hazards are likely to be somewhat less serious in a case like the
> one giving rise to the present inquiry, where cross-examination
> can inquire into the source of the testimony, and test its truth and
> genuineness.

---

14. *Id.* at 465.
15. The Restatement does not state that its listing of permissible methods is exclusive, nor does it number them.
    Though this "tenth method" is not identified in the Restatement, it is consistent with method 3 (revealing
    other testimony or evidence).

*RTC v. Bright*,[16] is a very interesting case involving two former savings and loan executives named Bum and Boots. The appellants were two lawyers who had been disbarred from the trial court, and their law firm disqualified, because they had asked a witness to consider adding material to her affidavit that she had not provided herself in the interview. When she initially resisted, the lawyers explained their understanding of events and tried to persuade her to change her affidavit. The witness refused the changes and later described the encounter to lawyers for the defendants. In the lawyers' appeal, the circuit court reversed and made this distinction:

> It is one thing to ask a witness to swear to facts which are knowingly false. It is another thing, in an arms-length interview with a witness, for an attorney *to attempt to persuade her, even aggressively, that her initial version of a certain fact situation is not complete or accurate.*[17]

The guiding principle, as always, is obtaining truthful testimony based on the witness's personal knowledge or opinions. To ensure that happens and to avoid the hazards discussed in Opinion 79 the lawyer needs to politely challenge the witness throughout the preparation session. An effective technique is to interject by asking if the witness is "comfortable" in testifying in a particular way. The lawyer then needs to use her skills in evaluating the witness's demeanor and candor in responding to the lawyer's suggestions.

# CONDUCT THAT IS UNETHICAL IN WITNESS PREPARATION

## Do Not Facilitate or Condone False Testimony

Every trial lawyer knows that telling a witness to lie is not only unethical; it is also a crime. Title 18 U.S.C. § 1622 outlaws procuring or inducing another to commit perjury: "Whoever procures another to commit any perjury is guilty of subornation of perjury, and shall be fined under this title or imprisoned for not more than five years, or both." The crime consists of two elements: (1) an act of perjury committed by another (2) induced or procured by the defendant. Subornation is only infrequently prosecuted, probably because of the ease with which it can

---

16. RTC v. Bright, 6 F.3d 336 (5th Cir. 1993).
17. *Id.* at 341 (emphasis added).

now be prosecuted as an obstruction of justice under either 18 U.S.C. § 1503 or § 1512,[18] which, unlike § 1622, do not require suborner success as a prerequisite to prosecution.

The Model Rules cover false testimony or evidence extensively.

Rule 1.2(d) prohibits a lawyer from counseling or assisting a client in an act the lawyer knows to be fraudulent or criminal. Rule 1.0(f) defines "'[k]nowingly,' 'known,' or 'knows'" as "actual knowledge of the fact in question." However, "[a] person's knowledge may be inferred from the circumstances."[19] *Id.*

Rule 3.3(a)(3) prohibits a lawyer from knowingly offering false evidence. This rule further provides that if the lawyer later learns that information provided to the tribunal is false, she must take "reasonable remedial" measures which may include, if necessary, telling the court. If a lawyer does not "know" that evidence is false but "reasonably believes" it to be false, she may still present it to the court,[20] but she is not required to do so.[21] Comment 8 concludes by stating that "although a lawyer should resolve doubts about the veracity of testimony or other evidence in favor of the client, the lawyer cannot ignore an obvious falsehood." Thus, the ultimate test seems to be obviousness.

Rule 3.4(b) prohibits a lawyer from falsifying evidence or counseling or assisting a witness to testify falsely. Comment 1 to this rule includes the acknowledgment that our adversary system contemplates that evidence in a case will be "marshalled competitively" and that fair competition prohibits improperly influencing witnesses.

Rule 8.4(c) prohibits a lawyer from engaging in "conduct involving dishonesty, fraud, deceit or misrepresentation."

Finally, Rule 8.4(d) prohibits conduct that is prejudicial to the administration of justice.

Where does this leave a lawyer who does not have actual knowledge that a fact is false but reasonably believes it to be false? May she elicit that in a witness's testimony? The comment to Rule 3.3(a)(3) suggests the answer is "yes." But, considering the circumstances that led the lawyer to her reasonable belief that the fact is false, do those same circumstances support an inference that the lawyer had actual knowledge? May the lawyer resolve her doubt in favor of her client, or does her reasonable belief require further investigation? Does it depend on what a judge or ethics hearing referee believes to be an "obvious falsehood"? The careful lawyer

---

18. 18 U.S.C. § 1503 ("whoever . . . *endeavors* to influence, obstruct, or impede the due administration of justice . . .") (emphasis added); § 1512 (b) ("whoever . . . corruptly persuades another person, or attempts to do so . . . with intent to influence . . . the testimony of any person in an official proceeding . . . ").

19. "Reasonable belief" or "reasonably believes" when used in reference to a lawyer denotes that the lawyer believes the matter in question and that the circumstances are such that the belief is reasonable. MODEL RULES OF PROF'L CONDUCT R. 1.0(i) (2008).

20. MODEL RULES OF PROF'L CONDUCT R. 3.3 cmt. 8 (2008).

21. MODEL RULES OF PROF'L CONDUCT R. 3.3 cmt. 9 (2008). However, cmt. 9 makes clear that an exception exists in criminal cases where the lawyer may not refuse to offer the testimony of a client that the lawyer reasonably believes to be false. "Unless the lawyer knows the testimony will be false, the lawyer must honor the client's decision to testify."

who reasonably believes that proposed testimony or other evidence is false should conduct further investigation. If, after further investigation, the lawyer continues in the reasonable belief that the information is false, she should decline to offer it in evidence. If the false information is urged by the client and the client persists, the lawyer should consider withdrawal.[22]

## Do Not Obstruct Another Party's Access to Evidence

Under Model Rule 3.4(a) a lawyer shall not obstruct another party's access to the evidence and may not counsel or assist another person to obstruct access. This issue most often comes up in the context of alleged prosecutorial misconduct.[23] The American College of Trial Lawyers in its Code of Pretrial and Trial Conduct provides that "[a] lawyer should not obstruct another party's access to a nonparty fact witness or induce a nonparty fact witness to evade or ignore process."[24] The Code of Pretrial and Trial Conduct of the American College of Trial Lawyers has an entire section on access to fact witnesses and evidence, and it provides that a lawyer should never tell a fact witness to hide herself or leave the jurisdiction in order to avoid testifying. This Code also takes the position that, although a lawyer should not tell a fact witness not to cooperate with opposing counsel, she may tell the witness that he has no legal duty to talk with opposing counsel unless compelled by a subpoena or court order.

Model Rule 3.4(f) prohibits a lawyer from asking a person other than a client to refrain from voluntarily giving relevant information to another party unless:

1. The person is a relative or an employee or other agent of a client; and
2. The lawyer reasonably believes that the person's interests will not be adversely affected by refraining from giving such information.

Asking a witness to take a vacation during trial is one way to deny access to the other side; another way is to tell them to forget or to "dummy up." Either way, it is forbidden.[25] Advising a witness to falsely claim a lack of memory can even lead to a perjury prosecution. In *United States v. Barnhart*,[26] the court affirmed a perjury conviction where the defendant had told investigators that he had a "real bad memory" and had been told by a friend to "get dumb."

---

22. Model Rules of Prof'l Conduct R. 1.16(b)(2) provides that a lawyer may withdraw if the client persists in a course of action that the lawyer reasonably believes is fraudulent.
23. *See, e.g.*, Bennett L. Gershman, *Witness Coaching by Prosecutors*, 23 Cardozo L. Rev. 829 (2002), http://digitalcommons.pace.edu/lawfaculty/126/.
24. The Code of Pretrial and Trial Conduct may be found at http://www.vawd.uscourts.gov/media/3143/pretrial_and_trial_conduct.pdf.
25. *See* Christopher T. Lutz, *Fudging and Forgetting*, Litig. 10, 11 (Spring 1993).
26. United States v. Barnhart, 889 F.2d 1374, 1376 (5th Cir. 1989).

# RESPONSIBILITIES REGARDING NON-LAWYER ASSISTANCE

Model Rule 5.3 requires lawyers using outside consultants to make reasonable efforts to ensure that the person's conduct is compatible with the professional obligations of the lawyer. In other words, the trial lawyer cannot use a witness consultant or another witness to coach the witness in ways the lawyer cannot. The attorneys in the *Ibarra* case failed to heed this admonition.

# CONCLUSION: "TAMPERPROOF" YOUR WITNESS

Ethically, there is a right way and a wrong way to prepare a witness, and the trial lawyer needs to know the rules. Timidity grows out of a lack of understanding, and the trial lawyer cannot be timid in preparing a witness to testify (or, for that matter, anything else). She has an ethical obligation to advocate for her client when she meets with the witness. The witness expects that, the client deserves it, and the ethical rules permit, if not mandate, it.

Fortunately, there is a safe harbor. It's called the truth. By reminding the witness to tell the truth, and by using her skills in evaluating the witness and his ability to convey the truth, the lawyer can effectively prepare the witness to give helpful testimony in a manner that serves her client's interest.

# PART II

# Beyond the Basics

## CHAPTER 3

# "Framing" the Case

## Preparing the Witness for Her Role in the Picture

### *W. Scott O'Connell*

## OVERVIEW

Trials involving commercial disputes require the distillation of complex relationships and associated obligations into a comprehensible, compelling, and persuasive trial narrative. Just as brevity is the soul of wit,[1] simplification is the soul of a trial. "Keeping it simple stupid" is the great struggle in every case. Usually there is more information than a juror can process. Sticking to what information persuades is essential.

Law school prepares attorneys for many things. Thinking like an average juror is not among them. Understanding how jurors will evaluate the facts and legal issues in your case is mission critical information. Framing facts and legal issues properly is essential for success. Knowing the frames that will persuade a jury and those that won't may determine whether you win or lose.

These frames are built and supported, in part, by *effective* witness testimony. As a younger attorney, I thought *effective* witness preparation was simply *thorough* preparation. Over time, however, tying preparation to case frames and impactful themes has proven to be the difference-maker in witness performance. Witnesses simply do better on direct and cross-examination when they understand the frames

---

1. *Hamlet*, Act II, Scene 2, 86–92.

of the case and the themes that support them. Quantity of information is replaced by quality.

This chapter examines effective strategies for determining impactful case frames and associated witness preparation to maximize the persuasive benefits from such frames.

# IDENTIFYING WHAT YOU DON'T KNOW

Thinking critically at all times about proving the elements of a case is what trial lawyers do. Too often, smart attorneys can become enamored with facts or issues that are simply too dense, complex, or inaccessible for typical jurors. In every case, there are limits on what one can expect the jury to consider, evaluate, process, and decide. Understanding these limits is essential for effective witness preparation. Jury research helps define those limits. It is dangerous to assume to know how a jury will process facts and issues. Observing that process through a focus group of prospective jurors—a surrogate jury—takes away the mystery and helps the trial team focus on the presentation of the case. Success starts by knowing what you don't know.

# LEARNING WHAT YOU DON'T KNOW

In complex commercial cases, it is often essential to test facts and issues through a jury research exercise. Focus group research with mock juries is an invaluable tool. There is simply no substitute for getting real reactions from a surrogate representative jury to the facts, witnesses, evidence, demonstratives, and arguments. Discovering jury biases, attitudes, and expectations about the case, the parties, the claims, and the evidence informs on the packaging and presentation of the case.

All jurors have underlying biases, attitudes, and expectations. Some are so strongly held or pernicious that there may be a basis to challenge the seating of the prospective jurors. Others are less so but may become important drivers during the deliberation process. These biases, attitudes, and expectations are important to understand because they often influence in material ways whether a representative juror will accept your theory of the case. The ability to persuade is informed by these biases, attitudes, and expectations. This is often the space in which tough cases are won or lost. These are also issues on which witnesses must be prepared.

Putting your case to a focus group of surrogate jurors helps identify the biases, attitudes, and expectations of jurors. That information informs what information you must provide as part of your burden of persuasion.

A baseline inquiry that informs on all presentation decisions is how the surrogate panel perceives your client. What juror biases and expectations need to be addressed in the presentation of the case about your client and the products or services it provides? If you are defending a financial services company in claims arising from a consumer transaction, for example, it is helpful to know what level of engagement and interaction jurors believe is necessary of the company to have acted reasonably. Answers to this may inform how much you address the atmospherics of the company's relationship with consumers as opposed to the actual conduct at issue. Knowing the starting point of juror attitudes informs on how long a journey the burden of persuasion may be. It also informs on what themes are winners, and on those that are not.

Because cases are presented largely through witness testimony, all of this discovered information informs on witness preparation. The preparation process is where much of the lessons learned through jury research needs to be put to work. Witnesses need to know the boundaries of the frame—what information is impactful and what is not. All too often, the wealth of information learned through these valuable processes is not effectively utilized to help witnesses perform optimally.

## Discovering What Jurors Want to Know

Focus group reaction to your facts, theories, evidence, and witnesses is by itself invaluable. But equally important is learning from the mock panel what they needed to hear, see, and understand to be persuaded. Pushing the mock jury from mere reaction about your case to active thinking about what may have helped in the persuasion process often yields powerful insights. Asking jurors about what was missing from the presentation helps identify the evidence and witnesses that may help persuade. The absence of gap-filling evidence or information that jurors really want to hear indicates that the trial team needs to take on and inoculate the omission. In either circumstance, knowledge of this important juror feedback strengthens the case presentation.

When pushing these jurors for what impressed them or what was missing, listen carefully to what they say. Their insights may become the most important themes to press at trial. Comments such as "I did not believe a word he said" may drive a thematic focus on credibility; "Her lack of attention caused the issue" may warrant a thematic focus on carelessness; "It was his job to get this done right" may drive a theme of accountability. All of these statements are meaningful windows into a juror's thought process. Building a trial narrative solicitous of these themes may be the difference-maker in a verdict for or against your client.

Rigorous application of the jury research helps to ensure that all facts and issues are reviewed through the proper framework. This information obtained from the jury research should impact all decisions about the case. Every exhibit, witness, demonstrative, and argument should be evaluated for its ability to meet the bias, attitude, and expectation identified. Through consistent review of the case through the lens of the jury research, the trial team can focus its themes and theories and deliver consistent and powerful messaging to meet its burden of persuasion.

# ROUNDTABLE THE CASE: AN ALTERNATIVE TO JURY FOCUS GROUPS

Many cases simply cannot justify the investment associated with jury focus groups. When that is the case, convening a roundtable of firm colleagues to present and test themes, testimony, and evidence is often a useful alternative. Though not the same as involving jurors from the likely demographic pool, having colleagues participate in such an exercise provides independent review and assessment. Again, it is common for the trial team to become too close to the case, which can cloud objective assessment and informed risk analysis. Independent views can help the trial team to remain grounded and focused on the strengths of the case and to be well prepared for the weaknesses.

In a firm-based roundtable exercise, it is essential to promote an environment of candor. Rigorous honesty is essential for the exercise to yield useful information. Assembling a group that feels constrained to simply affirm the trial team's choices is pointless. Assigning one or more colleagues to actively question and closely analyze aspects of the theory of the case, witness testimony, and evidence may help expose weaknesses and the strategies to deal with them. In the end, it is essential that the case be appropriately battle-tested through this exercise. Neither the client nor the trial team benefit if the exercise lacks rigor and thoughtful analysis.

# USING WHAT YOU LEARN TO FRAME THE CASE

In complex cases, the trial team must provide the jury with a frame through which to organize, analyze, and weigh the evidence. The frame serves as a lens through which you want the jury to evaluate and judge the case. It helps jurors focus on what is important. The testimony and evidence within the frame is—according to the focus group or roundtable research—necessary and persuasive.

The frame encompasses the theory of the case as well as the supporting evidence and testimony. For example, in a typical negligence case, the defense may focus on the plaintiff's contributory negligence or comparative fault as its theory of non-liability. The resulting frame might be "plaintiff's actions caused the damages claimed in the case." The frame includes all of the evidence and testimony about the plaintiff's actions and their causal link to damages. As a matter of the trial presentation, the information within the frame becomes the focus of the information presented. Where possible, the supporting information is grouped together, emphasized through appropriate repetition and bolstered by demonstrative aids or graphics. The matters outside the frame—things that clutter or distract from focus on the impactful information—are screened out or de-emphasized to the maximum extent possible.

A useful trial preparation exercise is to identify all of the information on which the trial team wants to focus to animate the thematic frame. This will include evidence and sponsoring witnesses, anticipated trial testimony, anticipated cross-examination, admissions of a party opponent, answers to requests to admit, and interrogatory responses. Often, I capture this information quite literally inside a drawing of a frame. Items to be de-emphasized or jettisoned completely are captured around the outside of the frame. For me, the resulting work product is a useful tool to organize examinations, to prepare witnesses, to choreograph evidence and to create trial graphics designed to maximize the persuasive impact of the thematic frame.

## PREPARING WITNESSES USING THE FRAME

As trial counsel, your overarching job is to tell a compelling and persuasive story. Aristotle taught that the essential aspects of persuasive argument are ethos (character and credibility), pathos (emotional appeal), and logos (logic and reason). I add to this essential list another important consideration: impressio (impression on the jury). Because there are practical limits on the quantity of information a jury can process, focusing on the most impactful is very important. Preparing witnesses to address and emphasize these impactful areas is where the proverbial rubber meets the road. Effective witness testimony is essential to a compelling and persuasive story.

The thematic frame helps organize the information that is impactful. For that reason, it is a very useful tool for witness preparation. Focusing on the testimony that a witness will offer in support of the frame is time well spent. Often testimony is offered simply on a chronology with the belief that it will help the jury process the sequence of events. Sometimes such an approach is unavoidable. Other times, once the chronology has been established through other witnesses—and underscored by appropriate trial graphics—presentation of evidence based on the thematic frames is more impactful. Presenting the facts supporting the thematic frame in succession often adds to the impact of the evidence. This impact can be lost when the chronology of the underlying facts requires that you switch between and among different thematic frames. Staying concentrated on a specific thematic frame enables the jury to process this information as connected and additive to each other. Experience teaches that this type of concentration deepens the jury's understanding and grows exponentially the persuasive impact of the information.

# PUTTING THESE PRINCIPLES TO WORK: SOME PRACTICAL EXAMPLES

## Case Example 1: Frames in Defense of a Theft of Trade Secret Claim

A foreign software company sues a former employee located in the United States who joins a rival software company. The former employee is not bound by any restrictive covenants with the foreign company. Nevertheless, the foreign company sues the former employee claiming that he was privy to certain trade secrets and that such secrets would inevitably be disclosed to the new employer and rival company.

Jury testing revealed skepticism as to whether there were legitimate trade secrets in dispute and, if so, whether the former employee knew the information at a level that would jeopardize any value if the high-level information was revealed. Among other things, the claimed trade secret was a proposed functionality to be developed in the software as part of a business strategy. The new functionality was announced to the market. The former employee has no responsibility for developing the new functionality and did not have access to the code that would run this functionality. The former employee did have knowledge about expected delivery dates for aspects of the functionality based on business planning discussions. The evidence was contradictory on whether these dates were treated as a trade secret and maintained as confidential.

There was juror concern generally that a former employee could cause damage by disclosing confidential information to a rival. Further, some jurors were focused on the circumstances under which the former employee was hired away by the new rival.

From this research, undermining the validity of the trade secret claim was among the most persuasive arguments. A resulting frame for the defense was "No trade secret; No case." This frame contained all of the evidence and testimony that undermined the claimed trade secret. This included, among other things, testimony about the availability of the claimed secret information in the marketplace, the lack of novelty in the alleged secret, the lack of special know-how to make the alleged secret more lucrative to the plaintiff, and the lack of efforts and diligence to protect the alleged secret from disclosure.

Preparation of each witness focused on the information she or he had on these topics. The preparation was less of a question and answer session and more of a discussion on the supporting information. Through this discussion format, we were able to cover areas of emphasis and likely cross-examination. By the end of the discussion, the witness had laser focus on the areas of strength in the case, clear understanding of the areas of cross-examination, and a strategy for emphasizing that no trade secret existed.

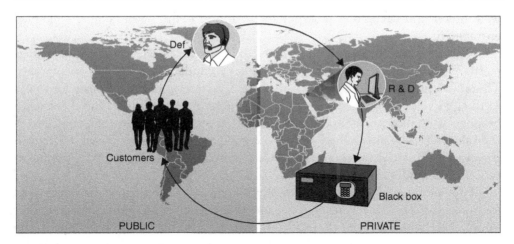

Figure 3.1    The witness testimony focused on the fact that the defendant never had access to information that could be considered confidential.

This information in the frame on which preparation focused included: (1) the software enhancement was announced to the market; (2) the deadline for the enhancement delivery was not confidential; and (3) the former employee had no access to the software being developed abroad by the coding team. Trial graphics underscored the fact that all software coding was being done by a research and development team abroad and that the former employee had no access to this information, as it was developed in the company's self-described "black box" (see Figure 3.1).

## Case Example 2: Frames in an Unfair and Deceptive Trade Practices Claim

A company with a chain of beauty salons sued a hair-care products company for improper termination of a distribution contract. Under the distribution agreement, the products were permitted for resale to customers through salons only that agreed to maintain certain requirements. The distribution of the product through this exclusive high-end channel helped build and sustain the "brand." The hair-care company, having concerns about whether the salons were complying with this requirement, sent a purchaser into the salons to try and purchase for resale on the gray market. The purchaser made clear that this was the purpose of the bulk purchase—to see if the salon would violate its distribution agreement. Notwithstanding this disclosure, the salon company sold the product to the purchaser. Because of this improper sale, the hair-care company terminated the distribution agreement with the salon company. The salon company sued claiming that misrepresentation of the purchaser concerning the intended resale of the product in the gray market were unfair and deceptive trade practices. In effect, the salon company claimed entrapment.

Research revealed that jurors were indeed bothered by the allegation of entrapment. Without more, the hair-care company's conduct was viewed unfavorably. There was, however, more to the story. The diversion of product from salons sales to the gray market was a major scourge on the hair-care industry. These exclusive products were showing up in discount chain stores at a lower cost than available in the salons. This reality caused salons to complain and caused material dilution to the brand. This additional context made a material impression on how the jurors processed the information.

The resulting frame was not simply that the salon company was terminated for breaching a contract; rather, it became that the salon company damaged other salons and the product brand through improper sales that had to be stopped. The evidence within this frame included brand protection requirements within the contract, information provided to salons about the harms of diversion, advertising in trade publications about the harms of diversion and the need to report it, and the product coding developed for each unit in order to track sales and stop diversion.

Whereas the salon company wanted to focus its case simply on the claimed entrapment to make an improper sale, the hair-care company needed to focus on the overarching problems of product diversion, the many harms resulting from such unauthorized sales, and the need to "police" the market for the benefit of all other salons as well as customers of the product.

Preparation of the corporate officer in charge of the contract focused on the distribution agreement, the restrictions on permitted sales, and the salon attributes necessary to remain an authorized seller. This representative discussed the consistency of this provision in all similar agreements and the benefits to salons for such uniformity. Preparation of the account representative focused on the education provided to all salons on the problem of product diversion and the ways in which the hair-care company was working to eliminate this activity. Preparation of the product security professionals focused on the coding applied to all units so that sales in the gray market could be traced back to point of diversion. The preparation of the security professionals also focused on the anonymous tip received about the improper sales of the salon company and the decision to send a purchaser to the salon company to see if it would engage in an improper sale.

This frame was punctuated with trial graphics taken from trade publications about the industrywide problem of product diversion. These visuals underscored the frame that efforts to locate and stop product diversion were necessary and the conduct at issue was not unfair or deceptive. This fulsome context of the diversion issue, the salon company's knowledge of this issue, and the specific contractual obligations swamped the claim of entrapment.

## Case Example 3: Frames in Breach of Fiduciary Duty Case

Minority shareholders in a closely held business sued the majority shareholders to try and seize control of the business. The minority had provided loans to the business and was upset that the majority refused to pursue a certain transaction and failed to provide working capital to grow the business and repay the loans. Rather than comply with the requirements of the operating agreement, the minority engaged in multiple examples of self-help to try and seize functional control of the business. The minority shareholders ultimately claimed that the loans were in default. This default became the basis for the legal proceedings and the effort to secure legal control of the company.

Although the minority engendered some sympathy because of the loaned money at risk, many were bothered by the minority owners' complete disregard for the corporate formalities and terms of the operating agreement. The minority misrepresented that it had certain authority and approvals to act on behalf of the closely held business. Finally, the actions to put the loans in default, though permissible under the applicable notes, were viewed as not "partner like" or not "fair" given the totality of the circumstance.

The resulting frame for this case became "joint ventures have joint duties, which the minority owners failed to fulfill." Within the frame were all of the minority shareholder actions that undermined the closely held business or that elevated the minority owners' interests over the business. In addition to highlighting on the unauthorized actions of the minority owners to act on behalf of the corporation, the evidence focused on otherwise legitimate actions that were in the minority owners' interest but were otherwise harmful to the closely held business.

The witness preparation focused on the closely held business as being a joint undertaking with obligations on the majority and the minority. The witnesses described the roles and responsibilities of each owner as detailed in the operating agreement. The witnesses then addressed all of the minority's actions that violated the operating agreement and that interfered with the success of the business. The concept of joint obligations and duties became a compelling frame through which all of the evidence was presented.

## Case Example 4: Contribution from an Alleged Joint Tortfeasor in Wrongful Death Case

The estate of a deceased worker killed while unloading a flatbed trailer of heavy equipment brought a wrongful death suit against the transportation company and the equipment manufacturer who packed the open trailer for shipment. The estate claimed that both companies were negligent: the manufacturer for the way the trailer was packed and the transportation company for the way it was unpacked.

The transportation company settled with the estate and sought indemnification and contribution from the manufacturer.

Although not a complex commercial case, this example demonstrates how dramatically the trial strategy of a case can change when parties settle out. When the estate was pursuing claims against both companies, the ability to have the two defendants go "hammer and tong" against each other was constrained. Such conduct would only add to the estate's recovery in the matter. Accordingly, much of the case focused on the comparative fault/contributory negligence of the decedent.

Once the claims with the estate concluded, the dynamics between the two remaining defendants changed in material ways. The frame of the case changed from a focus on the decedent and his conduct to "It was the driver's fault." The evidence in the frame focused on all the things the driver did and did not do that were the actual and proximate cause of the injury and death.

Witness preparation focused on what the driver did, and should have done, onsite at the time of the accident. Whereas the transportation company tried to focus on the alleged improper loading of the trailer, the manufacturing company was able to highlight all of the things that could have stopped the accident from occurring if the driver was properly trained and paying attention. The manufacturing company witnesses were able to highlight the ways in which loads shift during transport and the actions that the driver needs to take in order to ensure that the load is transported safely. The witnesses were effectively able to detail scores of examples along the shipping route where the driver had inspection responsibilities in order to maintain a safe load. In response to most of the questions asked, these manufacturing company witnesses were able to punctuate their answer with an omission by the driver to identify an issue sometime before unloading. In the end, efforts to put the liability back on the shipper were ineffective. The trier of fact concluded, in fact, that is was the driver's fault.

# CONCLUSION

The thematic frame helps jurors analyze and process the case you want them to decide. By sticking to the issues that are within the frame, you eliminate clutter and bring real focus. Using this frame to prepare witnesses enables them tell a better, more compelling story. In trial work, compelling narratives are persuasive. Empower your witnesses to be more compelling and persuasive; set the frame for your case and prepare your witnesses for his or her role in the frame.

## CHAPTER 4

# Fear and Arrogance

## Witness Preparation of the Meek and the Mendacious

### *Honorable David T. Schultz*

I tried my first jury trial—a two-week, multiple fatality, railroad grade crossing accident case—as a third-year lawyer in the state Attorney General's office. I vividly remember opening the doors to the courtroom in rural Minnesota, terror-stricken as the realization raced across my brain: "[Expletive], I do not even know which table I am supposed to sit at." I dealt with my fear in the typical lawyerly fashion—I swallowed it and walked into the courtroom.

Several days into the trial I watched as my main witness—a state railroad crossing engineer—did the unthinkable on cross-examination. After each answer he looked over at me from the witness box, shrugged his shoulders and raised his eyebrows, as if to say to me "Was that answer okay?" True story. Miraculously, the jury returned a verdict for my client, not on negligence but on causation.

It is not that I failed to prepare my witness. I did. I prepared him on what to do and what not to do; we reviewed the engineering studies for the crossing at issue; we went over his testimony several times. Of course, I did not specifically tell my witness please do not look at me and shrug *after every answer*. Nope; I did not specifically address that behavior.

But more fundamentally, I had not addressed the underlying cause of my witness's inexplicably bad behavior on the stand—his fear. Just as I had been seized with fear when I opened the courtroom doors, my witness had been seized with fear from the moment he learned he was going to testify at trial. But unlike me, who wanted to be there, my witness desperately wanted to be anywhere else but in that courtroom. And I, novice as I was, did not even recognize, much less address, his fear until it was horrifyingly too late.

As I have reflected upon that experience in the years since, I have come to believe that recognizing and directly addressing fear, and its twin, arrogance, are critical first steps in the proper preparation of any witness. Though all lawyers know this at an intuitive level, many fail to address it directly or, if they do address it, they do so with pat responses that do little to address the problem and indeed, may worsen it. This chapter attempts to deal with fear and to offer simple, practical techniques for helping your witnesses conquer—or at least survive—their fear.

# THE PROBLEM OF FEAR

Fear produces one of three responses—fight, flight, or paralysis. Left unaddressed each of these reactions can have devastating consequences at trial or in a deposition. The witness whose response to fear is to fight can be combative, arrogant, or simply unlikeable. A witness whose instinct is flight will engage in any number of destructive behaviors, from the unconscious shrugging of shoulders (the flight to his lawyer's protection) to the shrinking posture and downcast eyes (the flight away from the opposing counsel, the judge, the jury). The witness who suffers paralysis—the deer in the headlights—will give the opposing counsel whatever he or she wants just to be done with the ordeal.

But fear is not all bad. Properly harnessed, fear is a powerful motivator. To paraphrase Gordon Gekko "Fear is good. Fear works. Fear clarifies, cuts through and captures the essence of the will to survive." At the end of witness preparation the properly prepared witness will master his flight response or even his paralysis. You can—indeed must—instill a fight response. But it must be the proper fight response—one that teaches the witness to fight for the truth—his truth—and his reputation, well-being, and the material issues in the case. It is important to recognize that though the goal is to win, a win is not making the other lawyer look stupid or to launch zingers at them, but to tell one's story in a truthful, credible, straightforward manner.

# UNCOVERING THE WITNESS'S FEAR

## Get to Know Your Witness

The first step to helping your witness master his fear is to uncover it. Some authors who have addressed this topic characterize fear as simply or mainly a matter of performance anxiety—if you can get the witness comfortable with the setting and the process, he will overcome his fear of public speaking.[1] Having overcome their performance anxiety, all will be fine. This approach fails to get at issues underlying fear of public speaking which are often more intractable and which the dynamics of testifying may tap into.

I begin each witness preparation session by getting to know the person who will testify: what are her likes and dislikes; where did she grow up; what is her family situation. The lawyer needs to know the person to understand a particular reaction to the whole process of testifying in a lawsuit. For example, I represented a product failure analyst in a product liability matter. It was apparent from the moment I met him that he was cautious to the point of timidity. For the first two hours of our preparation, we talked about what he liked and disliked about his job, what was the most rewarding moment of his career, what was the least. Through this discussion it emerged that he felt guilty for not having discovered the particular failure mechanism at issue years earlier when he had tested a returned product. His testing could have uncovered the problem; but it was never interpreted that way until years later when—in hindsight—it could (and would) be understood differently. He had written up the testing in his lab notebook and now—when he was on the verge of retirement—he not only felt guilty but feared he would be fired and/or lose his retirement. That issue and those fears became the focus of a significant portion of our preparation time. At the end of this exercise, these fears and guilt had been addressed and directly assuaged. Only then was the witness able to understand and incorporate the instructions and substantive information necessary to make him an effective witness.

In another case, the company witness who had been involved in the accident that resulted in the plaintiff's husband's death came into our preparation session hostile and withdrawn. After much discussion the picture emerged of a man fearful of authority. He had grown up with an authoritarian father; more important, he worked for an abusive, short-tempered drill-sergeant-like boss. The trial process was just another opportunity for this witness to be beaten down by authority figures—the judge, the opposing counsel, even the court reporter who might yell at him to speak more clearly. Uncovering his fear of authority led us to devising techniques for taking back his dignity.

In the case of the railroad witness described earlier, our debriefing after the trial led to an important insight. The witness was not in fact a degreed engineer, though his job title implied such. He was the last of a generation of technical specialists who had come up through the ranks by learning on the job. (All of this was known, of course.) The department he worked in was now populated by degreed engineers

---

1. Studies show that a large percentage of people fear public speaking; estimates range from 8 percent to at least 38 percent. *See, e.g.,* 2015 Chapman University Survey on American Fears, https://www.chapman.edu/wilkinson/research-centers/babbie-center/survey-american-fears.aspx (last visited Aug. 26, 2017). Some authors claim that Americans fear public speaking even more than they fear death. *See, e.g.,* GLENN CROSTON, THE REAL STORY OF RISK, Ch. 8 (2012).

who had far better academic credentials than the witness. He felt inadequate at work; frequently interpreting questions from co-workers as being second-guessed. His biggest fear for the trial was that his (perceived) inadequacy would be exposed, which led him to need continual reassurance while testifying.

These examples are but a few illustrations of the centrality of getting to know your witness as a person. Investing that time at the front end of the witness preparation process will better equip you to recognize—and then deal with—the fears and insecurities that the prospect of testifying is tapping into for your witness.

## Talk about Fear Directly

Without fail—and particularly with educated professional witnesses—I will ask them directly "What is your biggest fear about testifying in this case?" (Beware the witness who sneers at the very notion that they might experience such fear—more on them later.) This tool is very powerful and affirming. First, by starting with the assumption that the witness has fear, the question communicates to the witness that fear is normal and expected; it is okay to be apprehensive or even terrified. Since admitting fear is taboo in corporate culture, failing to ask about it may confirm in the witness's mind that he or she should be embarrassed to be afraid. Left "undiagnosed," fear can interfere with information processing. It can make it difficult for the witness to focus on the more substantive aspect of preparation. And, of course, you lose the opportunity to allay fears that can be easily addressed, if known.

When I ask witnesses to identify their biggest fear about testifying, I am struck by the array of responses. Some common themes emerge however:

- I am afraid that if we lose the case I will be blamed/get fired.
- I am afraid the company will make me say things that are untrue.
- I am afraid certain embarrassing information will come out.
- I am afraid the jury/judge will not like me.
- I am afraid I will forget what I am "supposed to say."
- I am afraid the other lawyer will make me look stupid.

The list goes on, but the point is obvious. These fears are easily dispelled, but only if you talk about the fear itself. It is not enough to give the witness instructions that implicitly address the fear (e.g., "All you have to do is tell the truth") because the witness may not make the connection or may not use the tool in its most effective way.

For example, you might think that telling a witness to just "tell the truth and let the chips fall where they may" addresses his fear of being fired or fear of forgetting what they "are supposed to say," but until you address the fear itself your witness is not fully prepared to hear and understand the guidance you are giving him. Take, for example, the witness who is afraid of being fired. Consider having his or her supervisor come in to assure the witness his job is safe—completely. This will allow the witness to set aside the fear (assuming his or her supervisor is helpful and cooperative). The witness who fears being forced to lie can be assuaged by assuring him that the company only wants the truth and that you as the lawyer will not let him lie. And, of course, witnesses suffering from various forms of stage fright can be acclimated through various techniques. But, first and foremost get the fear on the table. Talk about it in a nonjudgmental manner and tell the witness you will give him tools to address/avoid the issues he fears.

## Acclimating the Witness to the Process

Much witness anxiety is simple fear of the unknown. Your witness may never have been deposed or testified at a trial before or, if they have, they may had a bad experience. Things that you take for granted are a mystery to them, including such mundane details as whether they can take a restroom break. It is important to demystify the process by explaining it in great detail. You should cover the following:

- Where to park;
- When to arrive;
- What to wear;
- What to bring or not bring and why;
- Who will be at the testimony (show them a picture if you have one);
- What the various participants' roles are and what to expect from them (this includes the court reporter, judge, and jury);
- Where they fit into the case (see Chapter 3, "Framing" the Case: Preparing the Witness for Her Role in the Picture);
- Communication techniques; and
- Any special needs they have or need to manage.

If you can, take the witness to the place she will testify—whether it is the courtroom where the trial will proceed or the conference room where they will be deposed. (This argues in favor of having your witnesses deposed at your offices rather than your opponent's. The opposite strategy is to have all witnesses deposed on the opponent's home turf, making them all less acclimated to the physical environment. On balance, I prefer to eliminate as many sources of anxiety as possible even if it may assist the opponent's witness as well.)

You must prepare your witness for the substance of his or her testimony and how best to deliver it. That particular topic, however, is beyond the scope of this chapter (see, e.g., Chapter 3).

## Empower Your Witness

Empowering your witness is a critical step in allaying his or her fear, whatever its origin. The process of empowering the witness consists of two distinct but interrelated actions. First, give the witness control over his testimony. Second, give the witness control over the opposing attorney. I give my witnesses control by reference to their oath; the witness must fully understand his job is "to tell the truth, the whole truth and nothing but the truth." Understanding this seemingly simple oath is key to empowering your witness.

- **Tell the truth.** The truth is that witnesses do not always know or remember the answer to a question. Instill in your witnesses a genuine appreciation for giving accurate testimony and letting the facts as the witness knows them speak for themselves. "I do not know" is a perfectly acceptable truthful answer when it is accurate. Many witnesses believe they have to have an answer to every question posed but do not realize that "I do not know," is an answer. The witness's obligation is to provide a truthful answer, not to provide information which he does not have. Similarly, "I do not remember," which is distinct from "I do not know" is a truthful answer. "What did Mr. CEO think of that?" "I do not know." "What did he say about it?" "I do not remember." Letting the witness understand that telling the truth means only providing an accurate answer based on what he knows and remembers relieves anxiety over believing he is responsible for providing information.

- **The whole truth.** Witnesses can and should be empowered to provide a fully responsive answer even when the opposing counsel is trying to prevent that from happening. In a deposition setting the witness should be taught how to deflect the misleading or "reptile" questions by telling the whole truth. Consider this question:

  > Q: Was not the reason your company provided information to the FDA about your medical device so that the FDA could decide whether the device is reasonably safe and effective for marketing to the public?

  This reptile question appeals to deep-seated fears in the jury—the government was hoodwinked into approving your company's dangerously unsafe medical device.

  Telling the whole truth means answering tricky or misleading questions in a fair and thoughtful manner. At a deposition—or a trial—the witness can tell the whole truth in response:

  > A: Yes, it is important and that is exactly why my company provided thousands of pages of information regarding adverse events associated with this implantable device.

  Occasionally, the lawyer sometimes will insist on a yes or no answer. Arm your witness with a very simple truth—that the question posed cannot be answered yes or no. In my experience, if the question is unfair and the witness says it cannot be answered yes or no, most judges will take the view that "You have your answer, counsel."

In short, the point of this preparation—that the witness has taken an oath to tell the whole truth—empowers the witness to take control over the unfair or misleading question without feeling he is doing something wrong. (Of course, this form of empowerment must be accompanied by a well-understood caution against volunteerism. The obligation to tell the whole truth is to tell the whole truth in response to the question that is posed and no more.)

- **And nothing but the truth.** This part of the witness's oath empowers him to avoid guesswork and speculation. The truth is what the witness knows, has observed, or, if asked, what he heard or believes. The obligation extends no further. The witness who understands that his oath in fact *requires* that he not testify to things he does not know eliminates an area of fear and confusion.

# PREPARING THE ARROGANT, FEARFUL WITNESS

Occasionally a witness presents as utterly confident and unafraid. He may appear so sure of himself that he seems downright arrogant. So much so that you worry whether he can or will take instruction from you. The first step in preparing such a witness is figuring out whether he is genuinely overly self-assured or is merely masking his fear with bravado.

In the case of the fearful, arrogant witness (as distinct from the truly arrogant or narcissistic witness) good preparation requires that you first unmask the witness's fear so that it may be addressed and conquered in the manner described earlier.

So, how does one get the witness to open up or to even recognize his own fear? I think the process requires spending even more time getting to know the witness. The preparation takes a certain amount of empathy and intuition. Often it is not what the witness says, but rather what he does not say. If you yourself are not attuned to such emotion, involve someone who is—whether it is a colleague in your firm or a trained professional. In addition, if possible, talk to the witness's co-workers or supervisors. They may have insight into the person's character and psyche that helps you identify, reorganize, and ultimately address the fear that is blocking his ability to perform well and learn his role.

One technique for drawing this person out is to simply have him tell you his story of the event at issue and listen carefully. If the person is actually fearful but covers it with arrogance, the fear will leak out. In this role the lawyer's primary skill is the ability to listen and to provide affirmation. For example, in one case I encountered a highway maintenance worker who, despite not having received education beyond the tenth grade, presented as hostile and arrogant. He disclosed at the outset of our meeting that this whole exercise was stupid and a waste of his time and that *if* he decided to testify at all, he would not need my help doing it. Perfect. I had to find common ground with this witness and find it fast. When we found that common ground—we both had worked the same unusual job during summers in high school—we stayed on that common ground just talking about shared experiences for an hour. Once I had established rapport, I made myself vulnerable by explaining why I needed his help and what I was afraid would happen to me if I did not get that help. Once I—from his perspective, the intimidating, well-educated lawyer—made myself vulnerable it gave him permission to do the same. Having broken through his arrogant façade, we could identify and address the fear that lay behind it. He was afraid everyone would think him stupid. With that on the table I was able to persuade him that he was in fact the smartest guy in the room—he was the only one who actually knew what the facts were. Armed with real confidence, the arrogance vanished, the preparation proceeded and the witness gave clear and convincing testimony.

## PREPARING THE UNAFRAID, ARROGANT WITNESS

Some witnesses are truly unafraid of testifying because they are certain they know more than anyone else. They do not need preparation because they are the smartest people in the room. True narcissism is not an act; it is a personality trait or character feature, or, in extreme cases, a personality disorder. In preparing these witnesses you cannot intimidate, cajole, threaten, or instill fear in them. It will not work. If you try, you will succeed only in making them angry and/or convincing them that listening to your advice is foolish.

Who is this ever-so-fun witness? Often he is the CEO of your client company or the expert witness *you* hired. You need to work with him in a way that allows him to take your advice without realizing it was not his own idea. In some ways, the narcissistic witness is like a toddler—headstrong, stubborn, and unwilling (really, unable) to compromise. Fortunately, one technique parents use with toddlers also works with narcissists—redirection.

As one commentator has phrased it, "the challenge with [these witnesses] is to get them to answer questions with an external perspective that they can comprehend instead of speaking from their own internal frame of reference that the world finds so annoying."[2] So the expert witness who wants to dwell on every minutia or wants to patronize the jury can be redirected to think of trying to explain his testimony to a group of ninth graders. The hell-on-wheels CEO can be redirected

---

2. Douglas L. Keene, *I'm Better Than I Need to Be!: Preparing Narcissistic Witnesses*, 20 THE JURY EXPERT: THE ART AND SCI. OF LITIG. ADVOC. 1–4 (2008).

by asking him to testify as if he is speaking to his mother or father (whichever one he loves *and* respects).

The particular strategy you employ will vary with the facts of your case and the peculiarity of your witnesses. But, one thing is consistent, *you* have to adapt to *them*. Your goal is not to convince them you were right all along; your goal is to convince them that you see the wisdom of their approach.

# CONCLUSION

Fear is a normal, human emotion. It is, in a very real sense, what keeps us alive. Paradoxically, it is also considered shameful to experience fear and it is taboo to discuss it. As lawyers preparing witnesses to testify in court or in a deposition, we are taught how to provide instruction or how to use techniques that are designed to address fear. But seldom are lawyers taught to address fear head on—to identify it explicitly and to talk about it directly. The process of engaging in that discussion will not only make your witness a better witness, but it will also make you a better advocate.

## CHAPTER 5

# Tagging In

## Working with a Professional Trial Consultant to Assist with Witness Preparation

### *Jessalyn H. Zeigler*

### *Charles G. Jarboe*

When it comes to preparing a case for trial, in appropriate cases consideration is typically made to hiring an outside trial consultant to test counsel's opening and closing remarks, trial themes, the impact of select evidence, and potential juror reactions. But trial consultants can also bring significant value to the client in assisting with witness preparation prior to depositions.

Lawyers are experts in the law; trial consultants are experts in people. When the stakes are high or a critical witness may present particular challenges, counsel should consider whether additional resources would help persuasively communicate the client's story through a deposition, which may be presented to the trier in fact through video deposition testimony whether counsel for the deponent intended such or wanted such.[1] Trial consultants typically have backgrounds in psychology, social science, or other people-oriented fields. They are trained to understand how juries react to people and information.

This chapter is designed to assist counsel in determining whether and when use of a trial consultant may benefit the client. It also explores some of the concerns that may prevent lawyers from effectively using a trial consultant and the legal issues regarding discovery of the consultant's work.

---

1. *See infra* note 12.

# WHEN SHOULD LAWYERS CONSIDER USING A TRIAL CONSULTANT FOR WITNESS PREPARATION?

Unlike the United States, where failing to fully prepare your witness for testifying at deposition or trial could be malpractice, several foreign jurisdictions bar or severely restrict witness preparation practices.[2] There are no specific rules in the United States telling lawyers how they can or should prepare a witness, including the use of a professional consultant to assist in the preparation process; there are only general rules, such as prohibiting a lawyer from assisting a witness to testify untruthfully.[3] The American Society of Trial Consultants (ASTC) has published its own Professional Code that sets forth the main objective of any trial consultant hired to assist with witness preparation—"to increase witnesses' understanding, comfort and confidence in the process of testifying for deposition or in court, and to improve witnesses' ability to truthfully present testimony in a clear and effective manner"—and lists various ways consultants can work with witnesses and lawyers to achieve this goal.[4] Trial consultants do not script answers or censor relevant but harmful answers (nor should the lawyer).[5] They review case materials provided by the lawyer and come to agreement with counsel on the scope of their services, the roles of both counsel and consultant during mock examinations, and they work with counsel to establish realistic goals and expectations for the preparations.[6] Trial consultants often set up and provide feedback in mock examinations and practice sessions, assess and address a witness's communication strengths and limitations, work to increase a witness's familiarity and comfort with the process, and otherwise identify ways to increase a witness's ability to effectively communicate the facts.[7]

The specific preparation needs vary for each witness. A corporate executive witness might require help controlling tone or body language to avoid seeming aggressive or condescending, whereas a technical professional could require help communicating facts in a way that will be understandable for jurors. Many witnesses have never testified before and need extensive practice to be able to effectively communicate facts and handle cross-examination. When should counsel proverbially reach a hand outside the ring and "tag in" a professional trial consultant to assist?[8]

---

2. Elaine Lewis, *Witness Preparation: What Is Ethical, and What Is Not*, LITIGATION (Winter 2010), at 41, 41–42.

3. The ethics rules applicable to witness preparation are the subject of Chapter 10.

4. AM. SOC'Y OF TRIAL CONSULTANTS PROF'L CODE 30–35 (2013), *at* http://www.astcweb.org/Resources /Pictures/ASTCFullCodeFINAL20131.pdf (last visited June 29, 2016).

5. *Id.* at 32.

6. *Id.*

7. *Id.*

8. To help answer this question, the authors interviewed several very accomplished trial consultants to get their perspective. The authors are grateful to Aref Jabbour, PhD, consultant, Trial Behavior Consulting, Inc.; Katherine James, MFA, founding director, ACT of Communication; and Richard Jenson, president, Jenson Research and Communications, Inc. and former president of the ASTC.

## The Stakes Are High

Some lawyers hire a trial consultant to help prepare every witness in every case,[9] but this is neither feasible nor necessary for most cases and clients. Higher-stakes litigation—such as "bet the company" cases, large-verdict-risk cases, and "test cases" that could lead to serial litigation—should trigger a deeper consideration of whether to hire a trial consultant. In these circumstances, one bad deposition or trial performance can have devastating financial consequences. Clients should be more willing to engage these additional resources if they understand the need and value added by them.

The timing of hiring a trial consultant is affected by the importance and risks of each case. The earlier a trial consultant is hired and has an opportunity to work with the lawyer, the more the consultant can assist in crafting themes and messages, and, in turn, help witnesses present those themes and messages in language they are comfortable with when the time comes for them to testify.[10] This is especially true where there are many witnesses and there is a complex or technical story to tell.[11]

## The Troubling Witness

If the company CEO or crucial witness comes across as disingenuous, evasive, condescending, or combative in deposition, the testimony could show up in the opponent's opening statements or case-in-chief.[12] If the crucial witness displays those characteristics on the witness stand, opposing counsel will likely incorporate them as a central theme in closing. Similarly, witnesses who express reluctance about having to testify, who seem uncomfortable with their role or the process, or who do not seem to grasp how their testimony fits into the overall case can be equally dangerous because of their unpredictability. Lastly, some witnesses think they know how to win the case on their own or feel pressure to take the case on their shoulders without recognizing the risk of engaging opposing counsel in a losing battle during deposition or cross-examination.[13] This latter group of witnesses requires assistance adjusting their presentation style and must understand their role is simply to tell

---

9. E-mail interview with Katherine James, founding director, ACT of Communication (June 16, 2016) (on file with authors); e-mail interview with Richard A. Jenson, president, Jenson Research and Communications Inc. (June 21, 2016) (on file with authors).

10. E-mail interview with Aref Jabbour, consultant, Trial Behavior Consulting, Inc. (June 17, 2016) (on file with authors).

11. *Id.*

12. Depositions of party opponents and their officers, directors, corporate designees, and managing agents can be used for any purpose, including in the opponent's case-in-chief. Fed. R. Civ. P. 32(a)(3). Note that "managing agent" is broadly defined by courts, and the result means that your deponent, if in a position to make decisions on behalf of the company that are within that deponent's job description, may have his videotaped deposition shown at trial (or the transcript read if it was not videotaped) in your opponent's case in chief, even though he was not a 30(b)(6) deponent and even though he is available to testify live at trial.

13. Interview with Richard A. Jenson, *supra* note 8.

their part of the story and not to advocate a case position;[14] going through several mock examinations should prepare them to testify effectively.

Troubling witnesses are those whose ability to deliver clear, factual, and effective testimony is complicated by one or more of the following obstacles:

- **Personality Obstacles.** This includes issues with demeanor, tone, presentation, or anything unrelated to the facts and unique to the witness that risks being off-putting to the jury or otherwise distracting from the facts.
- **Fact Obstacles.** These are the witnesses most involved in the action or inaction that led to the litigation. Perhaps they said, did, or failed to do something that puts the client at risk. These witnesses may need extra help learning how to "own" the facts or put them in context in a way that the jury can understand and that produces empathy.
- **Communication Obstacles.** The facts are good, but the witness, despite presenting well, struggles to reformulate complex concepts in ways that are understandable or fails to grasp the differences between deposition or trial testimony and ordinary communication.
- **Emotional or Psychological Obstacles.** Human emotions are at the core of virtually all disputes and can affect witnesses in varying ways. For example, a witness might fear his job will be at risk if he does not perform well and "help" his employer's case; this is especially true of witnesses who oversaw or had deep involvement with the specific issues being litigated. Other witnesses may be very afraid of testifying or public speaking. The list goes on. Any of these emotional components can dramatically affect the clarity and effectiveness of testimony.

Each obstacle presents its own unique challenges. Emotional or psychological obstacles may be the hardest for a lawyer to detect and address because of the complexities of human behavior and conditioning. Personality issues are often easy to detect, but witnesses struggling with personality issues usually require more time and special effort to overcome them. Whereas lawyers are better equipped to help prepare clients dealing with communication issues or challenging facts, trial consultants deal with the nuances of communication on a daily basis. They should bring both the benefits of their educational backgrounds and of having seen firsthand how jurors react to information and people. In other words, consultants are trained to understand the audience.

When it comes to identifying troubling witnesses who need professional assistance, go with your instincts. If after first meeting the witness your reaction is that he is unlikeable or cannot explain significant facts clearly, or even after a deposition does not go well, consider hiring a trial consultant to work with that witness.[15] If

---

14. Richard K. Gabriel & Julie Fenyes, *What a Trial Consultant Can Teach You—Even If You Can't Afford to Hire One*, GPSolo, Oct./Nov. 2003, at 10, 14.

15. Interview with Katherine James, *supra* note 8.

after working with the witness you have a sense the witness—fact or expert—has too much certainty or too little certainty in how to testify, consider hiring a consultant to help bring them back to center.[16]

## The "B" Witness

It is easy to recognize when a witness handles testifying poorly in practice or deposition. It is similarly easy to recognize when a witness does a great job testifying. The "A" or "A+" witness stays focused on the message, accurately and clearly communicates the facts, and handles cross-examination with poise and focus. However, there are many times when a witness was just "okay," or even forgettable. An "okay" witness performance can be damaging because it is a missed opportunity to tell the client's story and bolster the case. In all but the most straightforward cases, each witness's facts build on the others to craft a complete story. When a piece of that story is forgettable or unclear, it can weaken the overall message.

Deciding whether to enlist a trial consultant for a "B" or "B-" witness can be challenging. For one, it may be difficult to identify these witnesses before they testify. Unless it is clear from practice sessions and interviews that a witness has obstacles to overcome, you may not know until the first time the witness is in the hot seat, which usually will be their deposition. If the witness gives a middle-of-the-road performance at deposition, counsel should consider seeking professional assistance before trial, particularly if the witness is crucial to the case. If all of your "B-" and "B" witnesses become "A" witnesses through practice and professional guidance, you may greatly improve the defense of and/or settlement value of your case.[17]

## The Freshman Expert

In a significant case, we hired the top expert in a very specific and emerging field to testify at trial. The expert had written books and taught classes on the subject for years, but had never testified. During a meeting among the trial team one night—not in a practice session—one lawyer asked the expert a cross-examination type question to test a statement the expert expounded. The witness became defensive and scolded the lawyer for his tone and questioning. Despite having been warned about, and prepared to deal with, cross-examination, when questioned off the cuff, the witness all-too-quickly retreated to behaviors that would have been damaging if played out on the witness stand. Thankfully, when the witness testified several days later, he handled cross-examination with ease. But this shows the unpredictability of those who are not accustomed to testifying. To reduce or even eliminate unpredictability, experts testifying for the first time should practice and be given special attention during preparation.

---

16. *See* interview with Richard A. Jenson, *supra* note 8.
17. E-mail interview with Katherine James, *supra* note 8.

Also, the way academics or experts normally communicate to a peer group or employer differs greatly from how they must communicate to a jury or other trier of fact. Sometimes lawyers can overcome these obstacles, but if there are preparation roadblocks and time and budget allow, hiring a consultant to assist in preparing the expert for how to communicate with the jury can pay tremendous dividends.

## Using a Consultant to Prepare for Depositions

Many lawyers only think of hiring outside consultants for trial preparation. But trial consultants can effectively assist attorneys with witness preparation at the deposition stage, and help cases get resolved early and beneficially to the client.

Cases are (more often than not) won or lost in discovery. Few lawyers who have settled a lawsuit or obtained a summary judgment after or during discovery will tell you that the deposition testimony did not materially impact the parties' decision to settle or the court's ruling on a dispositive motion.

### *Use of the Managing Agent's Deposition*

Furthermore, depositions are typically videotaped and your opponent may use that videotaped deposition (or its transcript if it was not videotaped) in their case in chief. Under the Federal Rules of Civil Procedure, the deposition of a "managing agent" may be used at trial in an opponent's case in chief. The Federal Rules state:

> Deposition of Party, Agent or Designee. An adverse party may use for any purpose the deposition of a party or anyone who, when deposed, was the party's officer, director, managing agent, or designee under Rule 30(b)(6) or 31(a)(4).[18]

Many lawyers may be surprised to learn that "managing agent" is typically broadly defined not by title, but by job function. Some courts have settled on a three-pronged test that considers the following central questions:

1. Did the corporation invest the person with discretion to exercise his/her judgment, as opposed to a common employee that only takes orders and has no discretion;
2. Could the employee be depended upon to carry out the employer's directions to give testimony if the employer is in litigation; and
3. Could the person be expected to identify him/herself with the interests of the corporation rather than those of the other party?[19]

---

18. Fed. R. Civ. P. 32(a)(3).
19. Reed Paper Co. v. Procter & Gamble Distrib. Co., 144 F.R.D. 2, 4 (D. Me. 1992) (quoting Rubin v. Gen. Tire & Rubber Co., 18 F.R.D. 51, 56 (S.D.N.Y. 1955)). *See also* Fed. R. Evid. 801(d)(2) (allowing admission of statements made by employees within scope of their employment). "[A] statement of an agent or employee may be admissible against the principal . . . but a proper foundation must be made for such a statement to show it was [made] within the scope of his agency or employment." Mitroff v. Xomox Corp., 797 F.2d 271, 276 (6th Cir. 1986).

## *Use of the Unavailable Witness's Deposition*

The deposition may also be used if the witness is unavailable. Under Federal Rules of Civil Procedure Rule 32(a)(4), a party may use for any purpose the deposition of a witness whether or not a party, if the court finds:

A. That the witness is dead;

B. That the witness is more than 100 miles from the place of hearing or trial or is outside the United States, unless it appears that the witness's absence was procured by the party offering the deposition;

C. That the witness cannot attend or testify because of age, illness, infirmity or imprisonment;

D. That the party offering the deposition could not procured the witness's attendance by subpoena; or

E. On motion and notice, that exceptional circumstances make it desirable— in the interest of the justice and with due regard to the importance of live testimony in open court—to permit the deposition to be used.

This means that you can use the deposition of a witness whose deposition you have taken even if it is your own witness, if that witness is unavailable. This lends another reason to make sure that the witness is well prepared and provides an outstanding deposition.

## *How a Consultant Can Add Value to Deposition Preparation*

Introspection is a good thing. We asked several leading consultants to identify how a non-lawyer trial consultant can assist with more effective witness preparation. The responses included the following:[20]

1. Most witnesses learn better from doing, not listening. Trial consultants can focus on a witness's mannerisms and performance from a human behavioral standpoint while the lawyer is engaging in mock examination.

2. They assist in focusing upon prioritizing facts and issues that are important to jurors.

3. They assist counsel and witnesses in placing emphasis on key messages. Memorization often causes witnesses to forget components of the answers and appear rehearsed. They can effectively teach a witness how to dissect and answer questions generally, to avoid witness panic if an unforeseen cross-examination question is presented.

4. They identify witnesses' emotions toward the case and feelings about testifying, allowing them to teach coping strategies to dealing with those emotions and feelings.

---

20. *See* interview with Aref Jabbour, *supra* note 9; interview with Katherine James, *supra* note 8; interview with Richard A. Jenson, *supra* note 8.

5. They listen to the lawyers' explanations of the deposition process to the witness, assessing the witness' understanding or lack thereof, allowing them to identify additional messaging/explanations to the witness.

Whereas we lawyers get to be very familiar with the case and the facts of the case, often our witnesses are less so. Trial consultants are trained in psychology and social science with significant experience with judges and juries, and can help ensure that witnesses understand both the facts and counsel's instructions. They also assist the witnesses in making sure the answers are being well-communicated, in an understandable fashion, and without facial expressions or gestures that may negatively impact the judge or jury's perception of the witness.

# DISCOVERABILITY AND CREDIBILITY ISSUES

Some lawyers may hesitate to enlist professional help due to concerns that the opposition may discover that the witness was given advice by, and practiced their testimony with, a professional witness consultant. Should opposing counsel present that at trial, the jury could perceive the witness as coached or tainted. According to the prevailing law, however, the substance of a trial consultant's advice is highly protected opinion work product. But the fact that a trial consultant was used to prepare the witness is discoverable. Even so, there is research suggesting jurors do not care that a witness had assistance preparing their testimony; in fact, jurors may even expect it.

## The Framework: Work-Product Doctrine and Attorney-Client Privilege

The work-product doctrine is codified in Rule 26(b)(3) of the Federal Rules of Civil Procedure. Similar rules exist in most states. Rule 26(b)(3) reads, in part:

> (A) *Documents and Tangible Things.* Ordinarily, a party may not discover documents and tangible things that are prepared in anticipation of litigation or for trial by or for another party or its representative (including the other party's attorney, consultant, surety, indemnitor, insurer, or agent). But, subject to Rule 26(b)(4), those materials may be discovered if: (i) they are otherwise discoverable under Rule 26(b)(1); and (ii) the party shows that it has substantial need for the materials to prepare its case and cannot, without undue hardship, obtain their substantial equivalent by other means.

(B) *Protection Against Disclosure*. If the court orders discovery of those materials, it must protect against disclosure of the mental impressions, conclusions, opinions, or legal theories of a party's attorney or other representative concerning the litigation.[21]

The work-product doctrine evolved from the seminal United States Supreme Court case of *Hickman v. Taylor*, where the Court first established the two-tier system of protection: (1) ordinary work product—discoverable only upon a showing of substantial need and the inability to obtain the information by other means without undue hardship—and (2) opinion work product—discoverable only in extraordinary circumstances, if at all.[22]

Recognizing that lawyers and parties rely on the assistance of investigators, consultants, and other agents to prepare for trial, the doctrine extends the opinions, conclusions, and materials prepared by a party's representatives, including consultants.[23] Though the text of Rule 26(b)(3) suggests it is limited to documents and tangible material, the doctrine also protects intangible material, such as communications, that would reveal the opinions or mental impressions of the lawyer or the party's agents.[24] However, facts contained in information protected by the work-product doctrine that are otherwise discoverable are not shielded by the privilege.[25]

In contrast to the work-product doctrine, the attorney-client privilege provides absolute protection from discovery. For the attorney-client privilege to apply, the communication must be made (1) in confidence; (2) between privileged persons; and (3) for the purpose of seeking, obtaining, or providing legal advice to the

---

21. FED. R. CIV. P. 26(b)(3)(A)–(B) (emphasis in original).
22. Hickman v. Taylor, 329 U.S. 495, 511–13 (1947); *In re* Sealed Case, 676 F.2d 793, 809–10 (D.C. Cir. 1982).
23. *See* United States v. Nobles, 422 U.S. 225, 238–39 (1975); *In re* Cendant Corp. Sec. Litig., 343 F.3d 658, 662–63 (3d Cir. 2003) (hereafter *In re Cendant*); FED. R. CIV. P. 26 advisory committee's note (note to 1970 amendment of Rule 26(b)(3) providing the "subdivision . . . protect[s] against disclosure [of] the mental impressions, conclusions, opinions, or legal theories concerning the litigation of an attorney or other representative of a party"). *See also* GREGORY B. BUTLER ET AL., *Discoverability of the Jury Consultant's Work, in* 4 SUCCESSFUL PARTNERING BETWEEN INSIDE AND OUTSIDE COUNSEL § 64:34 (Apr. 2016 Update).
24. *See In re* Cendant, 343 F.3d at 662 ("Rule 26(b)(3) itself provides protection only for documents and tangible things and . . . does not bar discovery of facts a party may have learned from documents that are not themselves discoverable. Nonetheless, *Hickman v. Taylor* continues to furnish protection for work product within its definition that is not embodied in tangible form. . . . Indeed, since intangible work product includes thoughts and recollections of counsel, it is often eligible for the special protection accorded opinion work product.") (quoting 8 CHARLES ALAN WRIGHT & ARTHUR MILLER, FEDERAL PRACTICE AND PROCEDURE § 2024, at 337 (3d ed.)). However, the work product doctrine would not protect intangible work product of a party or the party's employee. *See* Pacific Gas & Elec. Co. v. United States, Nos. 04-74C, 04-75C, 2006 WL 6735871, at *4–5 (Fed. Cl. Mar. 9, 2006) (discussing *In re Cendant* and other cases).
25. U.S. *ex rel.* Fry v. Guidant Corp., No. 3:03-0842, 2009 WL 3103836, at *4 (M.D. Tenn. Sept. 24, 2009) ("the attorney work product doctrine cannot be asserted to prevent disclosure of underlying facts that are otherwise discoverable"). The same holds true for the attorney-client privilege. *See* Upjohn Co. v. United States, 449 U.S. 383, 395 (1981) ("The [attorney-client] privilege only protects disclosure of communications; it does not protect disclosure of the underlying facts by those who communicated with the attorney.").

client.[26] The privilege extends to communications made between the client and agents of the lawyer hired to assist the lawyer in rendering advice, provided that the communication was made for the purpose of obtaining the lawyer's legal advice.[27]

The work-product protection and attorney-client privilege can both be waived if the protected information is voluntarily disclosed to a third party. However, unlike the attorney-client privilege, the work-product protection is not *necessarily* waived by disclosing the information to a third party. Disclosing work product to third persons does not waive the protection unless the disclosure was made in a manner that increased the risk of the adverse party getting the information and was inconsistent with the maintenance of secrecy of the information.[28]

The rules applicable to non-testifying expert witnesses also are relevant in this context.[29] Rule 26(b)(4)(B) insulates from disclosure the facts known and opinions held by an expert retained or specially employed in anticipation of litigation or to

26. *See In re* Sealed Case, 737 F.2d 94, 98–99 (D.C. Cir. 1984) ("The privilege applies only if (1) the asserted holder of the privilege is or sought to become a client; (2) the person to whom the communication was made (a) is a member of the bar of a court or his subordinate and (b) in connection with this communication is acting as a lawyer; (3) the communication relates to a fact of which the attorney was informed (a) by his client (b) without the presence of strangers (c) for the purpose of securing primarily either (i) an opinion on law or (ii) legal services or (iii) assistance in some legal proceeding, and not (d) for the purpose of committing a crime or tort; and (4) the privilege has been (a) claimed and (b) not waived by the client.").

27. United States v. Kovel, 296 F.2d 918, 922–23 (2d Cir. 1961) (former IRS agent hired to help attorney understand complicated tax story conveyed by client to lawyer, similar to the role of an "interpreter"; therefore, communications between hired consultant and client did not destroy attorney-client privilege). Similarly, for communications between a lawyer and a hired consultant to be privileged, the communication must have been made for the purpose of obtaining, communicating, or interpreting legal advice. *See, e.g.,* United States v. Ackert, 169 F.3d 136, 139–40 (2d Cir. 1999) (holding "a communication between an attorney and a third party does not become shielded by the attorney-client privilege solely because the communication proves important to the attorney's ability to represent the client" and finding that *Kovel* had no application to that case because the lawyer was not relying on the hired consultant to interpret information given to him by the client); ECDC Envtl. v. N.Y. Marine & Gen. Ins. Co., No. 96CIV.6033(BSJ)(HBP), 1998 WL 614478, at *8 (S.D.N.Y. June 4, 1998) (holding that while work product applied to documents disclosed to hired consultants, attorney-client privilege was waived as to the documents because "[n]one of the withheld documents contain technical information from plaintiff transmitted to a consultant to 'translate' for the benefit of plaintiff's attorneys. To the contrary, most of the documents appear to relate to test data that was either not confidential or did not originate with plaintiff."); *In re* Grand Jury Subpoenas Dated March 24, 2003 Directed to (A) Grand Jury Witness Firm and (B) Grand Jury Witness, 265 F. Supp. 2d 321, 331–34 (S.D.N.Y. 2003) (communications between lawyer and public relations firm hired by lawyer for the purpose of giving and receiving advice regarding the client's legal issues were protected by attorney-client privilege and communications between witness, her lawyers, and public relations firm were protected by the work-product doctrine); Calvin Klein Trademark Trust v. Wachner, 198 F.R.D. 53 (S.D.N.Y. 2000) (communications between public relations firm and lawyers regarding how to put a positive spin on successive developments in the lawsuit not privileged because they did not contain confidential communications from client for the purpose of seeking legal advice; waiver also found because public relations firm was not "interpreting" any information to the lawyers so they could render legal advice).

28. United States v. Am. Tel. & Tel. Co., 642 F.2d 1285, 1299 (D.C. Cir. 1980) ("[W]hile the mere showing of a voluntary disclosure to a third person will generally suffice to show waiver of the attorney-client privilege, it should not suffice in itself for waiver of the work product privilege.").

29. For an extensive discussion of the attorney-client privilege, work product doctrine, and other rules relevant to the discoverability of trial consultants, *see* BUTLER ET AL., *supra* note 23; Stanley D. Davis & Thomas D. Beisecker, *Discovering Trial Consultant Work Product: A New Way to Borrow an Adversary's Wits?,* 17 AM. J. TRIAL ADVOC. 581 (1994).

prepare for trial and who is not expected to be called as a witness at trial, unless Rule 35(b) relating to examining physicians applies or the opposing party demonstrates exceptional circumstances under which it is impracticable to obtain facts or opinions on the same subject by other means.[30]

## *In re Cendant Corp.* Securities Litigation

There are few cases addressing the discoverability of a trial consultant's activities. Only one federal appellate court has addressed the issue directly, and it did so in the context of a consultant (television host Dr. Phil) hired to prepare a witness for testifying at deposition. Applying the legal framework described earlier, the Third Circuit Court of Appeals, in the case of *In re Cendant Corp. Securities Litigation*, held that the advice of a non-testifying trial consultant hired to assist a witness in preparing for testifying at deposition was highly protected opinion work product; however, certain limited facts were discoverable, including that a consultant was hired.[31]

In *In re Cendant*, Ernst & Young hired Dr. Phil, then a consulting expert in trial strategy and deposition preparation, to help prepare a former senior Ernst & Young manager for his deposition. In the former manager's deposition, opposing counsel asked:

> "Have you ever met Phil McGraw?"; "On how many occasions did you meet with Phil McGraw?"; "Did you understand Phil McGraw to be a jury consultant?"; "Did Mr. McGraw provide you with guidance in your conduct as a witness?"; "Did you rehearse any of your prospective testimony in the presence of Mr. McGraw?"; "In the course of preparing for this deposition . . . did you review any work papers?"; "Did you select the work papers that you reviewed?"; "Did you ask anyone for the opportunity to review any particular work papers?"; and "Did you ask to review work papers on any particular subject?"[32]

Counsel for Ernst & Young objected, citing the work product doctrine and attorney-client privilege.[33] The Special Discovery Master found that Dr. Phil was a non-testifying expert retained by counsel to assist in trial preparation.[34] The Special Master then held opposing counsel could inquire into whether the witness met with Dr. Phil, the date and duration of any meeting, and who was present at any meetings, but they could not ask what Dr. Phil told the witness, whether testimony was

---

30. Fed. R. Civ. P. 26(b)(4)(D)(i)–(ii).
31. *In re* Cendant, 343 F.3d at 660, 665–68.
32. *Id.* at 660.
33. *Id.*
34. *Id.*

practiced, whether the meeting was recorded, whether the witness took any notes, or whether Dr. Phil provided any documents to the witness.[35] The district court overruled the Special Master, taking the narrow view that the work-product doctrine and attorney-client privilege should be limited to lawyers and only expanded to non-lawyers in limited circumstances, and reasoning that trial consultants are hired to provide their own advice, not the advice of counsel.[36]

The Third Circuit reversed,[37] noting that the work product protection "extends beyond materials prepared by an attorney to include materials prepared by an attorney's agents and consultants"[38] and holding:

> Litigation consultants retained to aid in witness preparation may qualify as non-attorneys who are protected by the work product doctrine. Moreover, a litigation consultant's advice that is based on information disclosed during private communications between a client, his attorney, and a litigation consultant may be considered "opinion" work product which requires a showing of exceptional circumstances in order for it to be discoverable.[39]

Cendant's counsel argued the jury was entitled to know the consultant's communications with the witness, as it would be entitled to know all things that may have informed the witness's testimony and that may impact the witness's credibility.[40] The court rejected this argument, emphasizing counsel's presence during Dr. Phil's communications with the witness and relying on Ernst & Young's assertion that counsel shared its mental impressions, opinions, conclusions, and legal theories with Dr. Phil because they expected the communications to remain confidential.[41] Accordingly, the disclosure of Dr. Phil's notes or the substance of his conversations with the witness and counsel would intrude into core opinion work product, which is only discoverable under extraordinary circumstances that had not been demonstrated.[42] The court adopted the Special Master's ruling as "essentially correct" but diverged on whether the witness could be asked whether his testimony was practiced or rehearsed. Although allowing the opponent to ask this question, the court cautioned that the inquiry "should be circumscribed."[43]

Because the court found the work-product doctrine prohibited disclosure of the substance of the consultant's work, including the consultant's advice and communications, it declined to address whether the attorney-client privilege also protected

---

35. *Id.*
36. *Id.* at 660–61.
37. *Id.* at 661.
38. *Id.* at 662.
39. *Id.* at 665 (internal citations omitted).
40. *Id.* at 666.
41. *Id.* at 667.
42. *Id.* at 667–68.
43. *Id.* at 668.

these communications.[44] However, one member of the panel wrote a concurring opinion to express their view that "the attorney-client privilege was operative when Dr. [Phil], the client [], and [Ernst & Young's] counsel were engaged in contemporaneous and simultaneous discussions concerning the instant litigation."[45] The concurring judge reasoned that it would be impossible to "carve out" from any three-way discussions among counsel, the witness, and the hired consultant any potentially non-privileged two-way communications.[46]

## Lessons for Practitioners

Aside from *In re Cendant*, there is a notable lack of authority on discoverability of trial consultant work. To date, there has been only one reported decision directly applying *In re Cendant* in analogous circumstances.[47] The Northern District of California expressly adopted *In re Cendant*'s reasoning and held the parties could only ask witnesses: whether the witness met with a jury consultant, the purpose of any such meeting, who was present, the duration of the meeting, and whether the witness practiced or rehearsed his or her testimony.[48] The court held counsel could not ask questions that would go toward discovering how the consultant told the witness to improve their testimony or any issues they identified about the witnesses' appearance or behavior (fidgeting, sweating, voice, demeanor, etc.).[49] The court expressed reservation about protecting "coaching a witness to act credible," but nevertheless found that line of questioning would distract from the factual issues and should be precluded under Federal Rules of Evidence Rule 403.[50] Regarding the attorney-client privilege, the court stated: "[i]f the witness is a 'client,' the substance of any communication between the jury consultant, the client, and the attorney is probably [attorney-client] privileged," but it made no specific ruling on the privilege's applicability because there were open questions about whether the witnesses qualified as "clients."[51]

Perhaps the dearth of authority on these issues reflects an implicit recognition among the bar that the activities of trial consultants are protected by the work-product doctrine, attorney-client privilege, and/or Rule 26(b)(4)(B).[52] *In re Cendant* suggests a strong work-product argument exists, but the law is less settled

---

44. *Id.* at 661 n.4.
45. *Id.* at 668.
46. *Id.* at 668–69 (citing Davis & Beisecker, *supra* note 29).
47. Hynix Semiconductor Inc. v. Rambus, Inc., Nos. CV-00-20905 RMW, C-05-00334, C-06-00244 RMW, 2008 WL 397350 (N.D. Cal. Feb. 10, 2008).
48. *Id.* at *2, 4.
49. *Id.* at *4. *But see* Davis & Beisecker, *supra* note 29, at 627 (expressing skepticism that consultant advice such as "don't fidget," "avoid pausing in mid-sentence," and "look at the jury while you are testifying" would be protected).
50. *Hynix*, 2008 WL 397350, at *4.
51. *Id.* at *3 (many of the witnesses were former employees hired as consultants at the time of trial preparation).
52. Additionally, the trial consultants interviewed for this chapter all expressed that instances of lawyers inquiring into whether a witness worked with a consultant are rare.

regarding the application of the attorney-client privilege.[53] Lawyers should research analogous attorney-client and work-product decisions in their jurisdictions to better understand how their local courts would treat these issues.

Whether courts will depart from the Third Circuit's ruling has yet to be seen, but *In re Cendant* provides some important lessons lawyers should follow to improve the likelihood that witness preparation sessions and the consultant's advice are subject to the attorney-client and opinion work-product protection. These include:[54]

1. Outside counsel should execute the engagement letter or agreement with the trial consultant, not the client. The letter or agreement should state the consultant is being engaged to help the lawyer more effectively provide legal advice to the client and to prepare for trial. It should also set forth a clear protocol for the consultant to send all communications or reports directly to the lawyer.

2. A lawyer should be present for all meetings and communications between the consultant and the witness.[55]

3. All communications and reports should have a notation that the information is protected by the attorney-client privilege and the work-product doctrine, although as every lawyer knows, this is not dispositive. Likewise, recorded preparation sessions *should* be protected from disclosure,[56] but it is

---

53. With respect to the attorney-client privilege, when a trial consultant is present during communications between the lawyer and witness, arguably, this additional presence is inconsistent with the intent the communication remain confidential. *See* David A. Perrott & Daniel Wolfe, *Out and Proud: Ethical and Legal Considerations in Retaining a Trial Consultant to Assist with Witness Preparation*, 22(1) The Jury Expert 54–62, at 59 (2010), *available at* http://www.thejuryexpert.com/2010/01/out-and-proud-ethical-and-legal-considerations-in-retaining-a -trial-consultant-to-assist-with-witness-preparation/. Similarly, as expressed by the district court in *In re Cendant*, the consultant's advice could be categorized as assisting with the provision of the consultant's own advice, not the legal advice of counsel, thereby precluding application of the privilege. *Id. See also* Blumenthal v. Drudge, 186 F.R.D. 236, 243 (D.D.C. 1999) (acknowledging the attorney-client privilege could be extended to non-lawyers in certain situations, but declining to apply to the facts because the consultant was hired to provide his own advice); United States v. Kovel, 296 F.2d 918, 922 (2d Cir. 1961) ("If what is sought is not legal advice . . . or if the advice itself is the accountant's rather than the lawyer's, no privilege exists.").

54. Butler et al., *supra* note 23; Perrott & Wolfe, *supra* note 53; Davis & Beisecker, *supra* note 29.

55. Communications between a hired trial consultant and the witness should be protected by the work product doctrine, even without counsel being copied or involved on the communication because work product protection extends to the lawyer's agents. However, this practice creates unnecessary risks of disclosure and should be avoided if feasible.

56. Butler et al., *supra* note 23. *See also* Davis & Beisecker, *supra* note 29, at 627. In one case from the Texas Court of Appeals that did not involve a hired consultant, the court recognized videotaped witness practice sessions generally contain information properly classified as work product, but ordered the trial judge to conduct an *in camera* review of the witness's recorded practice session with attorneys to determine whether the video contained the lawyer's strategy, evaluations of the strength and weaknesses of the case, or mental impressions, which would be subject to protection, or information that tended to "mold the witness's testimony," which would not be protected. S. Pac. Transp. Co. v. Banales, 773 S.W.2d 693, 694 (Tex. Ct. App. 1989). The witness submitted an affidavit swearing that "he never saw the videotape, nor was it utilized in any way after it was taken." *Id.* This ruling is likely an anomaly and could be attributable to the fact there were accusations that the witness was "independent," rather than a party, and that the attorneys were trying to shape this critical witness's testimony. *See also* Grenier v. City of Norwalk, No. X06CV000169483S, 2004 WL 3129077 (Conn. Super. Ct. Dec. 16, 2004) (attorney-client privilege waived because videographer was present during communications between the lawyer and client, noting "[w]hile the videographer was necessary for the videotaping of Johnson's statement, he was not necessary for Johnson to consult with her attorney. The attorney could have easily and effectively communicated with his client outside of [videographer's] presence.").

wise to make a statement at the beginning of a recording that the videotape is being used for work-product purposes and is covered by the work-product protection and attorney-client privilege.

4. Trial consultants should avoid giving witnesses documents to keep. They should also avoid giving documents containing generic advice or publicly available advice or practice pointers about testifying, as those documents could be discoverable.

5. Advise the witness that the purpose of the session is to prepare the witness for trial and not to practice or rehearse scripted testimony. Practice what the witness will say if asked whether he or she worked with anyone in preparing to give his or her testimony.

6. Do not allow the witness to bring notes or documents from the preparation sessions when they testify (unless subject to a valid subpoena duces tecum).

7. Consider filing a motion in limine to exclude evidence that a trial consultant was used.

Circumstances where counsel uses a consultant to help prepare a testifying expert for deposition or trial require special consideration. Though the same analysis just described applies, testifying experts must disclose their opinions and the data or information they considered in forming their opinions.[57] Thus, if an expert considers any information from the preparation session or from a report generated by the consultant to formulate her opinion, or states an opinion in a recorded practice session, disclosure could potentially be required.[58] Again, counsel would be well advised to research jurisdiction-specific law regarding the interplay of the rules on privilege and testifying experts.

Counsel should also use greater caution when using a trial consultant to prepare a non-party witness or non-retained expert, including former employees. These situations could be afforded no attorney-client protection, and they risk being subject to the lesser protection afforded to ordinary work product.

---

57. Fed. R. Civ. P. 26(a)(2)(B).
58. Perrott & Wolfe, *supra* note 53, at 56; Davis &. Beisecker, *supra* note 29, at 627–31 (mock examination of a testifying expert witness normally should be afforded opinion work product protection); Quinn Const., Inc. v. Skanska USA Bldg., Inc., 263 F.R.D. 190, 194–197 (E.D. Pa. 2009) (report of non-testifying expert may lose its protection from discovery if it is provided to a testifying expert and is "considered" by the testifying expert; in that case; court held the report of the non-testifying construction consultant was discoverable because although the testifying expert said he didn't rely on it in generating his expert report or opinions, he did review the non-testifying expert's report to obtain an "overview" of the issues in the litigation prior to conducting his own analysis); Synthes Spine Co., L.P. v. Walden, 232 F.R.D. 460, 463–64 (E.D. Pa. 2005) (noting the term "considered" is broadly interpreted and that the "overwhelming majority of courts addressing this issue [of discoverability of expert witness materials] have adopted a pro-discovery position, concluding that, pursuant to Rule 26(a)(2)(B), a party must disclose all information provided to its testifying expert for consideration in the expert's report, including information otherwise protected by the attorney-client privilege or the work product privilege").

## Do Jurors Care?

The discoverability of the fact a witness met with a trial consultant is not surprising; it is well established that the fact someone met with legal counsel generally is not privileged—only the substance of those conversations is privileged. The question then becomes: will the fact the witness prepared with a professional cause the jury to perceive the witness as coached or unduly influenced, such that it outweighs the benefit of using a consultant? Some empirical research suggests this might be a non-issue:

> A research project conducted by members of the ASTC involving more than 500 jury-eligible citizens throughout the United States found 73 percent of respondents believe preparing witnesses to testify is a good idea. Another 66 percent agree that it is appropriate for a witness to practice before testifying. Less than 15 percent of respondents believe that witnesses who practice their testimony have something to hide.[59]

Based on this research, it is probably safe to assume most people either expect or do not care that a witness practiced and prepared prior to testifying. Because many other factors indicate that hiring a trial consultant provides significant benefits, counsel should not base the decision about whether to engage a consultant's assistance on the overblown fear of negative jury perception. As a reminder, every case is unique. Opposing counsel's effectiveness in introducing the use of a trial consultant to the jury varies, and it may warrant introducing the fact preemptively in direct examination or moving for exclusion prior to trial.


# It's "All about the Benjamins." Or Is It?

Budgetary concerns are undoubtedly an important factor to consider when deciding whether to hire a trial consultant to help with witness preparation. But use of a trial consultant that results in an outstanding deposition for your client can make or break the case and result in an outstanding outcome for your client.

Clients hire lawyers for results: to get them from point A to point B. If lawyers believe a key witness may hamper their ability to effectively communicate the client's message for one of the reasons discussed, they should consider enlisting a professional witness consultant and discuss it with their client.

Witness preparation, including the use of a hired trial consultant, is an art, not a science. With heightened self-awareness and the recognition of the potential benefits of hiring a trial consultant, lawyers are better equipped to make the right decision and to articulate their reasoning to their clients.

---

59. Craig C. New, Samantha Schwartz, & Gary Giewat, *Witness Preparation by Trial Consultants*, 18 The Jury Expert 8–11, at 10–11 (Aug. 2006).

## CHAPTER 6

# Preparing the Company Witness for Deposition[1]

*Sawnie A. McEntire*

This chapter discusses preparing the "company witness" for deposition, and it addresses witness preparation for employees, officers, or corporate representatives whose testimony implicates the company or furthers its defense. Such witnesses will include employees who have factual knowledge concerning the underlying issues in a case, and they also include corporate representatives designated as so-called Rule 30(b)(6) witnesses.[2] This chapter explores the strategies and techniques for preparing both such witnesses for deposition.

The goal, of course, is to prepare every witness as an effective advocate for the company, and this goal is achieved in a variety of ways. Whether the witness is a lower-level employee or a formal corporate representative, the goals are the same. However, there are special considerations that pertain to 30(b)(6) witnesses

---

1. Selected portions of this chapter are borrowed from the book entitled *Mastering the Art of Depositions* by the same author, Sawnie A. McEntire, and are reprinted with the approval of the author and the American Bar Association.
2. Most jurisdictions provide a mechanism for taking depositions of a corporation or other business entity through designated representatives. Although the details of how this is accomplished may differ depending upon the jurisdiction, there are common denominators on how witnesses should be prepared to testify as a representative. Rule 30(b)(6) provides the procedure for scheduling and taking such a deposition under the Federal Rules of Civil Procedure. For ease of reference, therefore, all such depositions will be referred to as 30(b)(6) depositions.

because such witnesses have the additional burden of testifying to corporate knowledge extending beyond their individual knowledge.

Every witness should feel comfortable with the deposition process. Many witnesses, particularly beginner witnesses, may experience anxiety about their depositions, and they will need reassurance. Because some witnesses are complete strangers to the process, they may fear the deposition room as if it were a dreaded Star Chamber, and this fear must be defused. One way to accomplish this is to develop a bond of trust and reassure the witness that he or she is not alone, but part of a team. Another way is to equip the witness with basic "witness techniques." This involves a teaching process, and it is as important as preparing the witness on the facts of the case.

A witness well versed in good technique—how to listen and spot problematic questions, and the inferences created by such questions—is better equipped to handle even the most challenging cross-examination. Learning how to use good witness techniques helps witnesses when confronted with surprise questions or unexpected documents. Thus, witness preparations should not be limited to a mere review of documents or facts. Rather, the session should also be used to teach the witness how to manage tempo, handle documents, spot bad questions, avoid adverse sound bites, and convey trial themes. These basic witness skills become critically important when the witness is caught off guard or feeling pressure under the fire of an aggressive examination.

# DIFFERENT TYPES OF WITNESSES

The primary distinction between a 30(b)(6) witness and an "individual" witness is the scope of knowledge at issue in the deposition. Witnesses appearing in their individual capacities are deposed on what they personally know. However, corporate witnesses should understand that their testimony may concern areas where they have no personal knowledge and, accordingly, they must reasonably educate themselves on corporate knowledge concerning the relevant issues. This corporate knowledge frequently exceeds what the witness may actually know on a personal basis, and this means homework for the witness. The witness should devote sufficient time to understanding the larger issues and the key documents relating to a 30(b)(6) deposition.

As a general matter, a witness appearing in an individual capacity should be instructed to testify only upon personal knowledge, and speculation should be discouraged. The individual witness should be prepared to limit his or her testimony to what the witness actually knows; the corporate witness should be prepared to fully advocate the company's position, which requires enhanced witness skills. Again, most jurisdictions impose a duty on 30(b)(6) witnesses to undertake reasonable due diligence to prepare for such depositions.

The Federal Rules of Civil Procedure do not require that an entity designate the person or persons most knowledgeable about the topic categories in a 30(b)(6) deposition notice.[3] However, other jurisdictions may have more stringent rules. Therefore, an initial understanding of pertinent procedural rules is important. Indeed, if the procedural rules require that a corporate witness be the "most knowledgeable," then the witness selection process should focus on those employees or representatives who have the most factual involvement in the case or the issues giving rise to the case. There may be more than one such witness if the topics are broad and wide ranging.

Clearly, a witness may have knowledge concerning certain topics, but be unfamiliar with others. Regardless of the requirements of the rules, however, it is always helpful to identify witnesses who have some foundation in the underlying facts since this will provide a head start. This will simplify deposition preparations since the lawyer does not have to start from square one, which is always time-consuming. It is also helpful because the witness is not forced to engage in a memory exercise.

# FIRST ORDERS OF BUSINESS

Every witness is different, and each arrives at the deposition room from a variety of backgrounds and experiences. If a deposition involves a 30(b)(6) witness, the lawyer should participate in preliminary discussions to identify the best witness representative. The goal is to identify intelligent witnesses who are teachable, make good appearances, and can learn basic witness skills.

Every lawyer encounters different witness types. Some are highly educated; some less educated; some are natural advocates; some are challenged regardless of preparation. Some witnesses are veteran testifiers, and some are beginners. But, regardless of who they are, and regardless of whether the witness is a corporate witness or appearing in an individual capacity, a presenting lawyer should strive to establish rapport and trust with the witness. A healthy level of trust will reap significant dividends—the witness will feel more secure knowing that the lawyer will protect his or her interests, and the witness will be less anxious. A less anxious witness typically performs better.

One way to enhance a witness's comfort level involves an orientation to the deposition process. This is typically achieved by following some simple steps:

- Explain what will happen in the deposition room, who will ask questions, and what the lawyers' roles will be.
- Show the witness the deposition room so the witness has an opportunity to visually see where the deposition will occur, if possible.

---

3. QBE Ins. Corp. v. Jorda Enterprises, Inc., 277 F.R.D. 676, 688–89 (S.D. Fla. 2012) (The rules do "not expressly or implicitly require the corporation or entity to produce the 'person most knowledgeable' for the corporate deposition.").

- Explain the purpose of objections, and what the witness should do, if an objection is made.
- Reassure the witness that the case will not be won or lost on the witness's testimony alone; too much pressure on any witness is counterproductive; some witnesses will fold under such pressure.
- Teach the witness basic techniques for responding to different types of questions and how to spot problematic, ambiguous, or objectionable questions.
- If known, advise the witness concerning the personalities of the other lawyers so the witness is not caught off-guard by aggressive or confrontational behavior.
- Encourage the witness to take breaks when necessary to alleviate fatigue or stress.
- Remind the witness that the deposition is not a memory test, and that it is okay if the witness does not remember specific facts, and that it is always okay if the witness requests to see documents to refresh his or her memory.
- Provide the witness with a short course on deposition etiquette, attire, and posture; appearance is always important, particularly in video depositions.
- If applicable, explain how and why a video record is made, and instruct the witness on the best way to sit and respond to questions in the presence of the video camera.
- Show the witness how to assert control over the tempo of the deposition, and how to avoid being rushed into answering questions.

# THE DEPOSITION ROOM

The deposition room is not a Star Chamber, but a newcomer witness may not know this and will typically fear the unknown. Thus, every lawyer should provide the witness with a preview of the physical layout of the room, and how the cast of characters will be seated, including the witness, the examining lawyers, the court reporter, and the videographer. If not available, a proxy for the deposition room should be used; any conference room with a conference table typically suffices.

If possible, the witness should sit down at the deposition table and get a feel for how he or she will be seated in juxtaposition to the other participants and the video camera. Again, this orientation helps alleviate anxieties that come with the unknown. This is particularly helpful for less experienced witnesses.

# USING DOCUMENTS TO PREPARE THE WITNESS

A second order of business is determining what documents can (or should) be shown to the witness. There are different criteria involved for individual witnesses as distinguished from 30(b)(6) witnesses. As a general rule, and depending on the witness's involvement in the underlying facts, a lawyer should exercise restraint in how many documents are shown to an individual witness to prevent document fatigue. Of course, a corporate witness should be shown sufficient documents to fairly and reasonably prepare for the anticipated testimony, and that is why it is important for all lawyers to have a working knowledge of key documents so this process can be made efficient. Simply put, the lawyer is a teacher, and a teacher cannot instruct the pupil unless the teacher also knows the course materials. To be an effective tutor, the lawyer must be well versed in the facts, the issues, the defenses, and the documents.

What is shown to the witness may be discoverable under various discovery doctrines and, therefore, appropriate precautions should be taken to protect sensitive or "undiscoverable" documents. Such documents certainly include privileged communications, attorney work product, attorney notes, and sensitive documents not previously requested or produced during discovery. The lesson here is to be careful: *what is shown in the preparation room may not stay in that room.*

Document-intensive cases typically require substantial document review by fact witnesses with the lawyer acting as a tour guide of what is or is not significant. But, if documents are used during the presentation session to refresh the witness's memory, then these documents are likely discoverable depending on the rules of the relevant jurisdiction. Determination of discoverability is, again, not always an easy question. Thus, an important order of business is to first determine which documents may or may not be discoverable if shown to the witness. This should be resolved before any preparation meeting begins.

*Document fatigue* is a real problem, and the lawyer should be sensitive to the risk that a witness can become overwhelmed when too many documents are discussed or reviewed. No witness should be expected to review dozens, much less hundreds, of documents and then asked to absorb or memorize the contents of those documents. This would be a numbing exercise for anyone, and it can cause burnout and information overload.

For these same reasons, lawyers should be sensitive to not exposing a witness to excessive or extraneous facts. The witness may become confused and lose focus of key trial themes. In depositions, the witness also may confuse facts that the witness *actually knows* based upon personal knowledge with the knowledge of others. A witness appearing in an individual capacity is best prepared if instructed to limit his or her answers to only what is known, and the witness should not travel beyond this easily defined boundary. This is a general rule of thumb, which has passed the tests of time. Of course, there is an important exception to this rule when dealing with 30(b)(6) witnesses when the witnesses are required to be reasonably familiar with the knowledge of the entire company on the topics relevant to the deposition.

An education process clearly occurs when preparing a 30(b)(6) witness. The lawyer should make sure the witness is provided with all appropriate documents and themes relevant to the topic areas that will be addressed at the deposition, and one easy way to accomplish this is to provide the witness with a briefing binder. This binder, once completed, is a valuable tool that can be used by the witness when working with the lawyer or as individual homework.

A briefing binder typically includes key pleadings, discovery responses and documents, and other materials that provide essential background on the case. If time allows, the binder can also include a chronology to assist the witness if the case is factually complex or document intensive. However, once again, caution should be exercised. Since this binder is likely discoverable, nothing should be included in the binder unless the presenting lawyer is confident the binder will not be discovered. Some lawyers may even elect to produce a briefing binder at the beginning of a corporate deposition so the witness can use the binder as a reference tool during the examination.

A briefing binder should contain the most important (helpful) documents relevant to the examination, and these documents should be arranged either chronologically or by topic category based upon the topics set forth in the 30(b)(6) deposition notice. The witness should be encouraged to consult the binder as needed during an examination, and to refresh his or her memory on key events or key documents. Binders are a great psychological crutch, and will give the witness significant comfort during the deposition. Again, nothing should be placed in this binder unless it is helpful to the witness and the company. Clearly, no privileged, uniquely sensitive, or harmful documents should be included in the binder.

Every company witness should be exposed to sufficient facts to understand the background of the case and the witness's role in the case. For a 30(b)(6) witness, the witness should be exposed to key documents to understand the story line of the case and the topics that will be addressed during deposition. At a minimum, however, every witness should be familiar with those documents that the witness personally authored or received during the ordinary course of business. The lawyer should also segregate and review particularly helpful or "hot" documents.

It is a best practice to assume the witness will be examined with "hot" documents, that is, those documents prejudicial to the witness or the client's case. By preparing the witness with these types of documents, the witness is better prepared to handle surprise questions and will not appear caught off guard.

## Technique versus Content

Witnesses should not be forced to memorize numerous documents or detailed facts. No witness is a fact sponge—and this truism applies equally to corporate 30(b)(6) witnesses and individual witnesses. There is a frequent temptation to teach a witness too many facts, and this temptation carries risk. This is particularly so in large, factually complex cases that involve numerous documents.

An individual witness should be shown only those documents that the witness authored or received, or other "hot" documents that the lawyer knows will be used during questioning. The corporate witness should also be shown key documents that fairly respond to the corporate notice or are needed to provide the witness with a working knowledge of the company's position. Anything on top of this may have diminishing returns.

In a similar vein, no witness should be forced to memorize dozens of minute facts. Few witnesses can pass intense memory tests, and this memory challenge increases when the witness is exposed to the stresses of an aggressive cross-examination. A typical witness will stumble under such circumstances.

In lieu of force-feeding endless documents or factual minutia to a witness, it is a better practice to teach good "witness techniques." This is done by teaching methods on how to spot bad questions, difficult questions, and objectionable questions, and still provide answers that are positive and consistent with the company's thematic case. Once good witness techniques are grasped and understood, the handling of documents and difficult questions becomes less onerous. The witness will feel more comfortable and will gain important self-confidence.

# PRIMARY, SECONDARY, AND TERTIARY FACTS

Another helpful strategy is to "rank" facts by relative importance for each witness. Few witnesses need to know everything about a case, and many witnesses have limited factual roles. Thus, for individual witnesses, there are basically three categories of facts: primary facts, secondary facts, and tertiary facts. Again, an exception to this general rule is a corporate representative designated to testify on behalf of a corporate client on a variety of topics; more expansive preparations are required in that instance.

Ranking facts facilitate how a witness is educated about his her role in the case. Here are three ranking categories that the individual witness should understand to become better witnesses:

- **Primary facts** are facts that the witness *already* knows based upon personal, firsthand knowledge. The witness already "knows" these facts because the witness was directly involved in or personally observed the events or transactions at issue.
- **Secondary facts** are facts that are readily or easily inferred by the witness because of the witness's experience or training. The witness "knows" these facts because they are reasonably inferred from what the witness already knows from personal observation. These *inferred facts* are known to a witness because of the witness's experiences and relationships, and such facts

are based upon the witness's historical observations and do not constitute speculation.

- **Tertiary facts** are facts that the witness does *not* know, and *probably does not need to know*. To burden the witness with this type of information can cause information overload and fatigue. Again, the witness should not be forced to memorize dozens of facts outside of the witness's ordinary realm of knowledge.

# Personal Knowledge and Speculation

Corporate representatives are required to prepare for deposition by making reasonable inquiries into the facts so they are prepared to address preselected topic categories. Their duty to exercise due diligence is dictated by the procedural rules of each jurisdiction and, as such, these topic categories may include factual areas where the witness has no personal knowledge. The witness is, therefore, required to reasonably study and learn about the company's knowledge. With this singular exception, fact witnesses should be instructed to testify only on the basis of personal knowledge, and to not guess or speculate in their answers. Speculation is always risky and creates problems for the witness and the lawyers.

Individual witnesses should stick with what they know, and this instruction is made easy by focusing on how we, as human beings, typically gain and acquire knowledge. Simply put, personal knowledge is derived from our five basic physical senses, and from reasonable inferences from those senses, and every individual witness should be instructed on these simple realities:

- What did the witness hear?
- What did the witness see or read?
- What did the witness taste?
- What did the witness smell?
- What did the witness feel from tactile touch?
- What did the witness reasonably infer from what the witness saw, heard, felt, etc.?

If a witness does not "know" facts within this framework, then the witness *does not have personal knowledge*. If the witness does not have personal knowledge, then the witness begins to speculate, leading to objectionable or dangerous testimony. Thus, a preparing lawyer should instruct each individual witness to stay within this framework, and to not stray from what is known. The witness should be given the comfort that he or she can simply say "I was not involved, so I do not know" or "I never saw that document, so I do not want to guess." This is a best practice, and it avoids the hazards that accompany speculation or guess work.

# RESPONDING TO DIFFERENT TYPES OF QUESTIONS

A witness should be aware of the differences between open-ended questions and leading questions, and using examples of each during mock exercises will help the witness understand the differences. The witness should be specifically instructed to expect leading questions that are tough, aggressive, and challenging, and using concrete examples are an excellent teaching tool, exposing the witness to the tone, pace, and the barbed (sometimes confrontational) nature of an aggressive examination. This also will help get the witness ready—both psychologically and substantively.

Depositions are conducted using different conversational rules than in typical social settings. What is said and how something is said in everyday, informal conversation is not how a witness should conduct himself or herself during deposition. The witness must understand it is important to be more guarded in a deposition, and more careful in word selection to avoid misinterpretation or distortion by the other side.

Every witness should also be instructed to be careful in making sure that questions are clear and unambiguous. This is a difficult task for any person who does not have substantial experience in listening to the subtleties in questions, particularly under the spotlight of an opposing lawyer. It is difficult to train a person to do something that is unfamiliar and inconsistent with daily habits and routines. It is also natural for people to volunteer testimony by falling back into informal conversational patterns because it is familiar and they want to be viewed as cooperative. But, a deposition is anything but informal, and the witness should be reminded of this consistently. The witness should always act reasonably in the deposition room; but "volunteering" is neither required nor recommended.

The witness should become familiar with open-ended (or direct) questions that seek narrative or descriptive responses. The clear signal words for such questions are "how," "what," "when," "where," and "who." A witness also may be asked to "describe" or "explain" certain events. When responding to these types of questions, the witness should be mindful to not volunteer information not specifically addressed in the question. The answers should be short, concise, and to the point. If the witness goes beyond a disciplined answer, then the response may inspire new questions on new topics that the opposing lawyer never contemplated. Disciplined answers are always preferred over longer, undisciplined volunteer answers. This is true for both a corporate witness and an individual witness.

As a general rule, every witness should be instructed to limit answers, when appropriate, to "Yes," "No," "I do not know," or "I do not recall at this time." These are typical instructions that have been used with witnesses for many years. However, a witness should also understand that these brief answers may not always do justice to the testimony or fairly describe the facts.

A witness, particularly a 30(b)(6) witness, should be an advocate for the case, and he or she should be encouraged to supplement his or her answers as needed to make sure that a mere "yes" or "no" is not lifted out of context. Representing a party to the case, a 30(b)(6) witness has a responsibility to advocate the company's case and may need to elaborate on certain responses to make a point. This is particularly important when inflammatory or highly aggressive questions are asked. Again, a beginner witness will encounter difficulties in perfecting this technique, but practice always helps, and a mock examination can drive these lessons home. Practice questions help the witness understand how he or she can (and should) react to tough questions.

# IDENTIFYING LOADED QUESTIONS

Every witness should be taught to listen to each question carefully before answering, and to then make sure that the question is *fully* understood—that is, *every word in every question*. Emphasis should be placed on the notion that *all* words are important, and the witness must learn to exercise patience and not rush in responding. A witness should listen to each word in each sentence, and then make sure that he or she understands both the question *and* the inferences created by the question.

A refresher course in grammar is helpful. Sentences include different types of words with different purposes—nouns, pronouns, verbs, prepositions, adjectives, and adverbs. Each word type has a distinct grammatical function. Adjectives and adverbs give everyday language power and punch. Special nouns and verbs are used to communicate enhanced qualities or powerful messages. The key is to look for dramatic word play by the examining lawyer. If possible, and if time permits, the witness should conduct exercises in spotting "punchy," aggressive, or "loaded" words.

Creative lawyers use words to create drama—this is how they develop the pathos, logos, and ethos of their case. More specifically, this is where the emotional impact of a question is invoked, and the answer frequently becomes irrelevant because the jury message is embodied in the question itself. Some lawyers refer to this as the "sting" in the question.

Good trial lawyers use every opportunity to advocate their case, and this advocacy is frequently reflected in the barbed words or phrases in their questions, and how their questions are presented in both tone and intensity. Many good lawyers will have thought through their case, and will have developed an inventory of pre-planned "attack" words to communicate desired messages to the jury. The witness should be aware that such attack words literally alter the character of a question, the inferences created by the question, and any answers provided. Some examples follow:

| Noun | Adjective | Loaded Phrase |
|------|-----------|---------------|
| event | deadly | deadly event |
| accident | foreseeable | foreseeable accident |
| accident | tragic | tragic accident |
| danger | known | known danger |
| risk | foreseeable | foreseeable risk |
| risk | unnecessary | unnecessary risk |
| incident | unfortunate | unfortunate incident |
| incident | avoidable | avoidable accident |
| injury | terrible | terrible injury |
| death | needless | needless death |
| act | intentional | intentional act |
| transaction | dishonest | dishonest transaction |
| transaction | fraudulent | fraudulent transaction |
| conduct | careless | careless conduct |
| conduct | harmful | harmful conduct |
| conduct | secretive | secretive conduct |

Adverbs are like adjectives in the sense they are *word enhancers* used to convey heightened zest to action verbs. Here are a few examples that frequently find their way into aggressive questions. They can be quickly recognized as the "Y" words: *very, especially, hardly, likely, possibly, probably, dangerously, knowingly, intentionally, purposefully, carelessly, recklessly, maliciously, grossly, negligently,* and *poorly.* These are just a few examples, and the list goes on and on.

Every witness should be counseled to listen to each sentence, spot the drama words, spot the "Y" words, and make sure his or her answer defuses the barbed nature of the question. A mere "yes" or "no" to loaded questions may result in the witness's adoption of the opposing lawyer's dramatic characterizations, and the pathos and ethos of the opposing case. This is precisely what the opposing counsel intends by using loaded questions. Thus, every witness should understand that such characterizations are loaded to benefit just one side, and meant to harm the witness and the company. Every witness should be taught to have a heightened awareness to this word play.

When responding to loaded questions, every witness should be counseled to politely disagree with unfair descriptions or inferences built into the question. Again, by answering "yes" or "no" to these questions, the witness effectively adopts the lawyer's words. Alternatively, a fair response can be prefaced with a statement that the witness disagrees with the lawyer's characterizations, and then proceed with a specific answer. This technique is preferred since it diffuses the offensive nature of the question itself.

A witness may also rephrase the question in the response, making it clear the witness is eliminating unfair words or phrases, and then provide a specific answer. By qualifying responses in this manner, the sting of the question is removed. Again, every witness is different in terms of his or her ability to handle aggressive lawyers and their questions. Practice is always helpful and will enhance the witness's skill and comfort level. Practice is always the best pathway to success.

# IDENTIFYING COMPOUND QUESTIONS

Prepositions and conjunctions are also important words, and their use may signal compound questions. Whenever a question includes the word *and, either, or, neither*, or *nor*, then there is likely more than one subject in the question, and there are really two or more questions linked by a conjunctive or disjunctive word or phrase. Although compound questions are sometimes harmless, this is not always the case. Did the witness answer "yes" to the first part of the question or did the witness answer "yes" to the second part of the question? The witness should be taught to spot this type of double question and request the examining lawyer to break the question into distinct parts before an answer is provided. The witness can also ask the court reporter to restate the question, and this provides the witness with an additional opportunity to make sure all of the moving parts to the question are defined. It is good practice to do this even when the subject matter is benign since it forces the witness to practice technique, which improves overall performance when the going gets tougher.

# IDENTIFYING QUESTIONS THAT ARE *NOT* QUESTIONS

Many loaded questions are not questions at all, but simply declarative statements disguised as questions. In reality, the opposing lawyer is seeking to put words in the witness's mouth, and then seeks confirmation of these words by trying to force the witness to provide a simple "yes" or "no." A simple way to spot these questions are telltale phrases routinely used by most lawyers, and every witness should be counseled to be alert for these verbal red flags. These phrases invariably betray the fact that the lawyer is not interested in narrative testimony, but is seeking instead an agreement with the lawyer's spin, and this spin is frequently inflammatory and beneficial to just the opposing side. Here are some examples of these red flags:

**Signal Phrases**
*Isn't it reasonable that* . . . [declarative statement]
*Isn't it fair to say that* . . . [declarative statement]
*Isn't it correct to say that* . . . [declarative statement]
*Isn't it possible that* . . . [declarative statement]

*Isn't it probable that* . . . [declarative statement]
*Isn't it likely that* . . . [declarative statement]
*Would you agree with me that* . . . [declarative statement]
*Would it be fair to say that* . . . [declarative statement]
*Would it be reasonable to conclude that* . . . [declarative statement]
*Do you not agree that* . . . [declarative statement]

Sometimes the question is flipped—the phrase comes at the end of a declarative sentence. Under either scenario, however, such questions seek to corner the witness into a "yes" or "no" answer using the lawyer's words, and not the witness's words. Every witness should be familiar with this technique and exercise caution when answering. Every witness should also be counseled to explain his or her answer fully, and not feel restricted to just providing a mere "yes" or "no."

All witnesses need to understand they cannot be forced to answer questions without an opportunity to explain. Every witness should also be encouraged to at least request the right to explain an answer or, if he or she disagrees with the inferences created by the question, to say so plainly. This encouragement also inspires self-confidence since the witness knows that he or she can push back on the examiner, and is not forced to play a purely passive or defensive role in the deposition process.

# THE "POSSIBILITY" QUESTIONS

"Possibility" questions frequently surface in depositions, and they represent thinly veiled attempts to solicit admissions through speculation. Human nature is such that most witnesses want to be agreeable or cooperative with others in social settings, and they tend to engage in informal conversational habits. Trial lawyers know this, and they frequently lure the witness into conceding that all things are *possible*, even those things that may hurt the witness or the company. Therefore, before walking into the deposition room, every witness should understand that *all things are not possible*.

Some things are so improbable that, when fairly viewed, they are impossible. For instance, in the pale of human experience, we know with substantial certainty that the sun will rise tomorrow. Although not scientifically guaranteed, we have virtual assurance that a new dawn will rise tomorrow, and the next day, and every day thereafter. As we view the world, it is not possible that the sun will not rise, and this truth is based upon our collective, common sense experience.

Likewise, certain events may not be "possible" within the realm of a witness's personal experiences. Every witness enters the deposition room with a lifetime of learning and acquired habits and, based upon these experiences and habits, it may not be possible that he or she did certain things on a specific date contrary to established habits. This is so even if the witness does not have a distinct memory of what happened on a specific date.

Lawyers frequently try to take advantage of a witness's lack of specific memory to usher in "possibilities." But, even in the absence of any memory of distinct events on a specific date, the witness can reject "possibilities" because, like the sun not rising, the suggested event makes no sense based upon what the witness knows. Here is a simple, but effective way to teach this technique:

> During the preparation stage, ask the company witness to identify the one food that the witness dislikes the most. Then ask the witness what he or she ate on Mother's Day three years ago. It is a high likelihood that the witness will have no memory. Then ask the witness whether it is likely that the hated food was served and consumed on that date. Undoubtedly, the witness will say no. This is because of an established habit or custom that the witness personally observes. Some things are just not possible.

In a similar context, although a witness should not speculate as to what is in someone else's mind, a witness can reasonably (and fairly) infer facts from surrounding circumstances and personal knowledge of those circumstances. Here is an example of inferred knowledge:

> A witness might be asked: "Would you agree that it is *possible* that John Doe reasonably relied upon the financial *misstatements* in the summary pro forma?" The witness can legitimately answer: "No. That is not possible because John Doe had a team of auditors and outside financial experts who investigated the finances of the company for several days prior to the investment that John Doe made."

This is a particularly important concept for 30(b)(6) witnesses who are designated to testify to "corporate knowledge." By way of example, a corporate witness knows that it is not possible that the company is dishonest or deceitful because he or she works with people of great integrity. Again, some things are not possible because the "possibility" defies common sense due to the surrounding circumstances. A witness is entitled to reasonably infer facts that are dictated by common sense, logic, and the witness's personal experiences in life and with the company.

# SUMMARY QUESTIONS

Many lawyers use a technique of summarizing a witness's testimony, and then asking the witness to confirm the accuracy of that summary. The obvious goal is to force the witness to commit under oath that the lawyer's summary accurately reflects the totality of the witness's testimony with nothing more to be added or supplemented by the witness. All witnesses should listen for these types of questions, and appreciate that the lawyer is trying to "box in" the witness and eliminate further flexibility that the witness may need. Again, this is particularly important for a 30(b)(6) witness.

What is said in a 30(b)(6) deposition is typically binding on the company. Thus, it is important that the opposing lawyer not artificially abbreviate or limit the witness's testimony. The witness can legitimately condition his or her answers by indicating that the summary is based upon the witness' *current recollection*, and to make clear that the witness reserves the right to supplement the list as needed. This caveat allows the witness to supplement testimony at a later date, if necessary.

## DOCUMENT SOUND BITES

Every witness should be instructed on how to handle exhibits, and basic techniques apply equally to both individual and corporate witnesses. These techniques help the witness avoid harmful sound bites and enhance the witness's time management skills.

An examining lawyer may take a multi-page letter or document, and then artificially limit the witness's response to a solitary sentence or phrase. The obvious risk is that the lawyer is lifting the sentence out of context, whereas the entire document should be reviewed to place the pending question into fair context. All witnesses should be encouraged to read as much of the document as reasonably necessary to understand how the spotlighted sentence fits into the larger context. The witness should also be encouraged to resist any demand that just one sentence or a single phrase be considered without reference to the remainder of the document. Of course, the goal should always be the ascertainment of truth, and truth can be lost or distorted through an opposing lawyer's manipulation of words or phrases out of context.

An additional benefit of looking at the complete document involves time management. The witness should never feel rushed into answering any question at any time. Reviewing documents provides justification for taking more time to formulate an appropriate and truthful answer.

## FREEDOM TO PAUSE

Witnesses are not prisoners shackled to a chair. They have rights, and they should be reminded of these rights frequently. One such right is they can (and should) take breaks when fatigued or if they need relief from the intensity of the deposition room. Witnesses should also be reminded they have the right to speak to their lawyer. If they have a concern about a specific answer, they can always take a short break to discuss the issue with the presenting attorney. However, they should not overuse this privilege since it may be perceived as abusive or coaching.

Most jurisdictions (and also lawyers) frown upon breaks while a question is pending. The idea is that the witness should not be allowed to receive assistance after a question is posed, but not yet answered. Taking a break while a question is pending also sends a negative message. An exception, however, exists if the witness believes the question encroaches upon privileged communications. In such instances, the witness should be encouraged to make clear that he or she needs legal advice to determine if the pending question "can" be answered. The presenting lawyer should insist on this right.

Clearly, a witness may not fully understand the scope of the attorney-client privilege, and what communications are exempted from discovery. The "pause" button should be pushed when this confusion occurs to make sure the privilege is protected, and not waived. This same consideration applies to trade secrets or other highly confidential information. There may be legitimate concerns that a specific question calls for the disclosure of highly proprietary information, and the witness should consult with legal counsel on this point before answering such questions.

## UNDERSTANDING THE QUESTION

Ambiguity can be the enemy of truth. Therefore, a witness should be taught to listen to each question and make sure that a complete understanding of the question is reached *in his or her mind* before proceeding with any response. To do this, the witness should be taught to listen to *each* word in *each* question. If there is any doubt as to the intended meaning, then the witness should request that the question be clarified. If the presenting lawyer believes the question is ambiguous, then an appropriate objection should be made, and the witness should be taught to pay special attention to any question if an objection is lodged by the presenting lawyer.

An important lesson for every witness is that he or she is not required to answer vague questions. A deposition is not a test of whether the witness can interpret an opposing lawyer's meaning or decipher poorly crafted questions. No witness is required to answer questions that are unintelligible, and the witness is not required to guess at the meaning of a question. If the witness understands this important right, the witness will be more at ease and performance will be enhanced.

## MAKING MISTAKES

All witnesses—veterans and beginners alike—make mistakes during the course of lengthy depositions. This is inevitable because a deposition is, by definition, an antagonistic environment with lawyers, some very skilled, pushing and cajoling witnesses with word play. Mistakes will be made, and some mistakes may be "unforced errors" due to fatigue or distraction.

Thus, a presenting lawyer should make sure the witness does not get emotionally swallowed up by a mistake, and then lose focus or concentration for the ensuing questions. If a witness is preoccupied with an earlier misstatement, the witness's performance will drop rapidly, and this will compound the prior error. Professional athletes are reminded to not get caught up in slips or errors. A pitcher who has just thrown three balls with the bases loaded will likely walk the batter if dread creeps into his mental focus. Witnesses are no different, and should be reminded that it is okay to make mistakes and, even if an error is made, the error can likely be cured through later examination.

All witnesses should be reassured that the weight of the entire world is not on their shoulders. If they perceive that the case rises or falls on their testimony, they may stumble under the stress. Most mistakes can be fixed, and all witnesses need to understand this.

If permitted by applicable rules, a presenting lawyer should discuss any significant mistake with the witness during a break and advise the witness on how to correct the error if and when an opportunity arises. But, these breaks are also opportunities to bolster the witness's positive attitude, provide reassurance, and build morale. The witness should not be overly criticized during a break, but should be encouraged and reassured. Positive messages are always better than negative messages for a witness already fighting stress and self-doubt.

Examining lawyers, particularly less experienced lawyers, frequently ask questions that invite opportunities to correct a past error or mistake, and the witness should be encouraged to take advantage of these opportunities. In some cases, it may be advisable for the witness to state simply on the record that an error was made, and then ask for an opportunity to clarify the prior response. It is rare that the examining lawyer will refuse such a request.

# PACE AND TEMPO

Many skilled lawyers seek to control a witness through the tempo by which questions are asked, and experienced trial lawyers know that tempo control is important for a variety of reasons. Even the appearance of exercising control is important psychologically. Quick questions prevent a witness from regaining composure during difficult questioning. Rapid-fire questions keep a witness off-balance and may cause the witness to rush or stumble when answering. A quick change in tempo may have a similar effect. Lawyers sometimes use sudden changes in voice inflections to catch a witness off-guard. A sudden explosion of righteous indignation may startle a witness, and cause the witness to lose composure or concentration. Some lawyers even alternate between a slow pace and a quickened pace to remain unpredictable.

If the witness can predict a lawyer's tempo, then the witness gains comfort. But, if the tempo is unpredictable, the witness becomes more uncomfortable. A jury may later listen and view the video, and it will be intrigued by the rhythm and counter-rhythm of the examination. They will also see any insecurity or discomfort exhibited by the witness. The examining lawyer will certainly seek to control tempo since it communicates to the observer that the lawyer is in control. This makes the examination more forceful and persuasive, and also creates the impression that the lawyer is "winning" and that the witness is "losing."

A witness should be taught to "expect the unexpected," and every witness should understand that there are many ways that he or she can exert control over the pace of the examination. The witness should be reminded that depositions are not timed tests, and that they should take time to listen to each question and never feel rushed. After all, the deposition is important to all parties. The witness should not feel compelled to answer questions at a pace set by the examining lawyer. If the witness wants to slow down the pace, reduce the intensity, pause and think about the answers, then the witness should do so. This is true in all cases for all witnesses.

# Testimony about Documents

There are special techniques that witnesses can employ when reviewing documents in deposition, and this applies equally with regard to both the corporate witness and the individual witness. All witnesses should be encouraged to take time to read and understand all pertinent portions of a document and never feel rushed. The witness can simply tell the examining lawyer that he or she wants to read the *entire* document, and then use this time to make sure that the *context* of the question is understood. Of course, the opposing lawyer may protest and object but, unless the witness is acting unreasonably, the lawyer's protestations will not sit well with a court.

Again, the conduct of all participants in a deposition should be reasonable. This applies to the lawyers and witnesses alike. It would be unreasonable for a witness to insist upon reviewing a 50-page document to answer one question concerning a specific paragraph on a specific page. This will likely be viewed as stonewalling. In most cases, common sense suggests that the entirety of an extensive document does not need to be reviewed to place a single question into appropriate context. Accordingly, a witness should be counseled to always review enough of a document to make sure proper context is established, but to not abuse this privilege. Common sense is always the guide. Since many depositions are subject to time limits, the presenting lawyer can always offer to "go off the record" if a lengthy document needs to be reviewed. The converse is also true. The examining lawyer can insist to "go off the record" to preserve time while the witness is reviewing a lengthy document.

Witnesses should be taught to request an opportunity to see documents to refresh their memory. If one document is presented to the witness, but the witness wishes to see another document for context, then there is nothing improper in making such a request. Again, the goal is truth, and truth is seldom achieved through gamesmanship. Every witness should be taught that they can protect the record by slowing down the examination, exercising their rights freely (but reasonably) and never rushing into their answers. This includes a fair review of documents before responding.

By requesting an opportunity to see documents during an examination, the witness effectively shifts the burden to the examining lawyer. The tempo of the deposition is changed, and the witness begins to exert control over this tempo. The examining lawyer is then confronted with a dilemma. Either the document is shown to the witness as requested, or the examining lawyer ignores or refuses the request. If this occurs, the witness should be instructed to "stay the course" and re-urge the request to see the document before any further response is provided. If the examining lawyer still refuses to comply, the lawyer becomes the "bad guy." The witness has a justification to later amend or modify any response to the question; or, the witness can simply state that the question cannot be answered without looking at the requested documents.

# ADDITIONAL CONSIDERATIONS FOR CORPORATE REPRESENTATIVES

## Initial Steps

Upon receiving a 30(b)(6) deposition notice, the first order of business is to determine whether the topic categories are objectionable. If the topic categories seek information that is either privileged or immaterial, then appropriate objections should be lodged. In appropriate cases, the responding lawyer may wish to file a formal motion for protection. Clearly, the practitioner should consult the rules in each jurisdiction to determine whether objections (or motions) must be heard before the deposition begins. In some jurisdictions, objections may be filed and the witness may be tendered subject to these objections. Objections to the topic categories might also be necessary because the deposition is premature, the notice seeks highly confidential or privileged information, or the categories are vague, ambiguous, or overbroad.

## Witness Selection

A next order of business is witness selection. Larger companies with substantial litigation experience may have a pool of preselected witnesses depending upon the topics outlined in the deposition notice. However, this is probably the exception to the rule, and most corporate clients will not have this resource. Thus, in most cases, a witness selection process is needed to evaluate the demeanor, acumen, and skills of possible candidates.

Who represents a corporate client in a major deposition is important, and the lawyer should play a meaningful role in the selection process. It is not uncommon to start preparing a witness for deposition and then realize there is something amiss in the witness's background or a personality quirk that makes the proposed witness less than ideal. A corporate client may not be sophisticated concerning the attributes of an effective witness and, accordingly, the trial lawyer should help educate the client concerning preferred characteristics. If possible, the lawyer should help evaluate the potential candidates, and provide candid feedback during this evaluation. The witness or witnesses ultimately selected should be smart, knowledgeable, make a good appearance, and exhibit self-confidence.

Witnesses with prior deposition experience are typically preferred since this experience helps reduce the challenge of preparing a beginner witness on the mechanics of the process. Clearly, prior familiarity with the process accelerates preparations. A veteran witness is also less vulnerable to aggressive cross-examination, and will likely exude more self-confidence under pressure during an intense examination. On the other hand, a witness who is a complete stranger to the process may enter the deposition room with anxiety and fear, and may manifest negative emotions during the examination. Although there are always exceptions, a veteran witness is typically more calm and composed under fire. All of these intangibles are important because the 30(b)(6) deposition is an important opportunity to make a good impression. A corporate witness binds the organization with his or her testimony and, therefore, it is important that the best witness put his or her best foot forward.

One cautionary note is necessary with regard to veteran company witnesses. A company witness who has provided depositions on several prior occasions may have testimony "baggage" from earlier depositions. Such witnesses may have given prior testimony that is either unclear or inconsistent with the trial themes in the case at hand, and the presenting lawyer should seek confirmation whether there is any harmful testimony given in these earlier depositions. Rest assured that opposing counsel will make this effort, and it is always better to avoid surprises before it is too late.

## Witness Demeanor

Witness demeanor is always important. A corporate witness, who "represents" the company, personifies the company for all purposes at the deposition. Since such a witness will likely be the person providing first impressions, it is important these impressions are favorable. A strong, self-assured witness will present a strong, positive image to opposing counsel and will impact the opposing party's view of your case. As such, the witness should be evaluated as to physical appearance, credibility, and likeability. Again, this is how the pathos and ethos of a case are developed. Since the witness *is* the company in the deposition, he or she should be believable, likeable, and trustworthy. These are important components of jury appeal, and it should be assumed that every deposition will find its way into the courtroom and before the jury.

A corporate witness should preferably have some foundation in the background facts of the case. Again, this is helpful since familiarity reduces the challenge of educating the witness on important background facts, and it also avoids the risks of having the witness memorize facts. If a witness has no familiarity with the underlying transactions, occurrences, or issues in the case, the preparation stage will be more complicated and time-consuming. The burdens on the witness will be greater since the witness will be required to learn new subject matter. Thus, it makes good sense to identify a witness or witnesses who have some familiarity with the topic areas that the deposition will address.

Selecting a witness who has some connection to the case also makes more sense from a jury's perspective. A jury may question why a witness designated as a company representative has no connection to the underlying facts. A lack of factual connection will certainly be exposed by opposing counsel to cast doubt on the witness' and corporation's credibility. A lack of familiarity also may serve as the basis for a discovery motion if the witness is not prepared to fully testify on designated topic areas. These types of attacks are avoidable (or at least minimized) if the witness has a substantive connection to the facts of the case.

## Seniority

Another consideration in witness selection is whether the witness is *too senior* in the corporate hierarchy. The lawyer defending the deposition may wish to avoid exposing senior executives (such as a member of the board, the CEO, or the corporation's president) to rigorous cross-examination. An important balancing test is therefore required in making this decision. Depositions are time-consuming, and place burdens on both the company and its senior executives. Also, in larger companies, senior executives typically delegate tasks and responsibilities, and may not have direct involvement in the detailed implementation of those tasks. Therefore, the learning curve for senior executives may be significant if the factual details of job functions become an issue in the case.

Many states recognize what is referred to as the "Apex Doctrine," which allows a corporation to limit, if not prohibit, depositions of senior executives unless it can be shown that the senior executive is personally involved in the underlying transaction or event. The purpose of this doctrine is to prevent unnecessary burdens on senior executives where depositions are sought for purposes of harassment or if the anticipated testimony will have minimal relevance to the proceedings. Some of these same considerations apply to the selection process of a corporate representative and why senior officials should not be presented.

Senior executives typically rise in their respective companies because they are skilled and effective at delegating tasks. However, they often do not know the details of how these various tasks are undertaken. They look to the bottom line and for end results. If they devote valuable time to knowing all of the details, they will be less effective. They are expected to be "big picture" executives. Thus, it is often ill-advised to tender senior executives to testify because the opposing lawyer will use their lack of detailed knowledge to discredit or embarrass the witness, or cast doubt on the integrity of the company.

## Selecting Attorneys as Witnesses

It is rare that a corporate representative should be an in-house lawyer. Exposing corporate counsel to cross-examination invites myriad problems and creates potential challenges to privileged communications. Wherever possible, witness selection should *not include* lawyers or members of a corporate legal department.

## Nonemployees as Witnesses

In some instances, outside consultants can be used as a company representative if they are otherwise involved in the affairs of the company and in a manner relevant to the topic categories in the 30(b)(6) notice. The use of outside consultants, however, should be approached cautiously since it may cause a bad impression with the jury. The jury may be left wondering why there is no employee in the company available to testify in the case, and why an outside consultant was paid to testify. The use of outside consultants is generally less effective, and should be used only when necessary, and when no other appropriate witness can be identified within the ranks of the organization.

## General Topics for Preparing a Corporate Witness

Preparing a corporate 30(b)(6) witness is similar to preparing any other lay witness. Basic concepts related to witness technique, understanding questions, identifying unfair questions, and controlling tempo apply equally to a corporate deposition. However, there are some unique issues that should be addressed and they typically include the following:

- A review and understanding of the specific topic categories for the 30(b)(6) deposition;
- An understanding of the unique role of the corporate witness and the binding nature of the testimony on the corporation;
- The distinction between serving as a corporate witness and a witness with personal knowledge or involvement;
- Access to and review of critical documents;
- Access to and review of operative pleadings and written discovery responses;
- Independent research by the witness;
- Understanding key themes in the case; and
- Understanding key facts of the case.

## Sufficient Time to Prepare

Efforts should be made to make sure there is sufficient time is provided to prepare a Rule 30(b)(6) witness. Again, the rules of practice in many jurisdictions, including the Federal Rules of Civil Procedure, require that the witness (or witnesses) be reasonably prepared to discuss each topic category. If there are numerous topics requiring witness testimony, the preparation period should not be rushed or abbreviated. The court may become concerned if a witness undertakes no preparations or is obviously under-prepared. If the witness fails to review critical documents, or is otherwise unfamiliar with the contentions of the parties, the witness's credibility will be adversely impacted. This in turn hurts the company. The complexity of the topic categories, and the breadth of these categories, should dictate the amount of time required to adequately prepare the witness.

## Pleadings and Key Discovery

A corporate witness should be familiar with the underlying facts of the case and the parties' general contentions. A witness for a defendant corporation should be generally aware of the plaintiffs' claims and the key defenses of the corporate entity. If the witness appears unfamiliar with the nature of the plaintiffs' claims, he or she will be perceived as unfeeling or disinterested. This is particularly true in a personal injury or death case.

Similarly, a corporate representative for a plaintiff should be generally familiar with the plaintiff's claims. Otherwise, the witness will appear indifferent, and the legitimacy and seriousness of the claims will be undermined. Therefore, as a general rule, corporate witnesses should be familiar with operative pleadings in the case, and should have an educated foundation in the issues and the company's position. This promotes the impression that the company and the witness care.

A corporate witness should also be familiar with key discovery responses—particularly sworn interrogatory answers or responses to requests for admissions. Otherwise, the witness may be impeached by these responses to the extent these responses bear on the topic categories for which the witness is tendered.

## Chronology

Using a chronology with a corporate witness is always helpful, particularly if the case involves multiple documents and other significant external and internal communications. A chronology can be prepared by counsel, but it should be reviewed by the witness and the witness should personally confirm the accuracy of each entry by reference to underlying documents or other available evidence. The witness needs to be able to testify that he or she personally confirmed the accuracy of the chronology; otherwise, opposing counsel will foster the impression that the witness is spoon-fed by attorney work product.

Any chronology should be neutral in tone, and it should avoid controversial descriptions that invite examination. The goal is to provide a template to organize the witness's testimony and to assist the witness if the witness becomes confused concerning the timing of events, transactions, or occurrences. Once prepared and disclosed, the chronology may become a significant exhibit in the case. Therefore, every effort should be made to verify its accuracy before disclosure and use.

## Trial Themes

A corporate witness is just like a lay witness concerning the importance and use of trial themes during witness preparation. The corporate witness should have an understanding of the contentions of the client, and the client's thematic story line. This understanding is important to avoid conflicts in testimony. If the witness does not understand the ultimate objectives in the case, the witness is vulnerable during cross-examination. Moreover, the witness's testimony may unintentionally inhibit the client's theory of the case. If the witness understands the case objectives, the witness will be better prepared to respond to challenging questions.

## Review of Critical Documents

Typically, privileged documents that the witness did not author or receive should not be shown to the witness during the preparation process. However, key documents that either have been or will be produced in discovery should be used.

If the witness has not reviewed critical documents that bear on the topic categories, then the adequacy of the witness's preparations may be challenged. The witness should therefore have a working knowledge of the critical documents that a jury will likely see or consider. Anything less may expose the witness to unnecessary cross-examination and will create holes in the witness's preparations.

The bottom line is that the witness should have a working knowledge of key documents, and should be comfortable in his or her understanding concerning the contents of these documents as they relate to the topic matters for the 30(b)(6) deposition. This may require independent homework, and the witness should be prepared accordingly.

## Protecting Privileges

Depending upon the jurisdiction, any documents shown to a corporate witness during the preparation process may be discoverable. Therefore, the lawyer should exercise caution regarding what documents are shown to the witness during preparations. Likewise, the presenting counsel should monitor and be involved in the witness's independent inquiries and investigation. The witness should not be given carte blanche and an open-ended opportunity to contact colleagues or co-workers without some guidance from counsel. Otherwise, the witness may step into privileged areas creating the risk that privileged material becomes discoverable.

Most discussions between counsel and the company witness are likely protected as privileged and not subject to disclosure. Thus, one technique is to summarize the contents of privileged communications verbally. In that manner, the witness has not seen a specific document or documents that may be privileged. The witness should be reminded of the importance of preserving the privilege, and the witness should be instructed to not disclose any communications with counsel or any communication with co-workers investigating the case or the underlying incident. Such matters are protected as privileged work product under the rules of practice in many, if not most, jurisdictions.

# CONCLUSION

In summary, all company witnesses should be prepared to address the relevant facts, and a thorough review of the facts will be important to adequately prepare such witnesses for their deposition. However, learning good witness techniques is also important. Learning these new skills will help the witness cope with difficult questions and will inspire self-confidence. This will translate into substantially improved witness performance.

# PART III

## Expert Witnesses

## CHAPTER 7

# Preparing the Expert Witness for Deposition

*Jean L. Bertrand*

## INTRODUCTION

This chapter discusses preparing expert witnesses for deposition, as opposed to either (1) preparing non-expert witnesses for deposition or (2) preparing expert witnesses for trial. The two chapters following this one are devoted to preparing the expert witness for trial testimony, and I defer to those esteemed authors for detailed advice.

With non-expert witnesses, the goal of the defending lawyer at deposition is to minimize the amount of information given to the other side, while maintaining a clear and defensible transcript. With experts, in contrast, if there is no deposition testimony about a particular subject area, the lawyer runs the risk that the court will prevent testimony about that subject area from being heard at trial. Therefore, not only must a defending lawyer at an expert deposition maintain a clean and clear record and minimize extraneous information given to the other side, the defending lawyer must also make sure that all areas of prospective trial testimony are at least identified. In federal court and most state courts, expert witness disclosure forms are exchanged before depositions occur, and the disclosures can be used to list all the subjects on which the expert may testify. At deposition, referring the questioning lawyer to the disclosure form should be sufficient to preserve all areas of testimony for presentation at trial. As discussed more fully later in this chapter, a well-crafted disclosure form is important to the entire process of expert discovery.

Preparing an expert for deposition testimony is also very different from preparing him or her for trial testimony. Expert witness testimony is almost never presented at trial by way of a videotaped deposition and, therefore, the deposition is almost never the time for the expert to present his or her opinions the way he or she would present them at trial. Nor will the expert witness yet be ready to criticize the opposing party's expert's trial testimony, demonstrative aids, and so forth. At deposition, the overarching goal is to preserve the expert's full range of subject matter for trial without creating sound bites that can be used to impeach the expert, or make him or her look bad.

Thus, the goals for expert depositions are (1) to be sure not to foreclose an area of testimony at trial; (2) to avoid an impeaching sound bite; and (3) to leave open options for additional opinions or comments the expert might develop by the time he or she testifies at trial, in light of other evidence that may be generated in the meanwhile. In short, the goal for defending expert witness depositions is to avoid being painted into a corner. This chapter attempts to give some guidance on how to avoid that corner.

In order to expose the problems created by failing to do the right things at the right time, this discussion moves backward in time, in reverse chronological order.

## AT THE DEPOSITION

At an expert's deposition, both sides can observe the expert's demeanor, ability to respond to unexpected questions, and ability to think on his or her feet. These observations may help determine whether a party will be amenable to settlement, or will want to press forward to trial. Thus, the expert's performance at a deposition is vital to the interests of your client. Your expert should be instructed to dress as a professional, sit up straight, maintain eye contact with the examining attorney, and speak firmly. If you find your expert is volunteering too much, is not being responsive to the questions, or is using body language or a tone of voice that reveals a lack of confidence, you should not hesitate to ask for a recess.

You also should not hesitate to object to questions asked of the expert, as you would with any other witness. However, unlike the situation with a party witness, you are not allowed to instruct an expert witness not to answer particular questions, as the expert is not your client and in many jurisdictions there is no privilege that you can assert. (There is limited protection of draft reports under Federal Rule of Civil Procedure 236 and some state rules.) In egregious circumstances, such as where the questioning attorney is delving into the expert's private affairs beyond the level necessary to explore bias, you could suspend the deposition and seek relief from the court, but your complaint will not be well received unless the questioner's behavior truly is egregious.

Because the defending lawyer's role at expert depositions is so circumscribed, it is crucial that the expert be thoroughly prepared in advance.

# IMMEDIATELY BEFORE THE DEPOSITION

Just prior to the expert's deposition (the morning of the deposition or the previous day), is the best time to review with the expert the rules of the deposition process. If the expert has never been deposed before, you should explain the roles of the various participants, the impact the presence of the deposition reporter will have, etc.

Be sure the expert has in mind important dates, such as: when the expert was first contacted by counsel; when the expert was retained; when the records were received (and from whom they were received); when the expert formed his opinion(s) in the case; the date key tests were performed; and the dates of important events in the case.

## Expert, Pace Yourself

Emphasize to the expert that a deposition is not a conversation. Nor is it a lecture to college students, grand rounds in a teaching hospital, or a brainstorming session with a peer or colleague. Even with an experienced expert, it is helpful to remind him or her that the speed of conversation at deposition should be slowed well below the speed of casual conversation for three important reasons: (1) to accommodate the deposition reporter, (2) to make an accurate record, and (3) to allow time for thoughtful answers. Some experts will get the idea if you tell them to pretend they are playing a record at 33 rpm instead of 45 rpm, to illustrate the speed at which conversation should occur during a deposition. Unfortunately, not all of them can remember vinyl records. Regardless of the analogy, the point is important. Witnesses create a clearer, more accurate, and less troublesome transcript if they speak very slowly, as in, v-e-r-y s-l-o-w-l-y.

## Remain Neutral

Remind the expert immediately before the deposition to take pains to appear neutral and avoid openly advocating for the client. The expert will not be credible if seen to favor one side. The witness's role is merely to answer counsel's questions, not explain why your client should win.

## Limit Answers to the Question Asked

Another reminder that you should always bring up just prior to the deposition, no matter how many times the witness has been deposed before, is that the witness should be careful to answer *only the question asked*. Commonly, witnesses, and especially quick-thinking, highly intelligent, educated and successful expert witnesses, anticipate where the questioner is going and leap ahead to answer the question they think the questioner means to ask, rather than the question actually asked. This creates a confusing transcript at best and, at worst, can create a disastrous transcript.

## Prepare for the Standard Questions

Prepare your expert to expect that there are standard questions routinely covered at every expert deposition. Here is a list of the subjects routinely explored.[1]

- How the expert was retained in the case, including:
  o   How the expert was contacted;
  o   When the expert was retained;
  o   What the expert's assignment entailed; and
  o   Whether the expert executed an engagement letter.
- The expert's previous testimony and reports, including:
  o   All cases in which the expert has testified, both at trial and in deposition (this includes seeking information beyond the previous four years that Federal Rule of Civil Procedure 26 requires, as well as any testimony that the expert has given since his or her report was disclosed); and
  o   All cases in which the expert has drafted a report, including those cases in which the expert did not testify (if copies of these reports have not already been requested in discovery, copies may be requested at the deposition).
- Cases in which the expert has previously served as an expert, including:
  o   The number of cases an expert for the party who retained him in the present case;
  o   The number of cases as an expert for counsel in the present case;
  o   The number of cases as an expert for plaintiffs; and
  o   The number of cases as an expert for defendants.
- The expert's compensation for his or her work in the present case, including a discussion of:
  o   Billing records;
  o   Time sheets and invoices;
  o   Total compensation paid;

---

1. Adapted from Prac. Law., Feb.–Mar. 2016, at 74.

- o   Communications between counsel and the expert relating to the expert's compensation; and
- o   The percentage of the expert's income earned from performing expert services.
- What communications, if any, the expert had with other experts in the present case.
- Whether the expert used support staff in the present case, and, if so:
  - o   The names and roles of the support staff;
  - o   The qualifications of each staff member;
  - o   Their billing rates and total compensation paid;
  - o   How the expert communicated with the support staff;
  - o   What tasks the support staff performed; and
  - o   Whether the support staff performed any testing or calculations on which the expert relied.
- Whether the expert has updated any information on his or her curriculum vitae or expert report since it was disclosed.
- The documents reviewed by the expert in preparing the report, if any, including:
  - o   Who provided the expert with the documents reviewed for the report;
  - o   How the documents were selected;
  - o   What documents the expert considered and relied on when reaching conclusions; and
  - o   Any documents the expert reviewed but decided not to rely on, and why.
- The expert's preparation for the deposition, including:
  - o   Any meetings with counsel (how many meetings, who was present, and how long the meetings lasted); and
  - o   The documents that the expert reviewed or discussed with counsel.

## Expert, Beware a Series of "Yes" or "No" Answers

Just prior to the deposition, you should raise your expert's awareness of the typical tricks and traps questioners use. For example, it is common to ask the "primrose path" series of questions (leading the witness down the proverbial primrose path). The questioner begins with a very general question that has a very simple and obvious answer, either "yes" or "no." He or she then goes on to a second question, which is a bit more relevant to the case at hand, but still has only one very obvious answer, "yes" or "no." The questioner gradually gets the expert witness accustomed to answering questions exactly the same way, for example "yes," "yes," "yes," or "no," "no," "no." Then the questioner speedily asks the question he or she has been building to, where the answer is not obvious and is not simple, yet the witness often will say "yes" or "no" one more time, giving the questioner a good sound bite to use at trial.

## Listen for the End of the Question

Another typical trick the questioner may use is to modify his or her question at the very end by tagging on a qualifier, often in a quiet voice, even a whisper. The expert, who has likely been listening to the question carefully and is eager to prove his expertise with the answer, often answers without hearing or taking into account the sotto voce tag line. This can create very damaging testimony. Although the defending lawyer can try to undo the damage done by these trick questions with questioning of his or her own at the end of the deposition, it is much better if the damage is avoided altogether. Forewarned is forearmed.

## Explain Why You Know What You Know

To establish some easy cross-examination points for trial, questioners often run through a long series of "you are not" questions. Assume that your expert is, for example, a pathologist. The questioner will run through a litany of things the expert is not, for example, "you are not a pulmonologist," "you are not a radiologist," "you are not an industrial hygienist," "you are not an epidemiologist," etc. The easiest route for the expert facing these questions is to simply agree over and over again that he or she is, in fact, none of those other things. However, if the expert's opinions and testimony might be on the border of pathology and pulmonology, or pathology and epidemiology, the easy concession without explanation can be troublesome at trial. It is far better to suggest to the expert that he or she should never minimize or trivialize the scope of his or her expertise. For example, a pathologist could explain that although he or she does not treat patients directly, he or she frequently consults with pulmonologists as part of a team, and is knowledgeable about pulmonology. When preparing for deposition, remind your expert that a deposition is not the time to be modest.

## Stick with What You Know

A deposition is also not the time to moralize. The questioning lawyer may try to "turn" the expert to the other side by presenting the expert with a hypothetical question that assumes facts in favor of the questioner's client and is phrased to sound completely reasonable—so obvious, in fact, that there can only be one answer. For example, in a failure-to-warn case, plaintiffs' counsel may ask defense experts to agree that the right and moral thing to do is to always provide enough information to enable a consumer to make an intelligent choice whether to buy or use the product. By failing to take into account the science at the time the product was manufactured, and various other factors, the question assumes away the disputed issues. An expert witness who has been retained to testify about the subject of the question will of course know the answer is not a simple "yes." Knowing that, questioning lawyers ask this particular question, *not* of the expert with applicable expertise, but of experts hired to talk about other issues, perhaps even damages experts. Instruct your expert to be careful not to assume *any* question is so clear or *any* answer so obvious that it can be answered without careful thought. And remind your experts to avoid moralizing and stick to what they know.

## Do Not Bless an Author or a Treatise

Frequently, the questioner will ask the experts a series of questions regarding whether certain publications or authors are considered by the expert to be reliable authorities in his or her area of expertise. The uninitiated expert might see these questions as harmless and easy to answer, and agree that, for example, a particular journal is a reliable and authoritative text. Before the deposition, always explain that these types of questions can come back to haunt your expert if, at trial, the opposing lawyer is allowed to read an article which the expert may or may not have read before, and with which the expert may well disagree. If the expert responds by challenging the accuracy or reliability of the excerpt that has just been presented for the first time in open court, the opposing counsel will cheerfully remind the expert that he or she conceded at deposition that the journal was a reliable and trustworthy text. It is much better if the expert comes to the deposition prepared to answer questions about the authority of texts, journals, and authors by saying "it depends," thus leaving an opening to contest conclusions in particular articles.

## Expect the "Rule-Out" Gambit

Your expert also needs to be prepared to deal with a questioner who challenges the expert's conclusions by positing the opposite conclusion, and then asking, "but you can't definitively rule it out, can you?" Experts, particularly those trained in the sciences, are inclined to agree that the opposite view cannot be definitively ruled out once and for all. Yet in a courtroom, that concession may give the impression that the version posed by the questioner is plausible. The well-prepared expert will refuse to concede the opposing opinion cannot be definitively ruled out, instead saying something along the lines of, "although nothing is totally impossible, I would consider that to be extremely improbable."

## Push-Back on "Yes or No"

Some questioners will bully witnesses, even expert witnesses, at depositions. For example, they may demand, loudly, that the witness give them a "yes" or "no" answer. They are not entitled to demand that the expert answer "yes" or "no," but unprepared experts can be intimidated into concluding that they must choose one or the other answer. Then they will evaluate whether the correct answer is closer to "yes" or "no," and deliver the one-word answer the questioner is looking for, but which may not reflect the expert's actual beliefs or opinions. The well-prepared expert will know to refuse to answer such a command. Instead, the expert can say something like, "it would not be truthful to answer that question with either a simple 'yes' or a simple 'no.'" If the expert is then given the chance to explain, he or she should do so, but frequently the questioner will simply move on, having failed to achieve the sought after sound bite.

## Know Your File

An additional task to be done just prior to the deposition is to look over the expert's file to be sure all the paperwork is in order and suitable to be produced to the other side. At the time of deposition, the file should consist of the materials the expert actually received or reviewed, a list of other materials considered (if any), the witness's report if one has been prepared, and some summary notes of the witness's opinions and conclusions. The file should not contain scribbled notes of work-in-progress, questions the expert wrote for follow-up, or rough calculations. Nor should it contain substantive correspondence (by letter or email) regarding the expert's process of reaching his or her conclusions and opinions.

# A FEW WEEKS BEFORE THE DEPOSITION

At about the time the deposition schedule is set, you should have a conversation with your expert to be sure everything is going according to plan (discussed next), and the expert will be ready for the deposition. A personal meeting is preferred, but cannot always be arranged. If you are dealing with an experienced, good witness, a telephone conversation will suffice.

At this point in time, the expert should finalize any written reports, calculations, or test results; put them in a form appropriate to be produced to the other side; and review the file. You also should ask the expert to update his or her curriculum vitae to add any recent publications, speaking engagements, or other new material.

This is also the ideal time to discuss with the expert the substantive areas of questioning he or she can anticipate from opposing counsel at the deposition. Experienced witnesses may be better at anticipating the questions than you are. Reviewing past expert witness deposition transcripts of opposing counsel can help identify style, approaches, and questions likely to be asked. Now is also the time to get your expert's thoughts about questions you should ask the other side's expert(s).

If you are dealing with an inexperienced witness, you may want to hold a mock deposition at this point in time to better acquaint the expert with some of the traps and tricks he or she can expect, discussed in more detail earlier. Invite other lawyers or staff from your firm to sit in and comment on the witness's deposition skills, demeanor, etc. But do not videotape mock depositions, as in many states the tapes can be discovered by the other side.

If you have an expert who has poor witness skills, this should not be your first mock session. You should already have done at least one mock deposition if you are dealing with someone who does not feel comfortable in the witness chair.

## Before Disclosing Your Experts

Shortly before disclosing your expert witnesses, you should do all of the following:

- Discuss the opinions each expert expects to offer and make a clear outline of them for your own file. If written reports will be generated, make a clear outline of them as well.
- Ascertain whether your expert witnesses have good witness skills. The fact that an expert is experienced does not necessarily mean he or she is an effective testifier. An expert in a technical field of expertise may not be an expert communicator. If you have a witness who does not have good testifying skills, or an inexperienced witness, you should do a mock trial testimony session, and a mock deposition session, to test the witness' instincts in response to deposition questioning, direct exam, and cross-exam. This also provides an opportunity to teach the witness about some of the tricks and traps he or she can expect, described more fully earlier.
- In the course of preparing for the mock sessions, you can accomplish another goal of expert preparation, which is to anticipate the likely deposition strategy the other side will employ and outline the questions your witness is likely to be asked. Preparing for the mock session will force you to think about the case from your opposing counsel's point of view.
- This is the time to anticipate a potential *Daubert* or *Kelly-Frye* challenge to your expert, seeking to exclude the expert's testimony altogether, or limit it in some fashion. Federal courts follow *Daubert v. Merrill Dow Pharmaceuticals Inc.*,[2] as do most state courts. However, several states (notably California and New York) still follow *Daubert*'s predecessor, known as *Kelly* or *Kelly-Frye*.
  - o The *Daubert* test requires the trial court to act as a gatekeeper, evaluating several factors before deciding whether the methodology underlying the expert's opinion is sufficiently reliable to permit it to be presented to the jury. Factors to be considered under the *Daubert* test include: (1) whether the expert's methodology can be, and has been, tested; (2) whether the methodology has been subjected to peer review and publication; (3) the known or potential rate of error of the methodology; (4) the existence and maintenance of standards controlling the methodology and its operation; and (5) whether the methodology

---

2. Daubert v. Merrill Dow Pharmaceuticals Inc., 509 U.S. 579 (1993).

is generally accepted in the relevant scientific community. Cases since *Daubert* have set forth multiple other criteria for courts to consider.[3]

o   In California, the courts follow *People v. Kelly*.[4] Under the *Kelly* test, the judge must decide if the expert opinion is "grounded in a scientific theory or technique which is generally accepted as reliable in the relevant scientific community." The expert must have sufficient qualifications to testify regarding the scientific theory or technique, and the data used must be reliable. Note that if you will be presenting a new or controversial technique or theory, you may need to retain a second expert whose testimony will be limited to showing that the technique or methodology is generally accepted in the relevant scientific community.

• Finally, draft and edit the witness disclosure form along with each expert to be sure he or she understands the scope of testimony you expect.

## "Plenty of Time" Before Disclosure

Every case is different when it comes to the scope and extent of expert testimony. And some cases proceed at a much faster pace than others. Therefore, it is difficult to pinpoint just when "plenty of time before disclosure" is, and it certainly will vary from case to case. Despite that difficulty, it is crucial to be well along in your expert witness preparation "plenty of time" before disclosing experts.

By "plenty of time before disclosure," you and your expert should have had enough interaction so that you have a good idea what opinions the expert will be presenting. Now is the time to refine them and determine if additional work needs to be done. You and your expert also should anticipate, together, what the other side's substantive response is likely to be to your expert's opinions, and what experts and counter-opinions the other side is likely to present.

At this point in time, be sure you are not essentially asking the expert to substitute for the role of the fact finder or the court. In most jurisdictions, including California, an expert is not permitted to opine on the conclusions which the judge or jury must make. For example, in the California case of *Summers v. Gilbert*,[5] the lower court was reversed because the trial judge permitted an expert to opine that one of the defendants was legally responsible under the non-delegable duty rule. The appellate court noted that the judge had the obligation to instruct the jury in the law and could not allow an expert—even a qualified lawyer-expert—to usurp the judge's role. This "expert opinion" was nothing more than an attempt to direct

---

3.  See, e.g., General Electric Co. v. Joiner, 522 U.S. 136, 146 (1997) (excluding expert testimony where there was "simply too great an analytical gap between the data and the opinion proffered"); In re Paoli R.R. Yard PCB Litig., 35 F.3d 717, 765 (3d Cir. 1994) (excluding expert testimony where the expert "place[d] heavy reliance on unreliable . . . data.").

4.  People v. Kelly, 17 Cal. 3d 24 (1976), as expanded by People v. Leahy, 8 Cal. 4th 587 (1994).

5.  Summers v. Gilbert, 69 Cal. App. 4th 1155 (1999).

the jury to the ultimate conclusion: that the defendant must be held liable. This opinion is not helpful to the jury; on the contrary, it is an attempt by the witness to usurp the role of the jury. The court said:

> Reading [the expert]'s testimony in its entirety, we conclude that he was advocating, not testifying. In essence, cloaked with the impressive mantle of "expert," [the expert] made plaintiff's closing argument from the witness stand. This is a misuse of expert witnesses, and renders his testimony inadmissible under Evidence Code section 801.[6]

In similar California cases, expert opinion has been refused on the subjects of (1) whether there is probable cause to file a suit, (2) the legal interpretation of contracts, and (3) whether particular acts constitute negligence.

Note, however, that expert opinion on custom and practice usually will be allowed. For example, even though a lawyer-expert cannot testify as to the legal meaning of language in a contract, that same lawyer-expert can provide an opinion on the custom and practice in the business community regarding the meaning of that language.

California is not alone in excluding expert opinions on issues of law. At least eight federal circuit courts of appeal have held expert testimony on issues of law is not admissible.[7] The federal courts have uniformly held that allowing an expert to voice an opinion on an issue of law usurps the authority of the court:

> The basis of expert capacity, according to *Wigmore* (§ 555), may be "be summed up in the term 'experience.' But experience is hardly a qualification for construing a document for its legal effect when there is a knowledgeable gentleman in a robe whose exclusive province it is to instruct the jury on the law. The danger is that the jury may think that the 'expert' in the particular branch of the law knows more than the judge—surely an inadmissible inference in our system of law."[8]

The burden of proof is on the party proffering the expert witness to establish compliance with *Daubert*, *Kelly-Frye*, and other rules limiting the scope and extent of expert testimony. Anticipate that you may be called upon to meet this burden

---

6. *Summers*, 69 Cal. App. 4th at 1185.
7. See Nieves-Villanueva v. Soto-Rivera, 133 F.3d 92, 99 (1st Cir. 1997) (joining seven other circuits in holding that the Federal Rules of Evidence prohibit expert testimony on issues of law).
8. Marx & Co., Inc., v. Diners' Club, Inc., 500 F.2d 505, 512 (2d Cir. 1977) cert. denied, 434 U.S. 861, 98 S. Ct. 188, 54 L. Ed. 2d 134 (1977); see Burkhart v. Washington Metro. Area Transit Auth. (1997) 324 U.S. App. D.C. 241, 112 F.3d 1207, 1212 ("Each courtroom comes equipped with a 'legal expert,' called a judge, and it is his or her province alone to instruct the jury on the relevant legal standards.").

of proof well before the other side finds out who your experts are and what they will say.

"Plenty of time before disclosure" is also the time to investigate your experts the same way your opposing lawyer likely will. Do a Google search, and search social media sites such as Facebook, LinkedIn, Instagram, and Twitter for information on your experts. Search for blogs or other online publications to which the experts might have contributed. Search online databases that compile background information on experts, such as Westlaw's Profiler. You should also search for experts' previous testimony, and any *Daubert* or *Kelly-Frye* motions that might have resulted in exclusion of some or all of any experts' testimony. Review your experts' publications, and the publications that cite them. Make a determination as to whether the experts' published opinions are consistent with the generally recognized state of knowledge in the field. Verify that each expert's curriculum vitae is accurate. Ask your colleagues and any other experts you have interviewed if they are familiar with each particular expert, and his or her reputation.

Ask your experts if their testimony in prior cases could undermine their opinions in the instant case. Or better yet, review the transcripts of the prior testimony to see for yourself what they reveal. Even if prior testimony involves different legal issues or otherwise does not directly undercut your expert's credibility in the current case, reading the transcripts may help you to better understand the expert's testifying style so you can fix any bad habits.

Last, counsel should obtain copies of everything the expert has considered or reviewed in formulating his or her opinion. This step overlaps with the review of the expert report. It is always required by Federal Rule of Civil Procedure 26(a)(2), and typically (but not always) required by California Code of Civil Procedure Section 2034.250.

# PLENTY OF TIME BEFORE "PLENTY OF TIME"

Early in the case, when you are first considering the areas and scope of the expert testimony you may need, start searching for experts. Seek recommendations from your colleagues and others who might be familiar with the fields of interest. Search online for publications in the area and presentations given by experts in the field. Research major universities' websites for information about the relevant subject areas and leads on experts.

Once you have determined the types of experts you will need, consider how much time will constitute "plenty of time" for your particular case, and calendar the remaining steps in this process to allow sufficient time to prepare for expert depositions.

Consider retaining more than one expert in each field. Once retained, they will be unable to work for the other side. In a limited field of experts, this can give you a considerable advantage. Moreover, you may find that your first choice will not actually testify for one reason or another, and it is very helpful to have one or more consultants you can use as your second string. Narrow your choice of candidates based not only on their credentials and opinions, but also their personalities. You need an expert with sufficient witness skills to survive the deposition, and be persuasive to the judge and jury.

When interviewing prospective experts, ask difficult questions, such as the following:

- Have you ever failed to be qualified as an expert?
- Has your testimony ever been excluded or limited by a court?
- Do you have any relationship, past or present, with the other side, its employees, experts, or lawyers?
- Is there anything about your personal life that could cause problems, such as substance abuse issues, a contested divorce, personal litigation, restraining orders, bankruptcy, failure to complete a course of study, etc.?

Discuss the expert's fee structure. Determine how much of the expert's total income is attributable to litigation consulting and testifying work.

Show the expert only those documents you are prepared to show the other side. Some attorneys believe a lawyer can show a document to a friendly expert without that document ever becoming discoverable, because of an unspecified "privilege." But federal and California courts have squarely rejected this theory. Federal courts construe Rule of Evidence 612 (regarding refreshing a witness's recollection) to require the production of any documents that are used in deposition preparation "to refresh memory for the purpose of testifying."

Among the most complex issues in expert deposition preparation is balancing the need to familiarize experts with the facts of the case, specifically including documentary evidence, without creating discoverable material for the other side. This complexity derives from the tension between the protection afforded to the attorney's strategy under the work product doctrine, and the evidentiary rules requiring production of materials used to refresh witnesses' recollection. Discuss the expert's note-taking practices and explain that communications between you and the expert are not considered privileged and are therefore subject to disclosure to the other side. Explain how much deposition time can be wasted pursuing irrelevant rabbit trails if an expert's file is full of partially legible notes, initial thoughts, unattributed quotes, or incomplete calculations. Efficient experts take notes on sticky tabs (actual or electronic) the first time through the file, then later consolidate those notes, then use that consolidated-note document to prepare the report or outline opinions, and then finally discard the no-longer needed sticky notes and initial draft(s).

Experienced lawyers eschew written communications with their experts. As trial expert Michael Schwartz has said, "although one must always produce discoverable material, one need not create it."[9] Note that in 2010, the federal rules were substantially amended to expand work product protection for certain types of communications between an attorney and a testifying expert, but this protection is not found in all state rules of procedure.

Consider the future availability of the expert. Ask about the expert's general health, plans to move from the area, or scheduling of extended vacations.

Follow up the retention of every expert with a retention letter, drafted either by you or the expert. Be sure it outlines and limits the scope of the assignment, commemorates the fee terms (and costs reimbursable to the expert), specifies that payment is not contingent on the outcome, and emphasizes the expert's independence. Normally, the law firm or lawyer is the expert's client, not the litigant.

All of the actions discussed in this section are fair game for questioning at deposition. If you deal with them at the beginning of the relationship, preparing for the deposition will be much easier, and the deposition will be much less stressful.

# CONCLUSION

To properly prepare an expert for deposition, you need to begin long before the deposition is scheduled. Indeed, the most important work is done at the very beginning, when you select the expert—not only for his or her expertise but also for his or her witness skills. Perhaps equally important is the work you do to deselect experts who will not perform well at deposition, making sure to allow yourself enough time to recover from false starts and turn to your back-up consultants.

If you are in doubt about your expert's witness skills, do not hesitate to engage in a mock deposition exercise. If nothing else, it will improve your expert's comfort level with the process as well as his or her performance during the actual deposition.

Time spent studying an expert's subject matter expertise is time well spent in preparing for deposition because a good questioning lawyer will do the same. In order to prepare your witness, you need to know what the questioner is likely to have found, and anticipate what questions will be asked as a result.

Shortly before the deposition, educate your expert about what to expect, even if it is familiar territory to you (and even if the expert declares it to be familiar territory, as well). It never hurts to remind witnesses to listen to each question carefully, to listen to all of the question, to answer only the question asked, to speak slowly, to avoid the tricks and traps, and to leave modesty outside the deposition room door.

---

9. Matthew D. Taggart, *How to Prepare for and Manage the Depositions of Expert Witnesses*, Los Angeles Lawyer, July–Aug. 2012, available at https://www.venable.com/files/Publication/054e3a0c-beb4-4df6-8b01-702676c3f65f/Preview/PublicationAttachment/7ebebf43-daf5-4bbb-b6fb-72363eb381ff/Taggart_LA_Lawyer.pdf.

In complex litigation, clients demand high-level performance from their legal counsel and retained expert witnesses. All too often, counsel hires expert witnesses with minimal vetting or strategizing. This is risky. A good opposing lawyer can do serious damage at the expert deposition stage, and the damage may be irreversible. But intensive preparation beginning long before the deposition can minimize the risks inherent in the expert deposition process.

As discussed fully in the next two chapters, preparing an expert witness for trial testimony is a very different process. However, no matter how hard the trial lawyers work to prepare the expert to perform well before the jury, if the deposition preparation was inadequate the trial testimony will be worse than it could have been.

## CHAPTER 8

# Dancing with Antaeus

## Twelve Unusual Questions to Ask Your Expert

*John Jerry Glas*

*Raymond C. Lewis*

You don't win a trial with *their* expert. You win a trial with *yours*. So why is it that we spend so much time talking about the art of cross-examination and so little time talking about the science of direct examination? Yes, lawyers at cocktail parties brag that the direct examination of an expert is "like dancing," but they don't tell you what kind of dance, and they don't tell you anything about your dance partner.

Well, there is good news and bad news about your dance partner. The bad news is that many experts resemble Antaeus from Greek mythology. They know they are "giants" in their respective fields. They think they are half-god. They would rather kill a lawyer than dance with one. And they only remain invincible while they keep their feet on the ground. The good news is that a tango with a homicidal giant is *exactly* what jurors what to see.

Times have changed. Jurors are suspicious of trial lawyers and their handpicked experts. They do not want to hear your expert, in response to every question you ask, reply "that's absolutely correct, counselor!" They want a *real* conversation, and the last thing that lawyers and their experts should give them is a rehearsed or choreographed performance.

We need to rethink our approach to direct examination of experts or it will always be the most predictable, boring, and ignored part of trial. Toward that end, here are 12 rather unusual (often counterintuitive) questions to ask your expert during trial preparation—questions that represent a very different approach to direct examination:

- How can we make this more complicated?
- Why are you just sitting there?
- Who told you that you're funny?
- What is a good mistake I can make?
- What are they right about?
- What does the book say?
- How can we make their case better?
- What you got that theirs ain't got?
- What do you do all day?
- What are you really an expert in?
- Does Google agree with you?
- What do you have to say for yourself?

Forget everything you've been told about direct examination of an expert. Ask these unusual questions of your expert during trial preparation, and use what you learn during your direct examination. Help your expert grab the jury's attention, earn the jury's trust, and teach the jury what they need to know. Prepare yourself to tango with a homicidal giant, and prepare your expert to win the trial.

# How Can We Make This More Complicated?

Conventional wisdom says to "Keep It Simple Stupid." In general, that's good advice, and the acronym (KISS) is certainly easy to remember, but lawyers can forget the reason behind the rule and make the mistake of *only* presenting the simplest explanation or the simplest exhibit. Those lawyers can learn the hard way that, by "dumbing down" the material, you can unintentionally "dumb down" your expert and "dumb down" your argument. Or worse, you can commit the cardinal sin of appearing to talk down to your jury.

Jurors know more about science and medicine and *everything* than at any other time in history. They know there is more to the story, and they will be suspicious of your expert's folksy explanation. They do not want your expert to take the stand and read them *Shakespeare for Dummies*. They want your expert to take the stand and read them *Shakespeare* in the original Elizabethan dialect . . . and then read them *Shakespeare for Dummies*.

Every trial-prep meeting should start by asking your experts how they would explain the most critical concept or opinion: (1) to their most learned peers; (2) to college students studying in their field; and (3) to their next-door neighbor. Ask the expert to create demonstrative exhibits for each of the three audiences.

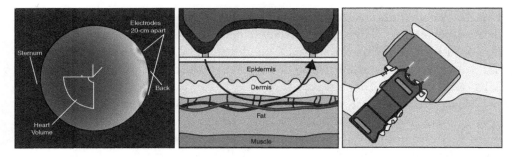

Figure 8.1 "He's smart."    Figure 8.2    "That makes sense."   Figure 8.3    "He's right."

At trial, solicit all three explanations and present all three exhibits. Use the first explanation and exhibit to demonstrate your expert's degree of understanding and experience (i.e., the "he's smart" exhibit). Use the second explanation and exhibit to make the concept more accessible to the jury (i.e., the "that makes sense" exhibit). Use the third explanation and exhibit to convince the jury your expert is correct (i.e., the "he's right" exhibit).

During the *State v. Nugent*[1] manslaughter trial, we had the challenge of explaining to Winn Parish (Louisiana) jurors the path of electrical current during a drive-stun by a TASER® Conducted Electrical Weapon (CEW). Contrary to what the opposing expert said, the current did not travel all over the body like lightning. It only traveled between the two contact points at the tip of the device, and it did not travel very far beneath the skin. When we met with our expert in bioelectricity, we asked him to show us the most accurate exhibit, and he showed us a finite element model (Figure 8.1)—which looked a lot like an atmospheric infrared image of earth and a little like the Imperial Death Star. We asked him for a simpler explanation, and he showed us a simpler visual graphic depicting the layers beneath the skin and using arrows to identify the path (Figure 8.2). But what we found the most persuasive was our expert's willingness to nonchalantly drive-stun a metal soda can *while holding* the metal soda can (Figure 8.3).

At trial, we provided the jury with all three explanations and we showed the jury both exhibits and the demonstration. During the next break, the bailiff walked-up to us and said, "I figured you were right for the past week, but I didn't really *get it* until I saw that can." Lesson learned.

## WHY ARE YOU JUST SITTING THERE?

Conventional wisdom says that an expert should take the stand and remain there until dismissed, but the days of listening to Abraham Lincoln and Stephen A.

---

1. State v. Nugent, No. 41,476, 8th Jud. Dist. Ct., Parish of Winn, La.

Douglas debate for hours are long gone. Jurors have shorter attention spans and are more visual learners. They crave movement and they need visual reinforcement. So do not just ask your expert to describe the location of L5-S1 on the lumbar spine. Tell your expert to stand-up and point to it on a model of the lumbar spine or on an MRI or on your back (or all three).

Make sure to practice your demonstrations with your expert. Do not just warn your neurosurgeon that you "may" ask him to stand up and point to the herniation on an MRI. Do not just "agree" that your accident reconstruction expert will stand up and draw the accident site for the jury. Tell your expert *you* are a visual learner and *you* need your expert to "show you" during the meeting. Never take the chance that you will blow up the wrong image (i.e., axial instead of sagittal MRI view), that your expert's drawing will omit a critical detail (like a median), or that your expert's handwriting will look like a toddler's.

There is a difference between *telling* a jury that your witness is a good doctor and *showing* the jury that your witness is a good doctor. Do not be satisfied telling the jury that your expert has been practicing for 20 years, let them *see* and *hear* what 20 years of experience looks like. If a finding from a physical examination is critical (i.e., finding of muscle spasm), have your orthopedic surgeon stand up and demonstrate on you how she routinely administers physical exams. Let the jury see and hear how professional and second nature an examination is for your expert. If a field sobriety test is the key to the case, let the jury see and hear the officer administer one to you. Watching your witness do what your witness does every day reminds the jury that your witness is an expert. Whenever possible, let the jury see your experts doing their job.

There is a reason why students love "show and tell." Do not be satisfied with having your expert explain what was tested, *show* them. If your expert analyzed a histology slide, let the jury see your witness "expertly" place a slide under a portable microscope, and hear your expert describe the steps involved in the analysis.

During the 2014 wrongful death jury trial in *Ward v. Jefferson Parish School Board*,[2] we faced the legal and emotional challenge of helping jurors determine what caused a child to die while at school. Instead of asking our expert to tell the jury what caused the death, we had our pediatric forensic pathologist bring to trial his microscope, the histology slides of normal heart tissue, several photographs of normal heart tissue found in textbooks (from his office), and the histology slides of the deceased child. During direct examination, we had our expert compare the textbook examples of normal heart tissue with the child's abnormal heart tissue, walk the jury through his process of diagnosing the child with a disease known as Arrhythmogenic Right Ventricular Dysplasia (ARVD), and explain to the jury how ARVD caused the terrible tragedy. Even though the jury still found the school partially liable for failing to monitor the child, one juror told us that

---

2. Ward v. Jefferson Parish Sch. Bd., No. 697-713, 24th Jud. Dist. Ct., Jefferson Parish, La.

our expert's methodical use of the tissue slides and textbooks succeeded in over-coming his personal skepticism about the existence and role of cardiac disease in causing the death.

During the 1999 capital jury trial in *State v. Whitten*,[3] we needed to prove that the defendant killed all four victims and lived with their dead bodies (daily forging checks in one victim's name) until the smell and flies drove him out of the house. But, by the time the bodies were discovered, the bodies were so decomposed that the best way to date the time of death was the age of the maggots that covered them. During our direct examination of our expert in entomology, we had our expert explain how he calculated the gestational period and age of the collected maggots while the jurors passed around a clear container of maggots. That one exhibit drove home to the jury what our entomologist did every day, made the tragic deaths more real, and made certain that our direct examination never became an academic exer-cise. It kept our feet on the ground.

# WHO TOLD YOU THAT YOU'RE FUNNY?

Conventional wisdom says that a lawyer should take a grumpy or difficult expert to the woodshed. But if you tell a curmudgeon to smile, his face will contort in unimaginable ways. If you tell a shy expert to make eye contact, he will make one of your jurors uncomfortable. You can't change your expert's personality during a one-hour meeting, nor should you try. Jurors do not expect genius to tolerate stupidity, and jurors do not expect hardened professionals to be warm and cuddly. If anything, jurors will be suspicious of brilliant experts who flatter ordinary lawyers.

The challenge is to discover your expert's real personality, and disabuse your expert of any ridiculous notions they may have about themselves. You know that friend of yours who *thinks* he is funny? How about that friend who *thinks* he knows everything? Or that friend who *thinks* he is a lawyer? Well, you need to figure out which one your expert is. Our job is to help our experts become who they *are*.

In the 2006 jury trial in *Swain v. RLI Insurance Company*,[4] a federal court case involving a trucking accident, we retained a gray-haired cardiologist who was unbe-lievably patient and kind toward me during our practice direct examinations, but was a nightmare to opposing counsel during his deposition. It was difficult to watch him bully the opposing counsel with one-word answers, pained expressions, and openly hostile criticism of well-intentioned questions. We quickly realized that the jury would almost certainly dislike and be suspicious of his Jekyll and Hyde routine, and we shared our concerns with our expert. He told us he could be "folksy" on the stand. We told him, "you don't have that club in your bag."

---

3. State v. Whitten, No. 393-956, Crim. Dist. Ct., Parish of Orleans, La.
4. Swain v. RLI Ins. Co., No. 05-cv-852, (E.D. La. 2005).

We made an executive decision. We asked our cardiologist to be cantankerous to *both* lawyers. We told him not to suffer foolish questions from *either* lawyer. The cardiologist nodded his head and smiled. Freed from having to pretend to be Mr. Nice Guy, he took the stand at trial, relaxed, and answered questions as if they were being asked by lazy medical interns. The jury loved him and agreed that the accident did not cause the plaintiff's subsequent heart problems. Turns out that a difficult witness is a trustworthy witness, and a little hostility or disagreement can go a long way in persuading jurors that your expert is objective and that the conversation they just witnessed was real.

Veteran high school teachers tell new teachers to "be yourself" in the classroom, and that is the best advice you can give your expert. If you are not a jock, do not try to be a jock on the stand. If you are not funny, do not try to be funny on the stand. And if you are not British, do not try to sound British on the stand. Like high school students, jurors will see through you, and they will eat you alive. Do not allow your expert to make the fatal mistake of acting the way they *think* experts should act on the stand or trying to become what they are not.

# WHAT IS A GOOD MISTAKE I CAN MAKE?

Conventional wisdom says to ask perfect questions and get perfect answers, but that is not how real conversations work. The first time you spoke with your expert, you did not ask every question perfectly nor did your expert flatter you and praise your understanding of the material. Your expert corrected you. Your expert read you something or drew you something. Somehow, your expert found a way to teach and persuade you. Recreate that real conversation for the jury, and ask your expert what are some "common mistakes" or "common misconceptions" you should address.

We have to stop asking the questions we want to ask our expert, and start asking the questions jurors would ask our expert. The goal of direct examination is not to take a juror's level of understanding and raise it to the level of your expert's understanding. The goal of direct examination is to take a juror's level of understanding and raise it to your level. The best way to do that is to allow the jury to experience the same learning curve you experienced (or a condensed version of it). Never deprive jurors of explanations and steps that helped you, and never ask jurors to make logical leaps no one asked you to make.

Every jury has a bias, prejudice, or misconception about some aspect of your trial (i.e., about a product, injury, diagnostic test, disease, etc.). When you identify that common misconception, do not try to disabuse the jury of it with a single, condescending question ("what if someone actually thought" or "what if someone stood up in opening statement and said . . . "). Most misconceptions are based on one or more true premises, facts, or metaphors. Let the jury hear your expert agree with the truth of those premises, facts, or metaphors. Then ask why, if that premise/

basis/metaphor is true, the common misconception is not also true. Let your expert correct *you* and explain it to *you*. Picture a juror who holds that misconception thinking, "hey, I was thinking the same thing" while your expert is agreeing with the premises, and "oh, I see why that isn't true" while your expert explains where you went wrong. Of course, that is easier said than done, and you have to be sincere in your curiosity and questioning or the jury will recognize the whole line of questioning is staged.

Be careful not to take it too far. Before the *Nugent* trial, every time we asked a question of our expert in bioelectricity, and he answered "yes," we got the feeling he was thinking "close enough." We became concerned that the jury would get the same feeling so we warned our expert that we were going to make mistakes during direct examination—but we didn't tell him when. It was up to him to listen carefully, and to correct every mistake—no matter how insignificant the correction.

Our expert welcomed the challenge and took our instructions to heart. During his direct examination, he corrected every rounded-off number, challenged every exaggeration, and contested every metaphor. Our direct examination quickly became a monumental challenge, and the wrestling match that ensued provoked laughter among the jurors and the following exchanges:

Q. I've shown a couple of witnesses this diagram, which shows the TASER X26 being applied to the chest of a person. Does this—Is this a diagram that you have seen before?

A. I have.

Q. Do you believe it to be accurate?

A. It is.

Q. [I]t shows the location of the two prongs on the chest of a person. . . . This would be looking down like this at [the] person if we were to literally take a, uh, slice, one slice out like this and then we were to rotate it. That's what it would look like?

A. Yes. Your –

Q. Looking down?

A. Your diagram is [being held] a little low. You want to be a little higher, become more, uh, pectoral muscle there and a little more of the heart.

Q. Okay. I didn't hold it at the right height, but it's a slice—

A. Yes.[5]

\* \* \*

---

5. *Nugent*, Trial Tr., Day 5 (Oct. 27, 2010), 33:30–34:18.

Q. And the taser the amount of energy is one tenth of one joule. Is that right?

A. That's correct.

Q. So if we're—If you heard the expression, that the dose is the poison,—

A. I've heard that expression.

Q. [I]f you say well, one Tylenol is not poisonous but if you were to have two hundred Tylenols, that could be poisonous?

A. Actually about fifteen will kill you.

Q. Right. Now, I—But I—Okay. But we're—

COURT REPORTER NOTE:

**Laughter in the courtroom**

A. And that's if you're not alcoholic.

Q. I'm gonna lose this battle. I'm gonna try. All right. Work with me. You're my witness. All right?

COURT REPORTER NOTE:

**Laughter in the courtroom**

Q. All right. I've been waiting how long to call a witness?[6]

\* \* \*

Q. So, you can say, "well, [can] Tylenol kill you." Well, yes. If you take two thousand Tylenol. But did Tylenol kill a patient? You would want to look at the actual Tylenol that the patient took?

A. That's correct.

Q. The same is true for electrical current. The question of whether electrical current can kill you has been decided. Right? I mean we know from lightning whether electrical current can be delivered to the heart. We know from defibrillators. Is that true?

A. Yes and may I correct something?

Q. Please.

A. It's not fifteen Tylenol. Fifteen grams of Tylenol, which will be thirty extra strength—

Q. Please.

A. —would be lethal.

Q. Please stay with me. All right?[7]

---

6. *Id.* at 30:24–31:12.

7. *Id.* at 31:23–32:7.

Plato did not want his students to play the fool, but he recognized the value of a good foil. That is the fine line that every trial lawyer must walk during direct examination. Never play the fool, but never miss the opportunity to play the foil, ask the questions the jurors want answered, and help your expert teach them by teaching you.

## WHAT ARE THEY *RIGHT* ABOUT?

Conventional wisdom says to avoid agreeing with *anything* an opposing expert says, but jurors are less suspicious of experts who are comfortable agreeing with parts of an opposing expert's testimony.

During the 2012 personal injury case of *Wilson v. Global Van Lines, LLC,*[8] we faced the challenge of addressing an abnormal post-accident MRI that was somehow sandwiched between two normal MRIs. During direct examination, we established that: (1) plaintiff's pre-accident MRI showed a normal cervical spine with normal curvature; (2) plaintiff's treating doctors interpreted the first post-accident MRI (taken at three months) as showing abnormal curvature; and (3) the plaintiff's second post-accident MRI (taken months later) was identical to the pre-accident MRI. Instead of asking our expert if the treating physicians were wrong to conclude that the accident caused abnormal curvature, we asked our expert if the treating physicians were *correct* when they read the first post-accident MRI as showing abnormal curvature. Our expert replied "yes," and that surprising answer got our full attention—which our expert held just long enough to explain that the cause of that abnormal curvature on that one post-accident MRI was the pillow positioned under the plaintiff's head (not the accident). If that case had proceeded to trial, we would have recreated that moment during direct examination. We would have allowed our expert to surprise the jury with the same "yes," and to teach them about the pillow while he held their full attention.

Always bring their expert's report and deposition testimony to your meeting with your expert. Show your expert everything their expert said and find out what premises, assumptions, calculations, and opinions are 100 percent accurate and complete. That is your real starting point because that is what jurors want to hear first. They want you to tell them *specifically* where the two roads diverge in the yellow wood before you ask them to choose a road to travel by. If you do not tell them, they may try to figure it out for themselves during jury deliberations—which you do not want.

## WHAT DOES THE BOOK SAY?

Conventional wisdom says to ask your experts for their opinion and not their sources, but that ignores human nature. When you are sitting at a blackjack table,

---

8. Wilson v. Global Van Lines, LLC, No. 12-173, 21st Jud. Dist. Ct., Parish of Tangipahoa, La.

the dealer (who is an expert at blackjack) doesn't tell you her opinion, she tells you "the book says to hit." And you do not hit 15 because Gina from Little Rock, Arkansas, told you to hit 15; you hit 15 because "the book says to hit 15." Similarly at trial, give jurors a reason to believe your expert by reading them textbook passages and showing them textbook examples that support your expert's opinions.

Before the *Nugent* trial, we noticed that the forensic pathologist supported his autopsy finding that the cause of death was sickle cell sudden death and his classification of the manner of death as accidental (versus homicide) by including a citation to a textbook. When we learned that the forensic pathologist found an image (microscopic photography) in the textbook of pre-mortem sickling that was identical to the sickling he saw when viewing the deceased's histology slides, we asked him to bring that textbook and that slide to trial. During our examination, the jury heard the following exchange:

Q. And did you bring that textbook with you . . .

A. Yes, I did . . .

Q. I see it . . . We can't miss it. It's huge . . .

A. Uh, the title of it is Spitz and Fisher's . . . Medical, Legal Investigation of Death . . .

Q. Could you turn to that page please?

A. And it's page eleven or six.

Q. Okay. So, literally . . . what you saw in microscopic examination is a textbook example . . .

A. Uh, that's correct . . . [9]

For the rest of the *Nugent* trial, we referred to the death as a "textbook" case of sickle cell sudden death, and the jury agreed.

The "textbook" scenario works both ways. During the *Ward* wrongful death case involving ARVD, the plaintiff's forensic pathologist correctly noted ARVD in her autopsy report but misdiagnosed it as "slight right ventricular dilatation" (RVD). During direct examination, our expert compared the child's histological slide with textbook images of ARVD and RVD to prove: (1) ARVD and RVD look nothing alike; and (2) the child's histological slide looked nothing like the "textbook" case of RVD.

Always ask your expert to show you what a textbook example looks like, especially when textbook examples do not support the opposing expert's conclusions. Proving that the present case is not a "textbook" case can be half the battle. Picture showing your expert MRI images of acute trauma from a textbook, and having your

---

9. *Nugent*, Trial Tr., Day 3 (Oct. 25, 2010), 18:15–19:16.

expert physically point to the edema in the textbook MRI images. Now picture your expert showing the plaintiff's MRI images, and physically pointing out where there is no edema.

## HOW CAN WE MAKE THEIR CASE *BETTER*?

Conventional wisdom says to discuss only the facts of your case with your expert, but jurors know that only the "really good" and the "really bad" cases go to trial, and they *want* to know which type of case they are deciding. Jurors often lack the knowledge and experience required to recognize "on a scale of 1 to 10" where a specific claim, defense, argument, or injury ranks; and the best way to teach them is to show them what a better claim would be or what a more severe injury would have been.

In a traumatic brain injury trial, have your expert respond to "gloom and doom" testimony about a subdural hematoma by explaining more severe injuries (that did not happen) like those involving mass effect, midline shift, or herniation. In a slip-and-fall case, your expert can attack the defendant's argument that the lighting was "reasonable" by discussing much better forms of lighting. Teach the jury what a much better claim/defense *would have been*, and the jury will learn why the current claim/defense is inadequate or untenable.

That trial strategy starts during the meeting with your expert. When you meet with your expert, find out what facts or circumstances *would have made* the plaintiff's case, or a defendant's defense, much better.

## WHAT YOU GOT THAT THEIRS AIN'T GOT?

Conventional wisdom says to never ask your expert to comment on *their* expert's credentials, and that is good advice. You should never have a doctor with a medical degree from Harvard comment on a medical degree from *any* other school. But if your expert has knowledge and experience their expert lacks, you need to bring it to the jury's attention at the start of your direct examination and you can do that without asking your expert anything about their expert.

Nothing is more effective during a jury trial than filling out a chart comparing your expert's qualifications with theirs. Days later, jurors may not recall what each row addressed, but they will remember *seeing* a column of "yes" for your expert, and *seeing* a column of "no" for theirs. If you want that visual seared into a juror's mind, you have to bring a draft chart to your meeting, roll-up your sleeves, verify that you can write "yes" on every row of your expert's column. You should bring that same chart to your deposition of their expert and get their expert to say "no" to the exact same questions.

During the 2015 wrongful death jury trial in *Ricks v. City of Alexandria, et al.,*[10] plaintiff hired a cardiac electrophysiologist who, during his deposition, made a number of startling admissions regarding his lack of knowledge and experience. At trial, during cross-examination, we showed the jury a chart and made the jury watch us write "no" in nine of eleven rows for the plaintiff's expert. And the two times their expert answered "yes" (despite saying "no" during his deposition), he had to exaggerate his experience. For example, the jury actually heard their expert insist he "researched" the product prior to his being hired when, while casually reading a journal, he read something about the product in an article. Which is like saying you are an expert and you have researched post-traumatic stress disorder because you read *American Sniper*. The jury was treated to this exchange:

Q.  Had you ever researched the effect of a conducted electrical weapon?

A.  Yes.

Q.  Prior to being retained in this case?

A.  It was part of published data that I had seen.

Q.  When articles came out you'd read them from time to time. Had you ever done a research project?

A.  I read the medical journals.

Q.  Had you ever done a research project?

A.  No.[11]

Fortunately, the *Ricks* trial ended with a directed verdict for the defense, and we never had to call our expert. But, if the trial had continued, the jury would have watched us start the direct examination of our expert by writing "yes" in every row of our expert's column during direct examination. The completed chart (which should be left on the screen or displayed for the entire direct examination) would have looked like the one shown in Figure 8.4.

Of course, what's good for the goose is good for the gander. You should expect opposing counsel to prepare the same type of chart, and you should ask your expert: "What's their expert got, that *you* ain't got?" Hopefully, your expert's answer will be "nothing." But, if there are significant differences in qualifications, you will at least have time to discuss those differences with your expert and to prepare a response.

---

10.  Ricks v. City of Alexandria, et al., No. 12-cv-349 (W.D. La. 2012).
11.  *Id.* Daily (Rough Draft) Trial Tr., Day 2 (May 3, 2015).

| KNOWLEDGE & EXPERIENCE: CONDUCTED ELECTRICAL WEAPONS | | |
|---|---|---|
| **When Hired:** | **Kerwin** | **Swerdlow** |
| Served on Scientific & Medical Advisory Board for TASER International, Inc.? | No | Yes |
| Served on Board for any CEW Manufacturer? | No | Yes |
| Published (first author) a peer-reviewed CEW scientific paper? | No | Yes |
| Published (senior author) a peer-reviewed CEW scientific paper? | No | Yes |
| Published any peer-reviewed CEW scientific paper? | No | Yes |
| Written *any* CEW scientific papers? | No | Yes |
| Retained an expert in a CEW lawsuit? | No | Yes |
| Researched effect of CEWs? | "Yes" | Yes |
| Touched a CEW? | No | Yes |
| Seen "in real life" a TASER M26 CEW? | "Yes" | Yes |
| In the broadest possible sense, did you have any exposure or experience with TASER CEWs? | No | Yes |

Figure 8.4    What Our Experts Got That Theirs Ain't Got

# WHAT DO YOU *DO* ALL DAY?

Conventional wisdom says to quickly establish your expert's qualifications, but jurors often define who a person is by what they do. Make sure the jury sees the big picture by asking your expert to tell you what a "typical day" or a "typical week" is like in their practice.

During the *Nugent* trial, we decided to tender one witness as an expert "in the field of emergency medicine" and "on the physiological effects of electronic control devices on the human body." Because our expert had conducted so many studies and published so many articles on the same product, we were concerned the jury would get the impression he was a "lab geek" or (worse) a "hired gun" who worked for the manufacturer of the product he researched and tested. To make sure the jury saw the big picture, we elicited the following testimony about a typical week in his life:

    Q.  If you would, please tell the jurors about your actual practice, what you do in the course of a week?

A. Uh, several things. I wear many hats. Uh, in the course of a week I spend approximately twenty-four to twenty-five hours, uh, actually taking care of patients in the emergency department. Uh, I probably spend, uh, twenty to twenty-five hours, uh, doing what's called EMS, medical direction. So, I provide, uh, administrative and medical director services to, uh, some of the law enforcement and, uh, fire department paramedic programs that are around our area, and I spend an additional twenty to twenty-five hours on, uh, research activities. So, my typical workweek is about seventy hours or so.[12]

Our expert's answer did not sound rehearsed, and his description of his typical work week emphasized he was neither a "lab geek" nor a "hired gun." We interviewed some of the jurors after they found our client not guilty of manslaughter. It was clear that those jurors realized our expert was a hard-working doctor who helped people every day, and they gave his testimony greater weight.

If a jury doesn't hear about your expert's practice, they may assume the worst. During the 2009 (paralysis) jury trial in *Craige v. Grundmann*,[13] we were faced with a classic battle of experts. Plaintiff's neurosurgeon testified that the plaintiff's paralysis was caused by trauma, and our neurosurgeon was going to testify that the real cause was unrelated transverse myelitis. During direct examination, plaintiff's counsel failed to ask their expert about a typical day. So, during our cross-examination, we made certain the jury heard that their expert did a *lot* of work for local plaintiff lawyers.

In contrast, during our direct examination, we asked our neurosurgeon to describe a typical day. The jury heard about his seeing patients, performing surgery, and preparing to present at an international conference. The compare/contrast was incredibly effective. Despite a sympathetic and paralyzed plaintiff, the trial resulted in a hung verdict (7–5) with the split jury unable to answer the very first question on the jury interrogatory: did the accident cause any injury?

## WHAT ARE YOU *REALLY* AN EXPERT IN?

Lawyers often assume they know the correct field in which to tender their expert. Please do not make that assumption. Make sure your expert agrees with the exact wording of every field in which he or she will be tendered as your expert witness. Your expert will always be the best judge of whether the field is too broad or too narrow.

Avoid tendering an expert as an expert in *doing* something. There is a difference between tendering your witness as an expert "in the field of cardiology" and

---

12. *Nugent*, Trial Tr., Day 6 of Trial (Oct. 28, 2010), 7:13–24.
13. Craige v. Grundmann, No. 06-12,739, Civ. Dist. Ct, Parish of Orleans, La.

"in open heart surgery"; between tendering your witness as an expert "in the field of economics" and "in calculating present value of future medical expenses"; and between tendering your witness as an expert "in the field of human factors" and "in analyzing the rise and run of stairs." Know whether courts in your jurisdiction have allowed experts in your witness's field to offer the type of opinions you will ultimately seek. If so, get the court to accept your witness in that field *and then* establish your witness's experience performing open heart surgery, calculating present value, or analyzing the rise and run of stairs.

Broader is not better. During a 1998 hearing challenging the constitutionality of a Louisiana criminal statute, a local law school student tendered his witness as an expert in the field of theology. Because he tendered the witness as an expert in the *entire* field of theology, which is broadly defined as the "study of God," the court allowed us to conduct an almost unlimited voir dire on the tender. We were allowed to question their witness regarding every religion (from Judaism to Islam), every theological work (from Plato's Timaeus to Hegel's Phenomenology of the Spirit), and every theological concept (from Aristotle's Unmoved Mover to Cartesian Metaphysics). After repeatedly admitting his ignorance, the demoralized witness could not remember the answer to our final question: "which Apostle replaced Judas?" The judge knew the answer (Matthias), and promptly ruled that the witness was *only* an expert as to the *specific* tenets of his *specific* faith for his *specific* church. By tendering too broadly, the student rendered his witness's testimony meaningless.

## DOES GOOGLE AGREE WITH YOU?

Conventional wisdom says to have the court instruct the jury not to search online, and you should definitely request a daily jury instruction prohibiting independent research,[14] but your client is not paying you to be an optimist. Always assume at least one juror will ignore the court's instructions. Prior to meeting with your expert, always perform relevant Internet searches regarding the injury, illness, product, or accident.

Do not allow the outcome of your trial to be determined in a basement apartment by a juror wearing pajamas and reading Wikipedia. Learn what Wikipedia

---

14. *See* Judicial Conference Committee on Court Administration and Case Management, Proposed Model Jury Instructions: The Use of Electronic Technology to Conduct Research on or Communicate about a Case (December 2009); *see* OneBeacon Ins. Co. v. T. Wade Welch & Assoc., No. CIV.A. H-11-3061, 2014 WL 5335362, at *10 (S.D. Tex. Oct. 17, 2014) ("As judges of the facts, you must decide this case based solely on evidence presented here within the four walls of this courtroom. This means that during deliberations you must not conduct any independent research about this case, the topics involved in the case, or the individuals or corporations mentioned. In other words, you are prohibited from consulting dictionaries or reference materials; searching the internet, web sites, or blogs; or using any other electronic tools to obtain information to help you decide the case."); *see also In re* Methyl Tertiary Butyl Ether (MTBE) Products Liab. Litig., 739 F. Supp. 2d 576, 610 (S.D.N.Y. 2010).

says. Learn what your expert would say about that Wikipedia entry. Maybe the Wikipedia entry discusses an earlier model of the product. Maybe the Wikipedia entry contains factually incorrect statements. Maybe the Wikipedia entry cites an inapplicable or discredited medical study. Consider the pros and cons of handing that Wikipedia page to your expert during direct examination and letting your expert "set the record straight." Never introduce a Wikipedia entry for the sake of attacking a Wikipedia entry during direct examination unless you are absolutely certain your expert can destroy it absolutely. When in doubt, leave the inadmissible prejudicial material out!

Remember that you can discuss the substance of the web page with your expert without physically showing the inadmissible hearsay document to your expert. Why take the chance that opposing counsel will argue that your showing the web page to your expert somehow rendered it admissible—even though your expert did not rely on the web page in reaching any opinions? Know how your court has ruled on this issue before you hand your expert anything.

## WHAT DO YOU HAVE TO SAY FOR YOURSELF?

Conventional wisdom says to ignore any blemishes to your expert's record, but it is imperative to steal opposing counsel's thunder during your direct examination. Sun Tzu's advice from *Art of War* rings especially true: "It is a doctrine of war not to assume the enemy will not come, but rather to rely on one's readiness to meet him; not to presume that he will not attack, but rather to make one's self invincible." If you know your expert's skeletons, you must assume opposing counsel knows them too, and what better way to be ready for that attack than to preempt it.

There is a reason why every politician and every corporation wants to "get ahead" of every story. Jurors will never forgive you for hiding something unfavorable about your expert during direct examination. You *must* be the one to bring it up. You *must* ask the tough question that opposing counsel was going to ask. And, your expert *must* directly, honestly, and fully address it with you.

Do not meet with your experts until you've researched your experts like you were going to cross-examine them at trial, and then (gently) cross-examine them when you do meet. Your experts may not know their skeletons are "out there" on the Internet or in published opinions. They may not fully understand how those skeletons could negatively affect the way jurors listen to their testimony. And they may be expecting you to object and the court to sustain your objection. Always show your expert what you found, and find out *how* your expert wants you to raise that issue during your direct examination.

Yes, it can be difficult to walk the line between "preparing" your expert and "scaring" your expert into not wanting to testify at trial. Never play devil's advocate so aggressively that you anger or alienate your expert during your meeting. Always approach the issue as if you are simply trying to make sure your expert's "side of the story" comes out at trial.

During the 2005 jury trial in *Pyles v. Weaver*,[15] we represented a gentleman's club on Bourbon Street that was being sued by a former entertainer for having inadequate security the night a patron threw a glass at her. Plaintiff sustained dental injuries, and additionally claimed a cervical injury and permanent brain damage. The night before we called our security expert to the stand, we checked "one more time" to make sure there were no negative published opinions about our security expert. We discovered that the Court of Appeals had just published an opinion in his personal lawsuit against a former employer in which our security expert claimed that he sustained . . . wait for it . . . permanent brain damage. Fortunately, we had time to meet with our (allegedly brain damaged) expert, and decide whether to discuss his lawsuit during direct examination or address it during redirect.

Four years later, during the 2009 judge trial in *Octave v. Sheriff Willie Martin, Jr.*,[16] the plaintiff retained the same security expert. Incredibly, during his examination, plaintiff's counsel failed to ask the expert about his personal brain damage lawsuit. So, during cross-examination, we challenged the expert's rather selective memory about the officer's testimony by asking (now paraphrasing): "Well, you've told us what you remember about the officers' testimony; but, in fairness to you, you do have *permanent* brain damage." Needless to say, opposing counsel came out of his seat like he was shot out of a canon. He objected that we were insulting his expert and all but demanded our immediate disbarment. The court calmly read the published opinion and overruled the objection. After our cross-examination, plaintiff rested and the court calmly granted a directed verdict to our clients.

Make sure your expert knows *when and how* you are going to be asking him direct examination questions about his skeletons to steal opposing counsel's thunder. Never surprise your expert with "stealing thunder" questions. Never raise an issue with an opposing expert before you know what your expert would say about that issue.

Before the 2015 jury trial in *Crayton v. Campbell, et al.*,[17] we realized both the plaintiff's neurosurgeon and the defense neurosurgeon had omitted from their expert reports any mention of the edema (swelling) in a lumbar MRI taken one year after the car accident—even though that edema was critical evidence of recent trauma. When we met with our expert, we showed him the MRI film, selected specific views to enlarge for the jury, and practiced direct examination questions about the extensive degenerative changes seen in the MRI. We also asked him about the significance of the edema, and explained why and when we would ask him one question to "steal their thunder" (i.e., "Why didn't *you* mention the edema in *your* report?"). Only after hearing his perfectly reasonable answer, did we decide

15. Pyles v. Weaver, No. 2001-15,258, Civ. Dist. Ct., Parish of Orleans, La.
16. Octave v. Sheriff Willie Martin, Jr., No. 28,753, 23rd Jud. Dist. Ct., Parish of St. James, La.
17. Crayton v. Campbell, et al., No. 704-421, 24th Jud. Dist. Ct., Parish of Jefferson, La.

to raise the issue during our cross-examination of their expert *and* during our direct examination of our expert.

# CONCLUSION

It is time we change the way we approach direct examination. Trial lawyers have to stop shining the spotlight on themselves and thinking of direct examination as an opportunity to prove they know the material "just as well" or are "just as smart" as their expert witness. That is hubris and hysterical. The purpose of direct examination is not to persuade the jury to trust the paid advocate who is asking the questions. The purpose of direct examination is to persuade the jury to trust the expert answering those questions. Shine the spotlight on your expert and let your expert win the trial!

## CHAPTER 9

# Queen's Gambit

## Preparing Your Expert for the Chess Match of Cross-Examination

### *Daniel J. Stephenson*[1]

## INTRODUCTION

> There are only two main principles in chess: safety and activity.
>
> — *Dan Heisman, United States Chess Federation National Master*

Trials are routinely compared to chess matches.[2] The expert witness, then, is your "queen." The expert has the greatest leeway to introduce evidence that will inflict damage on your opponent, and the greatest flexibility in terms of "moves." The expert can be the conduit through which facts are introduced, but unlike fact witnesses, the expert can also render opinions. Like the queen in chess, who can move diagonally and laterally, the expert in a trial can move multidimensionally. Trials are often won or lost on the testimony of experts.

Like the queen in chess, the expert also has to be adequately protected. The queen's mobility and value make her a prime target for harassment. One of the most common opening series of moves is called the Queen's Gambit (Figure 9.1), where pawns in front of both parties' queens are moved forward, then White moves an adjacent pawn forward. The "gambit" is that Black has to decide whether to capture White's pawn with his own. The capture (Figure 9.2) is a temporary victory, but it moves the capturing black pawn out of the line of protection of his queen. The "activity" (offense) has a corresponding effect on "safety" (defense).

---

1. I gratefully acknowledge the excellent contributions of Kathryn F. Abernethy.
2. *See, e.g.*, BOB BODEDE, CHESS AND CRIMINAL TRIALS (London: XLibris 2013); Roy Strom, *Illinois' Changing Trial Chess Match*, CHICAGO LAWYER (Feb. 2014).

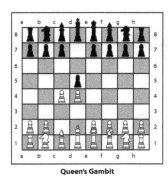

Queen's Gambit

Figure 9.1

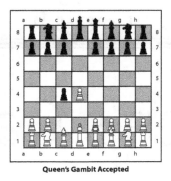

Queen's Gambit Accepted

Figure 9.2

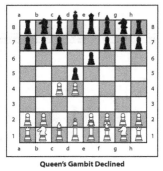

Queen's Gambit Declined

Figure 9.3

Naturally, Black does not always accept this move; his defense is called Queen's Gambit Declined (Figure 9.3), which emphasizes safety over activity.

If you are a lawyer and a chess lover, Gerald Abrahams might be one of your heroes. He was an English Barrister and accomplished amateur chess player who developed a move called the "Queen's Gambit Declined Semi-Slav Defense, Abrahams-Noteboom Variation." Chess, like trying cases, can be complicated.

Expert testimony always requires a strategic trade-off between safety and activity. When an expert covers a lot of territory effectively, he or she can do great damage to the other side's case. The queen can capture a lot of pawns by roaming the board. This very activity, however, can put her *en prise*—in a position to be captured. If your expert is vanquished on cross-examination, you may have very few moves left before the game is over.

Your opposing counsel will come after your expert with a vengeance on cross-examination. Some experts will succumb. Others will emerge with nicks. The best experts will emerge from cross-examination even stronger than when the direct ended. What is the difference? Clearly, some experts are just naturally better than others at handling cross-examination. Others are made better by good preparation. You cannot always tell who is going to be a "natural." Preparation of your expert witness for cross-examination could be the key to trial success.

Most trial lawyers have a standard set of points they emphasize with any witness they are preparing for trial: tell the truth; give the facts and don't speculate; give short and direct answers; and read the documents put in front of you before answering questions about them. Lawyers frequently practice the direct examination with the witness before trial. A good lawyer may also have a colleague that the witness doesn't know pepper the witness with cross-examination questions to give a feel for what cross will be like.

Although these are good starting points with an expert, the process of preparing for cross-examination does not end with the same drill you've put your fact witnesses through. Fact witnesses are only testifying to their personal knowledge—what they saw, heard, and did—and rarely are asked to carry a scientific or economic theory at trial. Lay witnesses also have the benefit of memory—everything they are testifying about is something that actually happened to them at some point in their lives.

An expert, on the other hand, is the centerpiece of your case on complex technical, scientific, or economic issues. The expert must not only teach the jury something new about science, mathematics, or economics, but must also convince the jury that her view on that subject matter is the correct view. Thus, the expert is more than just a witness; she is part teacher and part advocate. It is important that experts maintain their credibility on cross-examination, otherwise they have very far to fall in the jury's estimation. Expert preparation for cross-examination thus goes beyond, and is arguably more critical than, preparation of fact witnesses.

# DOES PREPARATION WORK?

It is a mistake to think that combination[3] is solely a matter of talent, and that it cannot be acquired.

— *Richard Reti, Czechoslovakian Grandmaster and "Endgame Artist"*

Lawyers are among the most skeptical people on earth. The skeptical lawyer says, "how do we know if preparing an expert for cross-examination makes any difference?" Before we launch into a study of *how* to prepare experts, it is appropriate to ask *whether* the exercise does any good. Can expert witness performance on cross-examination be improved?

A few studies have been done on preparation for cross-examination. They uniformly show that witnesses do better on cross when they're prepared, at least in certain areas like confidence, delivery skills, and nervousness reduction.[4] But there are few studies measuring the effects of *expert* preparation, and common sense suggests that experts should have fewer issues in those three areas.

Studies tell us some things that work with experts in front of juries. Examples of factors that affect expert credibility include the following:

1. Jurors are more persuaded by "likeable" experts than unlikeable ones, even when the content is the same.[5]

---

3. In chess, a "combination" is a sequence of moves, planned in advance, often initiated by a sacrifice.
4. Marcus T. Boccaccini, Trina Gordon, & Stanley L. Brodsky, *Witness Preparation Training with Real and Simulated Criminal Defendants*, 23 BEHAVIORAL SCIENCES & THE LAW, Oct. 11, 2005, at 659–87. *See generally* Tess M. S. Neal, *Expert Witness Preparation: What Does the Literature Tell Us?* in THE JURY EXPERT, AMERICAN SOCIETY OF TRIAL CONSULTANTS 44–52 (Mar. 2009).
5. Stanley L. Brodsky, Tess M.S. Neal, Robert J. Cramer, & Mitchell H. Ziemke, *Credibility in the Courtroom: How Likeable Should an Expert Witness Be?*, 37 J. AM. ACAD. PSYCHIATRY & L., 2009, 525–32; Tess M.S. Neal, Rosanna E. Guadagno, Cassie A. Eno, & Stanley L. Brodsky, *Warmth and Competence on the Witness Stand: Implications for Credibility of Male and Female Expert Witnesses*, 40 J. AM. ACAD. PSYCHIATRY & L., 2012, 488–97.

2. Confidence exuded by an expert is an asset up to a point—experts seen as arrogant or too assertive are less credible than "medium-confident" experts.[6]

3. On technical issues, the expert giving explanations in simple language is more credible than the same expert who delivers the same content with high-complexity lexicon.[7]

It seems logical that expert preparation could improve performance in one or more of these categories. What does experience show? My experience suggests that there are some "natural" experts who do not need to be prepped; others who will be disasters no matter how much preparation you give; and many in between who can be helped by focused preparation.

The late Dr. Robert Sansom was one of the naturals. He had degrees in engineering and economics, graduated first in his class from the Air Force Academy, and was both a Rhodes scholar and a Fulbright scholar. In the first of two trials between the same parties and lawyers, his testimony decimated the other side's case. In the second trial, the other side decided to try to rough him up. They went down his resume line by line, trying to find holes, but Dr. Sansom emerged from that questioning with even more credibility. When they asked him, "who did you represent in that case?" the answer was "the Queen of England." Another time it was "a consortium of five state governors."

The cross-examiner tried using loaded questions on Dr. Sansom. He deftly fended them off. He was asked "did your lawyers tell you to say that?" He smiled and said, "Mr. Young is an outstanding lawyer, but he doesn't know enough about EPA emission standards to tell me what to say." The jurors laughed. Mr. Young laughed. It was a plus. Dr. Sansom needed no preparation.

On the other end of the spectrum was Norman Hale (not his real name), a piloting expert in an aviation disaster case. Norman was an excellent pilot who knew the rules and techniques back and forth. He did a wonderful job on direct examination. On cross, however, he was such an agreeable guy that he couldn't help conceding major points, just because the cross-examiner suggested them. He wanted to please everybody. Our team knew this about Norman in advance and tried to rid him of it in our prep work. He agreed with the concept, like he agreed with everything, but intense preparation had no effect on Norman.

In between these two poles lie the majority of experts. I have seen numerous examples of experts who responded well to preparation, and I seen some who blundered in instances where preparation would have made a difference. In the sections that follow, I will discuss the areas in which expert cross-examination performance can be improved, and provide some tips on how to do it.

*Lesson to be learned: preparation is unnecessary or futile with some experts. A number, however, will respond positively to good preparation.*

---

6. Robert J. Cramer, Stanley L. Brodsky, & Jamie DeCoster, *Expert Witness Confidence and Juror Personality: Their Impact on Credibility and Persuasion in the Courtroom*, J. AM. ACAD. PSYCHIATRY & L., 2009, 63–74.

7. Joel Cooper & Isaac M. Neuhaus, *The "Hired Gun" Effect: Assessing the Effect of Pay, Frequency of Testifying, and Credentials on the Perception of Expert Testimony*, 24 L. & HUM. BEHAV., 2000, 149–71.

# SUBSTANCE: TRIPARTITE PREPARATION

Help your pieces so they can help you.

— *Paul Morphy, described by Garry Kasparov as "the forefather of modern chess"*

A good expert opinion, and good expert testimony at trial, rests on a tripod. The first leg of the tripod is the expert's knowledge, skill, ability, and qualifications. This may include research studies the expert has performed and papers the expert has written. It includes all of the fancy degrees and accolades that will dazzle the jury into believing that this expert is an authority on the matters on which he or she speaks. As the lawyer, your job is not only to find the expert with the best possible qualifications in the subject area, but to make sure that the expert's qualifications cannot be turned into a liability.

The second leg of the tripod is the expert's mastery of the specific facts of the case. This leg rests on the expert's careful attention to factual detail. Perhaps the expert compiled a database of all reported incidents similar to those alleged by plaintiffs in a class action. Perhaps the expert reviewed thousands of pages of financial documents and the relevant fact depositions. An expert who has not mastered the case facts, or has made a major oversight, is one whom the jury will not trust.

The third leg of the tripod is the scientific validity or industry acceptance of the expert methodology. This leg of the tripod is about whether your expert has tested the materials at issue in the case using a test widely considered scientifically valid, or whether the expert has used a test that is considered experimental. It is also about whether the expert is applying a well-known industry practice or is using a method that others in the field have counseled against.

Cross-examination will focus on kicking one of the three tripod legs out from under your expert. If any of the three legs fails, the expert topples; they have taken your queen. Your expert should be prepared to handle questions arising in all three categories.

# THE EXPERT'S QUALIFICATIONS

I failed to make the chess team because of my height.

— *Woody Allen, Actor and Film Director*

The first step in preparing your expert for cross-examination begins many months—or years—before trial, when you hire the witness. Retaining the right expert with the right qualifications for the case ensures that the other side will have great difficulty finding a weakness during cross-examination. It is equally important to ensure that your expert sticks to what he or she knows when formulating opinions in a case. There are countless cautionary tales of experts who succumbed to pressure to greatly exceed the scope of their qualifications when rendering their opinions in the case, only for their opinions to be excluded from evidence or blown up on cross-examination. If you need an actuary, hire an actuary instead of trying to cajole your accountant into filling the additional role. Similarly, pressing a cardiologist with little or no pediatrics experience into testifying about pediatric cardiology is not a sound plan of action when there are pediatric cardiologists who could more appropriately fill the role at trial.

Once you have retained the best expert with the right qualifications, your role in preparing the witness for cross-examination begins. You need to dig deep into your witness's background and prepare the witness for uncomfortable questions that may be lurking there.

One of the biggest oversights lawyers make when selecting experts and preparing them for cross-examination is not reading the witness's prior published books and papers. Many a trial lawyer has discovered only too late that her star expert witness co-authored an article published in an obscure trade journal 15 years ago that completely contradicts key points in the expert's report. You must find and probe your witness's life history, because your opponent is certainly going to do so.

An expert surprised by his own published work on cross-examination can quickly become a major liability in your case. For example: In a case about whether the explosion of a steam-driven turbine was a force majeure or within the reasonable control of the utility company, the utility had the country's preeminent water chemistry expert, Dr. Jonas, testify on its behalf. The turbine had exploded because of a "caustic incursion." Dr. Jonas opined that the utility had maintained reasonable controls over water chemistry. Dr. Jonas was a prolific author. Our team discovered in preparing to cross-examine him that he was a leading proponent of monitoring not just the quality of the water in power plants but the quality of *steam* that was being blown under pressure onto the turbine blades. The utility did not monitor steam quality. On cross, we confronted Dr. Jonas with article after article that he had written, arguing in favor of steam quality monitoring. After a while he became annoyed: "where did you find all these articles?" He fumbled for an explanation for why steam quality monitoring was not essential, but the explanation was too technical and nuanced for the jury.

*The lesson to be learned here: get your hands on everything your expert has written, spot the issues, and cover them in advance so the expert is not surprised on the witness stand.*

You should also go over your expert's resume with a fine-tooth comb, and with an eye on the news. As corporate scandals come and go in the United States, sometimes even the most honest and trustworthy expert will end up with the black stain of a fallen corporate giant on his resume. Though an unfortunate stint at the most hated corporation in America du jour is not reason alone to withdraw or refuse to hire an otherwise eminently qualified expert, the expert should be adequately prepared to handle questions about his experience at the corporation.

For example, after the Enron and Arthur Andersen scandals, a number of very honest and qualified damages experts suddenly found that the entries on their resumes detailing their experience as young accountants at Arthur Andersen became fodder for cross-examination—they were dragged through the mud of the Enron scandal in front of the jury. Those who were not well prepared to deal with this line of questioning looked at their shoes and blushed during this examination, and suffered accordingly. Those who were well prepared not only shifted the focus away from Enron, but also were able to further qualify themselves in the jury's eyes by pointing out valuable experience they had gained at one of the "Big Five" back in the halcyon days when there were five instead of four.

*The lesson to be learned: prepare your experts to explain apparent red flags in their resumes. A good explanation can make an expert look more credible.*

One of the stereotypes of experts is that they are "hired guns," who will say anything for a fee. Prepare your expert for questions about fees. In my experience, juries understand that experts get paid for their time and don't hold it against them. The expert need not be bashful about it if the rate is reasonable. Of course, you might think twice about retaining an expert with an outrageous rate, or one who spends most of his time testifying. If you decide to use such an expert, have a good explanation because it will certainly come up on cross. In many cases, you can tie the fee to the expert's eminence in his field.

*Lesson: be prepared for questions about fees.*

Finally, a well-known cross-examination strategy is to run through a litany of all the credentials the expert does not have, fields he never studied, societies he doesn't belong to. "Sir, you and your lawyer spent 10 minutes awhile back talking about all the things you are. But I'd like to start by talking about what you're not." As the list gets longer, some experts may appear to wither and become nervous. It is that reaction, more than the list, that will do damage to the expert.

*Lesson: the expert should be prepared to be unflappable, even when faced with a recounting of his every shortcoming in life.*

# PREPARATION ON CASE FACTS

A player surprised is half beaten.

— *Chess Proverb*

Experts can get expensive. Clients are sometimes unwilling to pay an expert $1,200 per hour to crawl through every document in the case. And some experts are too busy with their "real" jobs to examine thousands of documents, or simply may not relish the task. Though it is always a good idea to control expert expense by confining the scope of what the witness receives to that which is relevant to the subject matter of the expert's opinion in the case, it is important not to get too stingy. An expert who has not been given all of the potentially relevant facts of a case is easily tripped up on cross-examination.

When facts are available for the expert to gather himself, it is good practice for the attorney to encourage this. The research can be guided, of course. When the expert is researching public databases or medical journals, it is best for the expert to obtain the information directly instead of through the lawyer. In most cases, however, there will be case-specific information that the expert cannot get anywhere else than from the lawyer. What approach should you take in those cases? If you give the expert too much, it costs the client. If you give the expert too little, however, you run some well-known risks.

In an airplane crash case involving an interruption in power to a warning system, the airline put an MIT engineering professor on the stand—the late Dr. Thomas Lee. The airline dutifully produced several boxes of documents that were represented to be all of the documents reviewed by Dr. Lee. It became apparent in going through the boxes that only pro-airline documents had been presented to him. The airline's lawyers had not given him the documents that cut the other way. Similarly, the deposition transcripts sent to Dr. Lee were highly selective and pro-airline. In some cases, they had sent him only portions of depositions.

Dr. Lee was a true scientist, and he acknowledged on cross that the scientific process involves looking at *all* of the evidence, not just the evidence that supports your theory. He even elaborated on this, talking about how important it is to look at the seemingly contrary evidence and see if it can be reconciled. It was easy to lay this general foundation. Then Dr. Lee was forced to acknowledge the one-sidedness of the documents given to him. The lawyers who sent him the selected documents were easy to blame. It allowed us to highlight our side's good documents. "The lawyers didn't give you this?" "No." This line of questioning was easy and effective. It fell in our laps because of the way documents had been fed to Dr. Lee by the airline's lawyers.

*The lesson to be learned: give your expert relevant documents on both sides of the case. Prepare the expert in how to handle the "bad" documents.*

Similarly, when giving deposition transcripts to an expert, send the entire transcript. To save time and expense, it may make sense to contact the expert and direct her to a specific page range most pertinent to her analysis, but give her the option of reading other testimony around the topic. Don't allow the "selectivity" line of cross-exam to undermine your expert.

Even the most experienced witness can, in the heat of the moment, forget a minor fact or the source of a particular piece of data. Jurors understand this. Experts should be prepared to acknowledge that they do not have all the data at their fingertips at the moment, but can find the information if appropriate. This is much better than guessing. Most important, the expert should not be rattled or embarrassed by the fact that they she does not have a photographic memory encompassing all of the case documents.

As the lawyer, you should check and recheck your experts' understanding of the facts, and the documents or depositions on which they relied to derive their understanding. Additionally, you should check and recheck for mathematical errors in any calculations your experts make.

As an illustration, I had a case involving a Chicago utility that had entered into a long-term contract with a coal mine in Wyoming. There were minimum purchase requirements. A few years into the contract, the utility realized it had purchased too much coal. It began a program of claiming force majeure whenever it could in order to reduce coal deliveries. The coal company sued, questioning the legitimacy of the force majeure claims. One of the issues was whether the freezing of the Illinois River, causing the closing of the locks, was a force majeure event. The utility could have transloaded the coal further upriver, above the locks, but the utility claimed that the cost would have been excessive. The key testimony for the utility was from an economist at a Big Four accounting firm on the question whether the cost was excessive.

The expert was impenetrable in almost every way—highly qualified and experienced as a witness. However, my colleague discovered the night before the expert's trial testimony that he had made a mathematical error in his calculations. It was a simple error and it increased the extra cost number by 50 percent. In other words, if corrected, it would have reduced the cost calculation but it would not necessarily been fatal to the excessive cost argument. What happened next, however, was fatal. When confronted with the error on cross-examination, the expert immediately denied it in the strongest possible terms. He was visibly surprised. As the knife twisted, he became flustered. He blamed his female assistant, who was in the courtroom, and he demanded from the witness stand that she bring him a file folder. He had appeared to be the epitome of professionalism on direct examination, but on cross he became insufferably arrogant. The math error was his downfall, not just because he had made the error but because of how he reacted when confronted with it. He was destroyed by it, and his client lost the issue.

*The lesson to be learned: the lawyer presenting an expert should understand and double-check all mathematical calculations by the expert. Preferably, the lawyer should do this personally.*

## ANTICIPATING THE ATTACK ON THE EXPERT'S SCIENTIFIC METHODOLOGY

Chess is the art of analysis.

— *Mikhail Botrinnik, Three-time World Chess Champion*

Protecting your expert from cross-examination on the science or specialized knowledge underlying her opinion really begins when the opinion is formulated and reduced to writing. Stretching a witness beyond the *Daubert* limits—or even past the witness's personal comfort level—will inevitably come back to haunt you on cross-examination. All of the preparation in the world will not make a witness look comfortable on the witness stand if she feels her opinion strains professional credulity. If the witness cannot wholeheartedly support the science or methodology on which the opinion is based, it is better to find a different witness or focus only on those areas this witness can get behind than to push the witness to her outermost limits.

Assuming that the witness has not been pushed out of his or her comfort zone, the greatest trap to be avoided with respect to scientific theory is every person's tendency to want to say kind things about others. Your expert may be asked about the respectability or qualifications of a revered publication, institution, mentor, or colleague. This is just opposing counsel setting the trap. It is then "sprung" when the expert is confronted with the contrary scientific opinion of the very person, publication, or institution upon which she has just heaped glowing praise.

A good place to start in protecting your witness from this type of damaging cross-examination is to parse your witness's resume and written publications. Has your expert worked with a co-author in the past? Is the co-author known for a theory that might be damaging to your case? Has your expert worked at a company that would be likely to oppose your particular case theory? Did your expert contribute to any work at that company that might compromise her on cross-examination?

The best defense on this type of cross-examination is simply working with the expert to remove certain words and phrases from his vocabulary, and refusing to allow such words or phrases to be put into his mouth via leading questions. The expert should be wary of loaded terms like "authoritative," "preeminent," and "prestigious."

For example, in pharmaceutical cases experts often have to deal with studies published in the *New England Journal of Medicine* (NEJM). The NEJM is a widely respected medical journal, but it has certainly published studies that were deeply flawed. Experts are often asked to admit that the NEJM is a "respected journal." If the expert says no, she may lose credibility, but if she simply says yes, she may be giving undue credence to something published in the NEJM. An expert who hasn't thought about this beforehand might answer yes or no. The best path is to explain: the NEJM is highly regarded in general but being published in the NEJM does not mean that a study is credible. One expert scored points by saying he was "disappointed that the NEJM published this study without investigating its flaws."

One "methodology" line of questioning that is common on cross-examination is to query the expert about all the things she did *not* do or has *never* done. "Have you ever designed a product like the one in issue?" Or, in a personal injury case, "have you personally examined the patient?" Other common methodology questions include whether the expert's opinions were subject to peer review and whether the expert had been to the scene of the accident.[8]

Questions like these should be addressed in advance between the lawyer and expert. The expert may not have to sheepishly answer "no" on the witness stand. One solution is for the expert to do some work: visit the scene if it's practical. A type of peer-review can sometimes be obtained from a colleague. If the expert has no access to something, it can often be explained: "I wasn't able to examine Mr. Plaintiff, but my opinions relate to his condition at the time of the incident, and we have excellent medical records from that time period."

*The lesson to be learned: Think like the other side. What are the weak points in your expert's methodology? Can those apparent weaknesses be turned to strengths? Can some additional work shore up the weakness?*

## STYLE AND DEMEANOR

Why must I lose to this idiot?

— *Aron Nimzovitsch, Chess Master*

The tone of an expert's voice, the angle of her gaze, the cut of her jib, and other delivery factors can have a surprisingly large impact on the expert's believability. I will begin this section with a story. Our side had an expert who testified on the market price of steel in a breach of contract case. Though the expert did a great job on direct explaining the economic theory behind his analysis, opposing counsel clearly did not understand it. He asked the expert a series of bumbling and unintelligible questions that should have made the lawyer look like a complete idiot. The judge overruled multiple objections and required the witness to answer. Unfortunately, the expert got sheepish and embarrassed that he couldn't just give straight answers, and had to keep asking for clarification. Though the cross-examining lawyer should have been the one who looked like an idiot, the witness ended up looking embarrassed and a little evasive. Because of the expert's reaction, the jury likely came away confused about the entire exchange. Had this been anticipated, the expert could have been prepared to remain composed as opposing counsel stumbled around trying to grapple with the subject matter and find a real question.

*Lesson to be learned: prepare your expert to be unflappable even in the face of bumbling, incoherent questions.*

---

8. For a lengthy list of these types of questions, see Wendy L. Couture & Allyson W. Haynes, eds. Litigators on Experts: Strategies for Managing Expert Witnesses From Retention Through Trial 314 (ABA 2011).

When the cross-examiner cannot win on substance, she may try theatrics. Or she may just bumble. She may, intentionally or not, use confusing terminology. The cross-examiner may use loaded questions, or even insulting questions. You should prepare your expert to answer calmly, and to seek clarification politely when necessary, without getting rattled.

Researchers agree that good expert witness demeanor on cross-examination is both important to jurors and teachable.[9] Here are some specific points:

1. The expert should continue to be a teacher, even on cross-examination.
2. The expert should not change demeanors from direct to cross.
3. The expert should maintain appropriate body language.
4. The expert should be an active listener during cross-examination.

These are common-sense points, but important enough to be worth amplifying.

The best expert is one who teaches best. Psychology professor Dennis Devine says that from a juror's point of view, experts fall into three categories: (1) the benevolent educator; (2) the hired gun; or (3) the superfluous pontificator.[10] Only the first of these types is going to win over the jury. The other two could even damage your case.

"Teacher" is the best role for your expert, and it is important to maintain that role on cross-examination. The advice of one consultant: "relentlessly see the opposing lawyer as a struggling student who does not understand your subject, and needs patience and guidance."[11] Train the expert that when the oddball, confusing, or offensive question comes her way, the best approach is not to argue, but to teach.

An expert's change in demeanor from direct to cross can be deadly. This can make the expert seem like a hired gun. If an expert is polite and accommodating on direct, but then turns nasty on cross, he plays right into the opposition's hands. This is hard for experts to get right. As the example of the overly agreeable Norman Hale showed, you do not want the expert to be <u>too</u> accommodating. But it is important to stay respectful, especially when under fire. Use of phrases like "may I explain?" help set a good tone.

Body language by witnesses has been widely studied. It bears heavily on likeability and credibility. The expert should angle his or her body toward the jury. Other tips for experts: look at the cross-examiner when the question is being asked, but turn to the jury when the answer is given, at least when explaining something; never look at your side's attorney; lean forward slightly; and keep your hands on the

---

9. Stanley L. Brodsky, Testifying in Court, 2d ed. (American Psychological Association, 2013); Rich Matthews, *Expert Witness Testimony: Some Science and Some Art to Increase Your Value to Your Client*, The Expert Institute (Sept. 2, 2014), https://juryology.com/2014/09/02/expert-testimony-science-art-increase-your-value/, accessed May 5, 2016.

10. Dennis J. Devine, Jury Decision Making: The State of the Science 129 (NYU Press 2012).

11. Matthews, *supra* note 9.

arms of the witness chair or in your lap, not together or clenched, but occasional hand gestures are good.[12]

Active listening is essential. Opposing lawyers can slip phrases into their questions that mischaracterize the evidence. Although this may draw an objection, the expert should not rely on objections to sort out bad questions. Politely ask for a rephrasing or point out the mischaracterization. Lawyers also make mistakes with sloppy questions, and the good expert can turn these to her side's advantage. Some questions can open the door for the expert to reinforce a theme or repeat key aspects of the expert's direct testimony. Of course, active listening can also help the expert avoid the pitfalls that often come with answers to misunderstood questions.[13]

*Lesson to be learned: prepare your expert to be a benevolent teacher, even on cross-examination. Practice appropriate body language. Ingrain the art of active listening.*

## SPECIAL CONSIDERATIONS FOR THE VIRGIN EXPERT WITNESS

Every Pawn is a potential Queen.

*— James Mason, Actor*

Some experts do nothing but testify. They are susceptible to the line of cross-examination suggesting that the expert is little more than a professional witness. Yet other experts come to the case with absolutely no testimonial experience. These "virgin experts" deserve special care and handling when preparing them for trial. They can be outstanding witnesses. The very fact of their virginity as witnesses makes them, in some cases, very credible scientists, doctors, engineers, or economists in the jury's eyes. But there are things to watch out for.

First, lawyers must accept the fact that not all preeminent experts in a field will be good witnesses. Size them up in the selection process. If you have in mind that a potential expert is going to testify, don't just assess the expert's paper credentials. Assess personality—will jurors like this person? Assess communicability—can he or she say things in a coherent, understandable way? Is the expert too arrogant? Trial lawyers have instincts. Use them. If the most qualified expert in the world would be a disaster on the witness stand, take a pass.

---

12. Some good articles on body language are: Tess M.S. Neal, *Expert Witness Preparation: What Does the Literature Tell Us?*, 21 THE JURY EXPERT 46, 49 (2009), http://www.thejuryexpert.com/wp-content/uploads/NealExpertWitnessesTJEMarch09.pdf (last visited Oct. 23, 2017) and *Five Imperatives for Expert Witnesses: Effective Non-Verbal Skills Can Be Learned*, THE SYNCHRONICS GROUP May 6, 2016, http://www.synchronics group.com/articles/articles_5imperatives_p.htm.
13. *See* Steven Babitsky & James J. Mangraviti, *The 5 Traits of a Dangerous Expert Witness*, SEAK, Inc., http://www.seak.com/the-5-traits-of-a-dangerous-expert-witness/, accessed May 5, 2016.

Virgin experts can often use help understanding what happens at trial, getting comfortable with the courtroom, and improving their skills at communicating highly technical or abstract concepts to a lay jury. Mock cross-examination, preferably by a lawyer the expert has never seen, should be a priority for virgin experts. A jury focus exercise can help in some cases. Here is an example of a case where it helped:

A study reported a statistical correlation between an over-the-counter decongestant and hemorrhagic strokes. Thousands of lawsuits ensued. The defendants, manufacturers of cold medicines, argued that the decongestant did not, and could not, cause strokes. Our client retained a pharmacodynamicist (an expert in the movement and actions of drugs) who was extremely well qualified. The only problem was that he spoke in a thick Scottish brogue. You might be thinking that Scottish is pretty close to American English. We would have looked silly had we retained a translator. But with our Scottish expert, it became clear that he could be misunderstood in significant ways. For example, when he said "pure," it sounded like "poor." In the pharma world, that's a significant difference.

We worked hard with our Scottish expert's communicability. We worked on avoiding problematic phrases. We worked on presentation methods to ensure clarity. We could see the improvement. However, we couldn't control what would happen on cross-examination. After a lot of discussion, we decided to do a jury focus exercise with our Scottish expert appearing live, undergoing both direct and cross. He was great. The mock jurors thought his brogue was charming. It gave him confidence, but also experience, so he knew what worked and what didn't.

*Lesson: work with your experts on communicability—it can be improved. Mock jury exercises to test real witnesses can be valuable.*[14]

Finally, just as with a lay witness, an expert who has never previously testified might benefit from a field trip to the courtroom in advance of trial so that he or she can get comfortable with it. Ralph Murphy (not his real name) was an in-house aerodynamicist for an airplane manufacturer. He was one of the foremost authorities in the world, so we decided to have him testify as an expert in a crash case. The man was an accomplished scientist, but he had some rough edges. We thought it would be helpful to show him the courtroom where he would be testifying, so the day before his testimony we took him on a field trip to the courthouse. He wore his usual jeans and cowboy boots to the courthouse, which was fine because court was not in session that afternoon. As we passed through the U.S. Marshal station, one of the marshals waved a wand over Dr. Murphy's boot. It shrieked. The marshal reached in and pulled an 8-inch Bowie knife out of the boot. After a lot of explaining about who Dr. Murphy was (he didn't exactly look the part), the marshals agreed to let us leave and come back without the knife.

---

14. Mock jury exercises are generally conducted with consultants. This is the tip of the iceberg in terms of how consultants may help in witness preparation. For a thorough analysis, see the excellent chapter by Jessalyn Ziegler and Charles G. Jarboe—Chapter 5.

*Lesson: don't assume your virgin expert knows anything about testifying in a court-room. A visual tour of the courtroom is helpful. Cover details like how to dress and what to bring (usually nothing, especially not weapons).*

# CONCLUSION

A computer once beat me at chess, but it was no match for
me at kick boxing.

— *Emo Philips, Comedian*

In Shakespeare's play *King John*, the Queen Mother accuses Constance, the mother of a claimant to the throne, of wanting her son to be king so that Constance might "be a queen and check the world." That is the beauty of queens—they can travel the chessboard and create great havoc to the opposition. In the chess game of litigation, the expert witness can be the most valuable piece on the board.

The more damage your expert does, the more likely your opponent will cross-examine with guns blazing. The queen is a vulnerable piece, and her loss can be devastating. The ability of an expert to withstand attack can be improved with preparation. The astute trial lawyer should spend a significant amount of time preparing his expert for cross.

The game of chess teaches some principles that apply to cross-examination preparation. The best trial lawyers think two moves ahead. They use their pieces wisely and don't extend them too far without protection. They mistrust their opponents. They prepare for the worst. British author and brewer Charles Buxton put it well: "In life, as in chess, forethought wins."

# PART IV

# Criminal and Special Proceedings

## CHAPTER 10

# Dante's Guide

## Preparing the Grand Jury Witness

### *Jackson R. Sharman III*

In the year 1300, at age 35, the narrator of Dante's *Inferno* famously finds himself in trouble:

> *Midway in our life's journey, I went astray*
>
> *from the straight road and woke to find myself*
>
> *alone in a dark wood. How shall I say*
>
> *what wood that was! I never saw so drear,*
>
> *so rank, so arduous a wilderness!*
>
> *Its very memory gives a shape to fear.*

The grand jury witness finds himself or herself in a position not unlike that of the Italian poet at the beginning of his trek through the *Divine Comedy*. The federal grand jury is one of the most powerful, secret, and peculiar institutions in American law and culture. It is certainly the most one-sided and the one that most lay persons find runs counter to their civics-class understanding of American governance.

In the poem, Dante has a guide through hell: the Roman poet Virgil. When Dante asks to be saved from the first of three beasts with which he is confronted, Virgil does not spare Dante's sensibilities:

> *And he replied, seeing my soul in tears*
>
> *"He must go by another way who would escape*
>
> *this wilderness, for that mad beast that fleers*

*before you there, suffers no man to pass.*

*She tracks down all, kills all, and knows no glut,*

*but, feeding, she grows hungrier than she was."*

As lawyers for grand jury witnesses, we must do as Virgil does, and first off remind our client that, like the She-Wolf, the grand jury "tracks down all, kills all, and knows no glut."

Because the grand jury is distinct from other parts of the apparatus of the American legal system, and because its workings are obscure even to many lawyers, this note first touches briefly on what the grand jury is; where its powers lay; and what restraints there are upon it. In preparing your client for a grand jury appearance—indeed, in advising your client whether or not he or she should even testify before the grand jury—you will need a working knowledge of the institution itself.

After we lay this structural groundwork, we pass on specific thoughts to consider, questions to raise, and practices to avoid.

To start with the grand jury, we must start with the Fifth Amendment.

# A PROSECUTION TOOL

Under the Fifth Amendment to the United States Constitution, "[n]o person shall be held to answer for a capital, or otherwise infamous crime, unless on a presentment or indictment of a grand jury. . . ." Whether or not your client is to testify about something "infamous," the government must proceed by indictment if it intends to charge someone with a federal felony. A defendant has an option of waiving indictment and voluntarily being charged by "information," a charging document that is issued only by the Assistant United States Attorney (AUSA). Usually, an information is lodged when the defendant has negotiated a resolution with the government, agreed to plead guilty, and a guilty plea is being proposed to the court.[1] Historically, and in theory even today, the grand jury is "a protective bulwark standing solidly between the ordinary citizen and an overzealous prosecutor."[2] Although this observation may have been true at some point in English history, it is not true today. Today, the grand jury is a tool of the prosecution. Decades ago, Sol Wachtler, the former chief judge of New York state, famously observed that a prosecutor could get a grand jury to "indict a ham sandwich."[3]

---

1. FED. R. CRIM. P. 7.
2. United Sates v. Dionisio, 410 U.S. 1, 17 (1973).
3. Unhappily, Judge Wachtler later pled guilty to extortion and was sentenced to 15 months in federal prison. He was diagnosed with bipolar disorder, advocated for the mentally ill, and eventually had his law license restored. Novelist Tom Wolfe quotes Judge Wachtler's "ham sandwich" observation in *The Bonfire of The Vanities* (1987).

Unlike the "12 in a box" of a petit jury, a federal grand jury will have between 16 and 23 members. Sixteen members are required for quorum, and the grand jury can return an indictment only with the agreement of at least 12 grand jurors.[4] If the grand jury does not indict the target or targets that the prosecutor desires (an extremely rare occurrence), it is entirely permissible for the prosecutor to present the same evidence all over again to a different grand jury. In addition, after an indictment has issued, prosecutors may "supersede" (meaning to issue an amended or supplemental indictment on the same subject matter and addressing the same defendant or additional defendants).

## THE GRAND JURY IS SECRET

Federal Rule of Criminal Procedure 6 governs grand jury secrecy. Because its secrecy is one of the most powerful characteristics of the grand jury, and one of the most dangerous, the prudent lawyer should review Rule 6 with care.

## NO DEFENSE LAWYERS

The persons who may be present in the grand jury room are quite limited: "attorneys for the government, the witness under examination, interpreters when needed and, for the purpose of taking the evidence, a stenographer or operator of a recording device. . . ." A lawyer may not accompany his or her witness-client into the grand jury room. Counsel hangs out in the hall or a witness room and waits either for his client to take a break or to be excused when the prosecutors have asked all that they wish to ask. This rule is so strict that a parent may not even accompany a child who is subpoenaed to the grand jury.

## DISCLOSURE OF GRAND JURY PROCEEDINGS

Unless certain enumerated exceptions apply, no one involved in the grand jury session *except the witness* may "disclose . . . matters occurring before the grand jury."[5] Unfortunately, the definition of "matters occurring before the grand jury" differs from circuit to circuit. If a disclosure issue arises with your witness, there is no substitute for reviewing the law in your federal circuit. In some circuits, a grand jury witness is entitled to a transcript of his own testimony. In others, he is not.

---

4. FED. R. CRIM. P. 6.
5. FED. R. CRIM. P. 6(e)(2).

# CAN MY CLIENT TALK TO OTHERS ABOUT HER GRAND JURY TESTIMONY?

Your client may find his grand jury examination unexceptional or boring, but it is likely to be of great interest to others, especially those who may be subjects or targets of the grand jury investigation or the lawyers for other witnesses who are trying to get their own clients prepared. It is not uncommon for prosecutors and agents to discourage witnesses—sometimes, in strong terms that would get defense counsel charged with obstruction of justice or witness tampering, were defense counsel to do the same—from speaking to anyone about their grand jury testimony and especially from speaking to subjects or targets. Your client should be prepared for those kinds of instructions and should also be prepared to be asked about the identity of anyone they may have talked with concerning their grand jury subpoena or their testimony.

# "CAN WHAT I SAY GET ME IN TROUBLE?": GRAND JURY SUBPOENAS AND WITNESS PROTECTIONS

Under Federal Rule of Criminal Procedure 17, federal grand juries can summon witnesses and require production of documents (and other tangible items). In theory, the grand jury itself issues the subpoenas; in reality, they are issued by the prosecutor. Grand jury subpoenas, unlike trial subpoenas, may be served nationwide: there are geographical limitations within the United States. Failure to respond or appear, at least without a good excuse, is contempt.

The most important protection for a grand jury witness is to not testify. If she doesn't say anything, nothing she says can be used against her.

The second most important protection for a grand jury witness is the Fifth Amendment.[6] Unfortunately, businesspeople, public officials, professionals, and other white-collar types are loath to rely on the Fifth Amendment, concluding—with justification—that most people believe that one who invokes his or her Fifth Amendment rights is guilty of something.

The decision to invoke (or not) one's Fifth Amendment rights turns on the facts of each case, and a detailed analysis of Fifth Amendment strategy is beyond the scope of this discussion. Nevertheless, a quick review of basic Department of Justice (DOJ) policies, as set out in the United States Attorneys' Manual (USAM) is helpful for the witness who has been subpoenaed to the grand jury.

---

6. "No person . . . shall be compelled in any criminal case to be a witness against himself. . . ."

# WITNESS, SUBJECT, OR TARGET?

Much as Caesar divided all Gaul into three parts, all grand jury witnesses potentially fall into one of three categories: witness, subject, or target.

Of the three categories, the first and the last are the most clear.

A witness is akin to the person who was standing at the street corner when the car wreck occurred. They may be asked whether the light was red or yellow, or they may be examined about the speed of the vehicles, but there is no suggestion that they were driving, performed mechanical work on the cars, dashed out in the street to distract a driver, or had a financial interest in the death of a passenger. They are, literally, just a witness.

At the other extreme is a target. A target is an individual or a company that the AUSA believes has engaged in criminal behavior and, in turn, has decided to indict.

A subject is everyone else. "Everyone else" is not a very helpful definition, but that is the way the government looks at it, as we see in the USAM:

> It is the policy of the Department of Justice to advise a grand jury witness of his or her rights if such witness is a "target" or "subject" of a grand jury investigation. See the Criminal Resource Manual at 160 for a sample target letter.
>
> A "target" is a person as to whom the prosecutor or the grand jury has substantial evidence linking him or her to the commission of a crime and who, in the judgment of the prosecutor, is a putative defendant. An officer or employee of an organization which is a target is not automatically considered a target even if such officer's or employee's conduct contributed to the commission of the crime by the target organization. The same lack of automatic target status holds true for organizations which employ, or employed, an officer or employee who is a target.
>
> A "subject" of an investigation is a person whose conduct is within the scope of the grand jury's investigation.
>
> The Supreme Court declined to decide whether a grand jury witness must be warned of his or her Fifth Amendment privilege against compulsory self-incrimination before the witness's grand jury testimony can be used against the witness.[7] In *Mandujano* the Court took cognizance of the fact that Federal prosecutors customarily warn "targets" of their Fifth Amendment rights before grand jury questioning begins. Similarly, in *Washington*, the Court pointed to the fact that Fifth Amendment warnings were administered as

---

7. *See* United States v. Washington, 431 U.S. 181, 186 & 190–91 (1977); United States v. Wong, 431 U.S. 174 (1977); United States v. Mandujano, 425 U.S. 564, 582 n.7. (1976).

negating "any possible compulsion to self-incrimination which might otherwise exist" in the grand jury setting.

Notwithstanding the lack of a clear constitutional imperative, it is the policy of the Department that an "Advice of Rights" form be appended to all grand jury subpoenas to be served on any "target" or "subject" of an investigation. *See* advice of rights below.

In addition, these "warnings" should be given by the prosecutor on the record before the grand jury and the witness should be asked to affirm that the witness understands them.

Although the Court in *Washington, supra,* held that "targets" of the grand jury's investigation are entitled to no special warnings relative to their status as "potential defendant(s)," the Department of Justice continues its longstanding policy to advise witnesses who are known "targets" of the investigation that their conduct is being investigated for possible violation of Federal criminal law. This supplemental advice of status of the witness as a target should be repeated on the record when the target witness is advised of the matters discussed in the preceding paragraphs.

When a district court insists that the notice of rights not be appended to a grand jury subpoena, the advice of rights may be set forth in a separate letter and mailed to or handed to the witness when the subpoena is served.

### ADVICE OF RIGHTS

- The grand jury is conducting an investigation of possible violations of Federal criminal laws involving: (State here the general subject matter of inquiry, e.g., conducting an illegal gambling business in violation of 18 U.S.C. § 1955).
- You may refuse to answer any question if a truthful answer to the question would tend to incriminate you.
- Anything that you do say may be used against you by the grand jury or in a subsequent legal proceeding.
- If you have retained counsel, the grand jury will permit you a reasonable opportunity to step outside the grand jury room to consult with counsel if you so desire.

**Additional Advice to Be Given to Targets:** If the witness is a target, the above advice should also contain a supplemental warning that the witness's conduct is being investigated for possible violation of federal criminal law.[8]

---

8. USAM 9-11.151 (internal citations omitted).

# "If I'm the Target, Will I Be Subpoenaed?"

Although it is somewhat rare, a target of a grand jury investigation may be subpoenaed to testify:

> A grand jury may properly subpoena a subject or a target of the investigation and question the target about his or her involvement in the crime under investigation.[9] However, in the context of particular cases such a subpoena may carry the appearance of unfairness. Because the potential for misunderstanding is great, before a known "target" (as defined in USAM 9-11.151) is subpoenaed to testify before the grand jury about his or her involvement in the crime under investigation, an effort should be made to secure the target's voluntary appearance. If a voluntary appearance cannot be obtained, the target should be subpoenaed only after the grand jury and the United States Attorney or the responsible Assistant Attorney General have approved the subpoena. In determining whether to approve a subpoena for a "target," careful attention will be paid to the following considerations:
>
> - The importance to the successful conduct of the grand jury's investigation of the testimony or other information sought;
> - Whether the substance of the testimony or other information sought could be provided by other witnesses; and
> - Whether the questions the prosecutor and the grand jurors intend to ask or the other information sought would be protected by a valid claim of privilege.[10]

# "This Isn't Fair. I Want to Tell My Side of the Story."

Your client may be chomping at the bit to get in the grand jury room and "tell his side of the story." There are sometimes good reasons to advise your client to not do so, but, if he or she insists, note the DOJ policy on the subject:

> It is not altogether uncommon for subjects or targets of the grand jury's investigation, particularly in white-collar cases, to request

---

9. *See* United States v. Wong, 431 U.S. 174, 179 n.8 (1977); United States v. Washington, 431 U.S. 181, 190 n.6 (1977); United States v. Mandujano, 425 U.S. 564, 573–75 & 584 n.9 (1976); United States v. Dionisio, 410 U.S. 1, 10 n.8 (1973).
10. USAM 9-11.150.

or demand the opportunity to tell the grand jury their side of the story. While the prosecutor has no legal obligation to permit such witnesses to testify, a refusal to do so can create the appearance of unfairness. Accordingly, under normal circumstances, where no burden upon the grand jury or delay of its proceedings is involved, reasonable requests by a "subject" or "target" of an investigation, as defined above, to testify personally before the grand jury ordinarily should be given favorable consideration, provided that such witness explicitly waives his or her privilege against self-incrimination, on the record before the grand jury, and is represented by counsel or voluntarily and knowingly appears without counsel and consents to full examination under oath.

Such witnesses may wish to supplement their testimony with the testimony of others. The decision whether to accommodate such requests or to reject them after listening to the testimony of the target or the subject, or to seek statements from the suggested witnesses, is a matter left to the sound discretion of the grand jury. When passing on such requests, it must be kept in mind that the grand jury was never intended to be and is not properly either an adversary proceeding or the arbiter of guilt or innocence.[11]

# "WILL I HAVE TO TAKE THE FIFTH OVER AND OVER AGAIN?"

At the other extreme, your client, after discussions with you, may intend to say nothing in the grand jury room except "upon advice of my counsel, I invoke my rights under the Fifth Amendment of the United States Constitution and respectfully decline to answer your question." Normally, your client will not have to go to the grand jury and repeat those words for hours, although it can happen:

> A question frequently faced by Federal prosecutors is how to respond to an assertion by a prospective grand jury witness that if called to testify the witness will refuse to testify on Fifth Amendment grounds. If a "target" of the investigation and his or her attorney state in a writing, signed by both, that the "target" will refuse to testify on Fifth Amendment grounds, the witness ordinarily should be excused from testifying unless the grand jury and the United States Attorney agree to insist on the appearance. In determining the desirability of insisting on the appearance of such a person,

---

11. USAM 9-11.152 (internal citations omitted).

consideration should be given to the factors which justified the subpoena in the first place, i.e., the importance of the testimony or other information sought, its unavailability from other sources, and the applicability of the Fifth Amendment privilege to the likely areas of inquiry.

Some argue that unless the prosecutor is prepared to seek an order pursuant to 18 U.S.C. § 6003, the witness should be excused from testifying. However, such a broad rule would be improper and make it too convenient for witnesses to avoid testifying truthfully to their knowledge of relevant facts. Moreover, once compelled to appear, the witness may be willing and able to answer some or all of the grand jury's questions without incriminating himself or herself.[12]

# PREPARATION 101

In some respects, preparing a grand jury witness for his or her testimony is the same as preparing any witness for sworn testimony. Because of the peculiarities of the grand jury process, however, there are some aspects of preparation that would be odd in other contexts.

**Tell the truth.** Remind the witness to always tell the truth. Not only is it a good thing to tell the truth, the witness who lies, misleads, or obfuscates in the grand jury may face not only a perjury charge but a federal false-statement or obstruction of justice charge. Although it should be obvious, there are no exceptions to these federal criminal statutes for lying to protect children, friends, a spouse, or colleagues.

**Exercise discipline.** Because the witness in the grand jury room is without a lawyer, he or she must exercise unusual discipline. What do we mean by that?

**Listen to the question.** The witness must listen to the question with even greater clarity and focus than would be required in a deposition, hearing, trial, or any proceeding where his or her lawyer was available. There is no counsel present to lodge an objection (speaking or otherwise) or to force the prosecutor to ask a clear question. In addition, unlike a deposition, the witness can be questioned by virtually anyone in the room: prosecutors, an agent, and individual grand jurors.

**Prepare for multiple examiners.** Given the environment in the grand jury room, there is a premium on listening to the question and answering that question directly—and then stopping. Because there is no defense counsel present to sharpen the question, prosecutors can sometimes get lazy, obnoxious, or incomprehensible. Grand jurors rarely formulate concise or on-point questions.

---

12. USAM 9-11.154.

**Stand your ground.** A grand jury witness must also be prepared to stand his ground. A grand jury room can be an odd combination of hostility and lethargy. The confrontational or accusatory tone often found in grand jury examinations is foreign to most witnesses, most of whom have consumed a steady diet of television where prosecutors, agents, and police officers are the (very) good guys and the individuals they are pursuing are the (very) bad guys. Your witness needs to be reminded that the reason he has been subpoenaed to testify before the grand jury is because someone in law enforcement believes he has knowledge of a crime (or, at least, of a potential crime). Indeed, simply having mere knowledge of a potential crime is the rosiest situation for a grand jury witness. More commonly, the witness is a "subject" and the government believes that there is a possibility that the witness may have actually been involved in a federal offense.

Because prosecutors have unfettered sway in the grand jury room, they often exhibit frustration, skepticism, or sarcasm when confronted with testimony that is inconsistent with the government's theory of the case. This is difficult for the witness inasmuch as he or she frequently has no idea what the government's theory actually *is*. In any event, so as to stick to the straight-and-narrow of truth-telling, the witness needs to be civil but firm in his or her refusal to agree with a statement or assumption that the witness believes is simply not true, however much it irritates the prosecutor.

**Hold your testimony close.** Your client should be instructed, repeatedly, to not talk with anyone about his grand jury testimony before his appearance and to minimize his discussion of it after his grand jury appearance except with counsel. Both scenarios offer the government an opportunity to charge witness tampering as a means to gain leverage over a witness. In white-collar investigations, for example, the government is likely already convinced that a "conspiracy" of some sort has taken place. It is not a great leap to conclude that conspirators are still running around doing bad things such as trying to influence or change each other's grand jury testimony.

**Look through the government's eyes.** At this point, your client may protest that he or she is a law-abiding citizen and, if anything, wants to help catch the bad guys. No prosecutor or agent, your client says, would believe that he is a criminal.

Nod, then remind your client that although she may be a law-abiding citizen and possessed of a commendable desire to aid law enforcement, law enforcement does not think like your client. No one involved in the criminal justice system is engaged in a disinterested search for the objective truth. Prosecutors are no exception. They are building a case, assessing it, seeing how strong it is; they do not know your client, and they do not particularly care about him.

**This is not a business deal.** If your client is a businessperson, he should be reminded that many prosecutors and agents (although certainly not all) lack extensive experience in the business world. They do not have customers, employees, vendors, or patients. They do not have to undergo examination by stock analysts on conference calls or be called on the carpet before the CEO or the board because of a missed sales target or a clumsy merger.

For those reasons, any business activity, whether common or obscure, can to the investigatory eye seem potentially criminal. If the examining prosecutor professes to be shocked, for example, when the witness testifies that a check labeled "commission" was really a commission payment and not an unlawful kickback, he or she should be prepared to stick to his testimonial guns (if the witness in fact truthfully believes that it was a legitimate commission payment).

**Do not be afraid to take a break.** Remind the witness that she can leave the grand jury room at any time to consult with you wherever you may be stashed, either in the hall or in a witness room. As with witnesses in civil depositions, it is probably better if the witness does not seek to confer with counsel when a question is pending, but the witness's comfort, security, and privilege override everything. Nor does the witness have to say that she wants to consult with counsel. She can simply ask for a break.

**Debrief immediately.** Debrief your witness as soon as possible after the testimony. Doing so is sometimes difficult because the witness may want to have nothing more to do with a mildly (or greatly) unpleasant couple of hours, or the witness may think that the whole thing was much ado about nothing and not worth even memorializing.

Resist both impulses. Memory starts to fade within minutes after the witness leaves the grand jury room. Except under extraordinary or unhappy circumstances, such as your client's indictment, you will not get a transcript of what went on in the grand jury room. Your only hope is to get it from the witness's mouth. How you do so is of course a matter of personal style and preference, although one useful format is to memorialize the testimony in as close to a question-and-answer format as possible.

Despite the need for speed, do not debrief your witness anywhere near the grand jury room and preferably not in the courthouse. U.S. Attorney's offices, grand jury waiting rooms, and courthouse elevators and corridors are full of eyes and ears, both electronic and human, and it is not worth the risk.

Note in your memorandum the time that your client went in the grand jury room and the time he came out. The length of his examination may be relevant if you are comparing notes with other counsel for other witnesses. Make a note of which prosecutors and agents were in the grand jury room: just because only one came out to retrieve your client does not mean that there were not others in the grand jury room. You should also ask your client if the prosecutor at the outset identified you before the grand jurors as only a witness in the investigation. In that regard, it is good practice for you to ask in advance the AUSA to do so. Many do, but some do not.

In your memorandum, you may wish to expressly state at the beginning that the memorandum is based upon your notes, mental impressions, and legal theories arising from and relating to your client's grand jury testimony and, for that reason, your memorandum should be considered a draft and any conclusions tentative and subject to change. Should the privilege be lost or your memorandum fall into the wrong hands, such language may give you room to distance yourself from any content in the memorandum that turns out to be inaccurate or incomplete but hurtful to your client.

\* \* \*

In the *Divine Comedy*, the Roman poet Virgil's last words to Dante are "lord of yourself I crown and mitre you." With careful preparation, you will be able to say the same to your grand jury witness.

## CHAPTER 11

# Getting Ready for the Biggest Stage

## Preparing the Criminal Defendant Client to Testify

*John R. Mitchell*[1]

## INTRODUCTION

We have all seen depictions of criminal defendant clients testifying on television shows such as *Law and Order*, *The Good Wife*, *Matlock*, *Perry Mason*, and countless others. Depending on the story line, this testimony either leads to a moment of glorious vindication in which the client's innocence is irrefutably demonstrated, or, more often, the prosecutor's aggressive cross-examination leads to the complete destruction of the testifying client. These depictions tend to take place during the last five minutes of the show, leading to a drama-filled conclusion that cleanly wraps up the half-an-hour or hour-long program. In the end, we either see the client hugging his attorney or taken away in handcuffs. The satisfying conclusion leaves

---

1. The author would like to thank Mark B. Marein, Karen E. Rubin, and Douglas E. Grover for their thoughts on this subject and contributions to this chapter.

very little ambiguity, and we are left to return to our normal lives (until next week's episode).

These shows are geared toward entertaining the audience, and they focus on the most dramatic portions of the case. The preparation that goes into trying a case often gets cursory attention, and, rarely, does the episode show the preparation necessary to ready the client to testify. Simply put, the portion of the case dedicated to preparing your client to testify rarely makes good television. But in the real world, hours of analysis and preparation are the necessary ingredients to properly prepare your client for the biggest challenge of his or her life.

Deciding whether or not a client should testify begins the moment that client walks into your office. It is a difficult decision, and it should be constantly on your mind as you delve deeper into the facts and see how the case unfolds in trial. But, ultimately, the client must decide whether or not to testify.[2] This chapter discusses the preparation necessary to ensure that the client who decides to testify is as ready as possible when that time comes.

# Are You Sure You Want to Do This? Making Sure the Client Knows and Understands the Risks of Testifying

Criminal defendant clients rarely take the stand. There is an old adage used by the criminal defense bar that goes: *When considering whether a criminal defendant should testify, don't.* I have heard numerous similar warnings, including: *Never put your client on the stand; The best defense is no defense; When in doubt, squat;* and *Do not put your client on the stand unless you have exhausted every other avenue for victory.* There are a million variations of this common theme. Yet, these phrases did not come into existence because criminal defense practitioners like catchy phrases. Instead, these cautions come from the experience gleaned from years in the trenches, and all criminal defense practitioners have seen or heard of clients who sank themselves by testifying. Since the government must prove, in every criminal case, that the indicted defendant committed each and every element of the crimes charged by evidence beyond a reasonable doubt, the overwhelming practice is to not put clients on the stand.

But there are instances where the client may want to or simply has to testify. In those cases, there is simply no substitute for hard work. You must roll up your sleeves and put in the necessary time to properly prepare your client. This is not a one- or

---

2. Model Rules of Prof'l Conduct R. 1.2(a) (after consultation, the lawyer shall abide by the client's decision whether to testify in a criminal case).

two-hour conversation, or an afternoon at the office. Instead, preparing your client to testify often takes more time than the remainder of the case preparation.

The first step to preparing the client to testify is to make sure the client understands what he or she is giving up when deciding whether or not to testify. The client can only make this decision after you have together examined the potential jury instructions and your client's rights, discussed the potential for burden shifting, explored what the client hopes to gain from testifying, and determined if your client can handle the stress of testifying.

## Knowing the Jury Instructions: What Is the Jury Going to Hear about Your Client's Rights?

Countless legal treatises discuss a criminal defendant client's rights at trial. We are not going to review all of those protections here. But these rights have a practical application in the courtroom, and, in many cases, the jury will receive specific instructions that may set the basis for a powerful closing argument. In preparing the client to testify, it is important to make time to revisit these protections and explain to the client how they will be presented to the jury.

All criminal defendants enjoy a presumption of innocence and, as noted previously, each and every element of the crime(s) they are charged with must be proven against them by proof beyond a reasonable doubt. These two protections are among the bedrocks of our criminal defense system, and the court will *instruct* the jury about these protections and numerous others when it charges the jury:

(1) As you know, the defendant has pleaded not guilty to the crime charged in the indictment. The indictment is not any evidence at all of guilt. It is just the formal way that the government tells the defendant what crime he is accused of committing. It does not even raise any suspicion of guilt.

(2) Instead, the defendant starts the trial with a clean slate, with no evidence at all against him, and the law presumes that he is innocent. This presumption of innocence stays with him unless the government presents evidence here in court that overcomes the presumption, and convinces you beyond a reasonable doubt that he is guilty.

(3) This means that the defendant has no obligation to present any evidence at all, or to prove to you in any way that he is innocent. It is up to the government to prove that he is guilty, and this burden stays on the government from start to finish. You must find the defendant not guilty unless the government convinces you beyond a reasonable doubt that he is guilty.

(4) The government must prove every element of the crime charged beyond a reasonable doubt. Proof beyond a reasonable

doubt does not mean proof beyond all possible doubt. Possible doubts or doubts based purely on speculation are not reasonable doubts. A reasonable doubt is a doubt based on reason and common sense. It may arise from the evidence, the lack of evidence, or the nature of the evidence.

(5) Proof beyond a reasonable doubt means proof which is so convincing that you would not hesitate to rely and act on it in making the most important decisions in your own lives. If you are convinced that the government has proved the defendant guilty beyond a reasonable doubt, say so by returning a guilty verdict. If you are not convinced, say so by returning a not guilty verdict.[3]

But that is not the only favorable instruction provided to the defense, and courts routinely provide instructions to juries about a criminal defendant who chooses not to testify:

**7.02 A DEFENDANT'S ELECTION NOT TO TESTIFY OR PRESENT EVIDENCE**

(1) A defendant has an absolute right not to testify [or present evidence]. The fact that he did not testify [or present any evidence] cannot be considered by you in any way. Do not even discuss it in your deliberations.

(2) Remember that it is up to the government to prove the defendant guilty beyond a reasonable doubt. It is not up to the defendant to prove that he is innocent.[4]

These instructions are powerful reminders for any jury. And they readily resonate when the court tells the jury that "I instruct you that you must presume that the defendants, are not guilty of the crimes charged in the indictment."[5] Remembering that reasonable doubt "means proof which is so convincing that you would not hesitate to rely and act on it in making the most important decisions in your own lives," often requires an honest and frank analysis of what your client is going to bring to the case that cross-examination of the government's witnesses did not. Accordingly, the extent to which the client's testimony could impact that analysis is a critical fact to discuss with the client during the preparation phase.

In fairness, there is some debate as to the effectiveness of these instructions and whether or not juries actually listen to these admonitions. It would be naïve to think that some jurors would not think that the client had something to hide

---

3. Sixth Circuit Pattern Jury Instruction 1.00 (Sept. 9, 2015 version).
4. Sixth Circuit Pattern Jury Instruction 7.02(a) (Sept. 9, 2015 version).
5. United States v. Phillips, et al., Case No. 1:11-cr-00180 (USDC N.D. Ohio).

when not testifying. And, despite repeated admonitions from the court, jurors may still improperly consider the client's refusal to testify and hold it against him or her. Still, if the client stays off the stand, you know what the court will instruct the jury.

## Burden Shifting: Moving the Needle Toward Conviction

The jury instructions just described have determined the course and presentation of many trial defenses, and numerous defense attorneys have successfully argued that a case had reasonable doubt, leading to the client's acquittal. The review of those protections in necessary here because, when the client chooses to testify, concepts such as *clean slate*, *proof beyond a reasonable doubt*, and *presumed innocent* lose much of their impact. Instead, when a client testifies, the constitutional protections do not disappear, but juries tend to ignore these instructions and its focus becomes *who do you believe?*

This is only natural. After all, when faced with two different sets of facts, most people will pick one over the other. The government will present a series of witnesses—agents, lay witnesses, expert witnesses, cooperating witnesses, victims, and others—who will provide one version of the events. Your testifying client has to offer a competing version that is believable. The client must understand that it is his or her credibility that becomes the focus of the case when deciding whether or not to testify.

When faced with this question, I often rely on Mark Twain's immortal words: "It's better to keep your mouth shut and appear stupid (or guilty) than open it and remove all doubt."[6] In close calls, I think it best that the client does not testify.

## What Are You Trying to Accomplish?

So the most basic, yet most important, question for any criminal defense attorney contemplating putting his client on the stand is this: *what am I trying to accomplish?* When the client testifies, the government has a golden opportunity to "back-fill" and establish some of the elements of the crimes that the client was charged with (e.g., the client's presence at the scene of the crime, the client's receipt of damning e-mails, the client's knowledge of certain facts, the client's possession of stolen items, etc.). Moreover, if convicted, the judge may sentence a client whom they have perceived to have lied more harshly than one who did not testify.

Every defense has a theme, and the client's testimony must be in harmony with and advance that theme. The theme may be as simple as "I didn't do it" or, as seen in many white-collar criminal trials, more complex, substantive testimony about how acts that are not in dispute were not undertaken with any criminal

---

6. There is some dispute as to whether Twain actually came up with this phrase. Abraham Lincoln is alleged to have authored something similar: "Better to remain silent and be thought a fool than speak out and remove all doubt." Either way, I have very little hesitancy on relying on Lincoln or Twain in most situations.

intent. Frankly, your goal may be as simple as letting the jury see your client for who he is and letting the jury decide if he is the sort of person the government has demonized since opening statement. In those situations, the client must be able to show the jury that he is not a villain. Or if he or she has done bad things in the past, the client must be able to demonstrate that he or she was not a villain in the particular circumstances that brought the indictment. When testifying, the client risks putting his or her character front and center, especially when he has prior convictions.

So ask yourself: is there any evidence that must come *solely* from the client? If so, then the client may have to testify. But if there are other avenues that you can explore before putting your client on the stand, exhaust those first. But understanding and fully analyzing *why* the client is testifying, and how that testimony advances your theme, requires you to spend the necessary time with your client to ensure that the client understands what we are trying to accomplish and how it advances our theme of the case.

## Can My Client Handle the Stress?

Right after determining what you are trying to accomplish is determining if your client has the strength to advance the theme of the case. Some clients simply cannot handle the stress of testifying. They stammer, sweat, contradict themselves, do not explain things well, present poorly, endlessly talk, become confrontational, or recoil from confrontation and wilt under the pressure of a competent cross-examination. Moreover, many clients carry such baggage, like previous convictions, that putting them on the stand is more likely to hurt the case than help it.

Can your client handle this stress of both direct and cross-examination? Will the client's personality or past history cloud the jury's ability to hear and appreciate the testimony your client will offer? The answers to these questions require long analysis and an honest appraisal of the client, and any decision you make should be repeatedly revisited as the case progresses. These questions also require a full and frank conversation with the client. The client must understand that there is no "time out" during the cross-examination. But it's the client's life, and, ultimately the client's decision. But making sure that you discuss the stress of testifying with the client is an important part of the client's preparation.

# THE CLIENT DECIDES TO TESTIFY: GETTING READY

We've spent a fair amount of space reviewing some of the considerations a practitioner should examine and discuss with the client when deciding whether or not to put a client on the stand. Now it is time to get to the meat of the article and examine the best way to prepare the client for testifying.

# What Do We Need to Prepare For?

Now that you have a set idea of what evidence you need from your client and have also determined that your client can handle the demands of testifying, the focus turns to specific items that need to be addressed.

## *Proper Courtroom Attire and Appearance*

I am not married to the idea that a client must wear a suit to trial. After all, Michael Jackson famously arrived at court in pajamas and sat through his child-molestation trial in a variety of handmade, one-of-a-kind outfits.[7] Any attempt to dress Michael Jackson in more traditional courtroom attire would have been seen as an obvious attempt to pander to the jury. Clients are who they are, and while you can try to nudge them toward more traditional courtroom attire, you cannot change them.

Your client may be a biker, gang banger, war protester, tax cheat, embezzler, or any flavor of alleged lawbreaker. But all clients must wear attire that will enable them to testify as well as possible. If the client has never worn a tie before, then putting him in a tie may be an impediment to his best testimony. I do ask that my clients be clean, well groomed, and dressed in a manner that shows respect for the process. I believe that it is important that the client appears as professional as possible, but is comfortable enough in the attire not to distract from the examination.

# Preparing for Direct Examination

## *Establishing Your Client's Credibility*

Your client's credibility is the ultimate issue here, and a client that loses credibility with the jury will most likely be convicted. A key component of preparing the client for the direct examination is locating and having a plan for dealing with those components of the case or your client's background that could detract from his or her credibility. First, and most importantly, the client must understand the absolute obligation to tell the truth, just like every other witness.[8] The client must understand that you, as counsel, have ethical obligations to the court if you discover that the client is lying.[9] As a practical consideration, juries, in my experience, are remarkably good at spotting liars.

Locating those troublesome components of the case and the client involves an extensive background search into the client's past. It is vital that defense counsel knows and understands where the client is vulnerable to impeachment because of past convictions or indiscretions that will weigh upon the client's credibility. The

---

7. http://articles.latimes.com/2005/may/24/entertainment/et-tailors24.
8. *See* James Farragher Campbell, *Ethical Concerns in Grooming the Criminal Defendant for the Witness Stand*, 26 Hofstra L. Rev., 265–74 (2007).
9. *See* Model Rule of Professional Conduct 3.3 (Candor Toward the Tribunal), 3.4 (Fairness to Opposing Party and Counsel), and 4.1 (Truthfulness in Statements to Others).

client must be thoroughly interviewed, and Internet searches must be conducted to see what exists out there in the worldwide web. Facebook, Instagram, Twitter, and countless other websites may contain the client's comments and opinions on a variety of things, and certainly some of those can be used against the client. Has the client published anything? You need to know. Running down these issues can be burdensome, but this is essential to avoid an unwanted surprise during the client's cross-examination. Everything from employment applications to bad business deals must be explored so that the examining attorney can evaluate where the pitfalls lie.

This may seem like overkill, but this background knowledge is essential so that you can properly advise the client about questions that could potentially open the door to the client's unfavorable past or that would put the client's character at issue. The client must have a clear understanding of the potential problem that can arise, particularly when the client has previous convictions or has engaged in questionable, uncharged behavior.

This is also an important time to remind the client about the attorney-client privilege and the danger of a potential inadvertent waiver. The client should be instructed not to discuss any of the advice or strategy that you have discussed with him or her over the course of the representation.

### Direct Examination

Preparing for the direct examination is the easy part, and it starts with the rapport that you have developed with your client. Every attorney-client relationship, particularly in the criminal context, is based on the trust that the client has in the attorney and manifests itself in the rapport between the attorney and the client. Hopefully, by the time that the client is testifying, this rapport results in an easy give and take between you and the client. You ask questions during the representation, and the client answers and provides the information that you need. By then, the client should be able to answer your questions in a clear and concise manner. If he or she cannot do so, or you do not have a good rapport with your client, your client should not testify.

Direct examination should start with this easy give and take. You will be asking open-ended questions that allow the client to advance the theory of the case. Your questions should be of the who, what, where, when, how, and, most importantly, why variety. The client should be testifying, not you, and the jury will be able to assess your client's credibility by the manner in which the client answers your questions. Your job is to set the question so that the client can answer and advance the case theme. I always instruct my clients to answer the question posed and to provide the shortest possible answer. Cut to the chase, and answer the question.

I have heard countless coaches espouse the theory that players should "practice like they want to play." This is why rapport is so important. Your client has to trust you to ask the correct questions so that the information flows in a conversational and believable manner. Practice is a vital component to developing this rapport, and I always do practice direct examinations of my client when it is possible that he or she may take the stand. I don't do this to rehearse his or her answers,[10] but to make sure that the client understands that I know the necessary questions. These practice direct examinations take place months before my client ultimately testifies. Because the decision to put the client on the stand is constantly under review, the practice direct examination is a key evaluating tool to make sure that we are making the right decision.

## Answer the Question, Part I

On direct examination, the client answers the question that has been asked. A skillful examiner will be able to narrow and control examination, particularly with leading questions on cross-examination. Clients must understand that they will be faced with questions that they do not want to answer, both on direct and cross-examinations.

That is why the client must learn to answer the question asked. If it calls for a "yes" or "no," then that is the answer. No jury wants to hear the client drone on and on about superfluous matters.[11] Jurors want to know if they can believe your client. Working with the client to answer the question is critical. The client will appear honest and forthright, making for a more favorable impression on the jury.

If this comes naturally to the client, he or she should answer questions while turned toward the jury. Many testifying witnesses turn and look at the jury when answering questions, and there is no reason that the client cannot do the same.

## Dealing with Your Client's Troubling Background

Having done the background search described earlier, you should know where the pitfalls lie. Having practiced the direct examination with the client should make him or her aware of the questions that could result in opening the door or putting the client's character at issue.

Still, clients with a questionable past may want to testify. If there is a prior conviction that is admissible, then the client should be prepared to "own it." Troubling facts in the case must be dealt with in the direct examination, and the client must own the previous bad behavior. Protestations of previous conspiracies or bad luck will score no points with the jury and detract from the client's credibility.

---

10. Nothing will undermine your client's credibility faster than rehearsed answers or answers prepared by counsel. The client has to be able to explain things in his or her own words. Since the client's credibility is many times the ultimate issue, I avoid anything that will detract from it, especially answers prepared by counsel.

11. When the client drones on and on, the chance of the door opening to otherwise inadmissible impeachment material greatly increases.

# Preparing for Cross-Examination

Cross-examination is much more challenging, and there is no time limit. Jodi Arias, convicted in 2013 of murdering her ex-boyfriend, testified for 19 days, five were spent on cross-examination.[12] Preparing for the cross-examination can be much more time consuming than preparing for the direct examination.

## Using Mock Cross-Examinations to Your Client's Advantage

If the client has one advantage, it is the ability to control the testimony on direct examination. Stated another way, unless the client has provided a statement or a confession, the prosecutor is disadvantaged because the first time that he or she will hear the client's testimony is when the client testifies.

I believe that it is important to perform mock examinations, and that the mock cross-examination is critical to preparing the client to testify. First, the client will learn how the process works and can evaluate if he or she can handle the stress of cross-examination. Hopefully, this process will enable the client to become as comfortable as possible in the witness chair. Second, the client gains greater insight into how the examination will be conducted. Like any cross-examination, the mock cross-examination will focus on the problematic elements of the case. The bad statements, e-mails, documents, and the other components that the government is relying on will be used during the mock cross-examination to test the client's ability to honestly and convincingly answer questions. The client learns, in real-time, how to answer the damaging questions and will be forced to answer the tough questions. If the client has been through a thorough mock cross-examination (or two), then he or she will be prepared for the tough questions that could detract from his or her credibility.

## Answer the Question, Part II

Again, the client has to be prepared to answer the question. Rambling, run-on answers detract from the client's testimony and can cause juries to question the client's credibility. Even the most inexperienced prosecutor will score some points on the witness. After all, if there was not damaging information against the client, (presumably) he or she would not have been charged. Having the client withstand the prosecutor's broadside stemming from those tough questions is critical to establishing the client's credibility.

## Maintaining Your Cool

The best chance of your client losing his or her cool is on cross-examination. Cross can become heated, or, in some cases, even personal. It can turn argumentative, with both sides talking over one another. It can take great strength to maintain

---

12. *See* http://www.usatoday.com/story/news/nation/2013/03/13/did-arias-testimony-help-or-hurt/1986595/.

your credibility when someone is accusing you of being a fraud, wife-beater, or worse. Many cross-examinations are designed to get the client to reveal what the prosecutor thinks are his or her true colors (e.g., lying, lack of concern, violent tendencies, etc.) and the answers are less important than the client's behavior while on the stand.

Shakespeare famously wrote in *Hamlet* that "The lady doth protest too much, methinks."[13] These words ring true today. Loud, repeated protestations of innocence reflect badly on the testifying client. Calm, dispassionate answers enhance credibility. It is absolutely paramount that clients who are contemplating testifying understand that they have to keep their composure. This is the one chance that the jury has to hear the client's version of the events. Clients must understand that their testimony will sound better if told in a normal conversational tone, rather than a screaming match.

I tell my clients that the success of their examination can be gauged by prosecutor's behavior during their testimony. If your client is prepared, this is an opportunity to enhance the client's credibility at the expense of the prosecutor. When frustrated, the prosecutors often get loud and demonstrative, hoping to rattle the client. They often try to pick fights. If the client can maintain his or her composure, then the client's credibility will be enhanced. Mock examinations are the perfect vehicle for the client to practice maintaining composure. Do not be afraid to get in your client's face and turn up the temperature during the mock cross-examination; you would rather find out if your client can handle the heat then, rather than when on the stand.

## Preparing for Redirect

Rapport and trust matter most when cross-examination ends. The prosecutor may have scored some points. The client may doubt his or her performance. The jury may have started to question your client's credibility.

Because you have done mock examinations, the client understands that he or she does not have to try to fix everything while testifying. Instead, the client can wait until you ask the open-ended questions that free the client from the constraints of cross-examination. After being grilled with an unending series of "isn't it true . . . ," your redirect is the opportunity for the client to answer those questions that he or she could not while on cross.

## Preparing for Questions from the Jury

Today, many courts permit juries to ask questions. In one case I prosecuted, the testifying defendant was asked a question that had been submitted by one of the jurors.

---

13. *Hamlet*, Act III, Scene 2.

He was not prepared for that question, and he flubbed the answer, badly. While the evidence of his guilt was compelling, flubbing the question did not help his cause.

The client has to be prepared for this as well. If the client is comfortable doing so, he or she should turn toward the jury when answering a question from one of the jurors.

## Preparing to Use Demonstratives and Exhibits

If your examination requires exhibits, demonstratives, or a re-enactment, make sure your client knows that it is coming. Do not use an exhibit unless your client has seen it before. Any advantage you may gain is not worth the risk of an unprepared client that goes away from the theme. You will see sheer panic in your client's eyes if you show them something they have never seen before, for the first time, while they are on the stand.

# What Tools Can Help the Client Prepare?

When practicable, I like to use jury consultants. They are expensive, but, in my experience, more than worth it if your client can afford the cost. Many jury consultants have worked with criminal defendant clients before. Many others are well experienced in preparing corporate representatives for Civil Rule 30(b) depositions. This type of experience can be valuable in preparing your client to testify. Still, if you choose to work with a jury consultant, make sure that the consultant is retained by you, as counsel for the client, with a specific engagement letter so that you protect the attorney-client privilege.

Numerous other professionals can assist: private investigators, forensic accountants, auditors, and numerous other consultants. These professionals do not assist the actual preparation, but, instead, are critical in locating the numerous pitfalls that could arise during your client's testimony. Again, make sure that the engagement is structured to protect the attorney-client privilege.

# Conclusion

There is no one-size-fits-all client, just as there are no-one-size-fits-all criminal case. My comments here are designed to give you an idea of the issues you may encounter when deciding whether or not your client will testify. Some ideas may work; some may be rejected because they will not work with your client. But preparation is the key. Tailor your preparation to your client's personality and the facts of the case, and, if you have done the necessary work, you'll have given your client the best chance for success when taking the stand.

## CHAPTER 12

# Beyond the Courtroom

## Preparing the Witness for Internal Investigations and Administrative and Congressional Hearings

*Lewis S. Wiener*

*Ronald W. Zdrojeski*

*Meghana D. Shah*[1]

## INTRODUCTION

Witnesses are, simply, the heart of the story in any case. Witnesses are the vehicle through which the story of the case is presented, breathing life into facts that have been undiscovered or unknown. When witnesses are well prepared by a lawyer, the story unfolds with ease and the lawyer puts himself or herself in the optimal position to overlay advocacy on the client's narrative. Whereas much has been written about preparing witnesses for trial, there is limited guidance on preparing witnesses for testimony outside of the courtroom. As the need to interview individuals in other contexts increases, there is a greater likelihood of engaging in fact-finding and dispute resolution outside of the courtroom—for example, in administrative proceedings or internal investigations. Though some core

---

1. The authors wish to thank Brittany Cambre, an associate in Evershed Sutherland's litigation group, for her invaluable assistance with this chapter.

tenets of witness preparation apply regardless of the situation, it is vital to understand how these various settings may impact a practitioner's preparation and presentation.

Though the majority of the procedures and skills used to prepare witnesses for traditional litigation purposes are transferable to preparing witnesses for nontrial situations, some are not. The practitioner who can look beyond the courtroom, armed with an understanding of the distinctions between trial witnesses and witnesses in other contexts, will be best prepared to elicit the facts clearly and accurately, thus best equipping the lawyer to achieve the client's goals. To effectively prepare a witness for hearings or to effectively interview witnesses in the context of internal investigations, a practitioner must understand how the objectives are both aligned with and distinct from those at trial, how the audience is similar to and different from a jury, and which rules, evidentiary and otherwise, apply.

This chapter sets forth guidelines for a practitioner to consider in understanding these distinctions and preparing witnesses for testimony in three distinct nontrial contexts: (1) internal investigations; (2) administrative proceedings; and (3) congressional hearings.

# INTERNAL INVESTIGATIONS

Corporate scandals in recent years and the ensuing passage of Sarbanes-Oxley, Dodd-Frank, and other compliance-based legislation have resulted in an exponential increase in company-initiated internal investigations. Though once employed largely in the context of emergency incident responses or employer-employee disputes, the internal investigation has now become a staple of sound corporate governance. Companies initiate internal investigations for a wide variety of reasons, including responding to allegations of fraud inside the company, responding to increased regulatory enforcement in a particular area, assessing findings of a certain practice of a competitor, or simply ensuring compliance with the company's policies. The objectives of the investigation and a witness's awareness of its existence will heavily inform the practitioner's approach to witness preparation in the investigation context.

A threshold consideration in approaching witness preparation is the stage of the internal investigation. In the investigatory stage, the practitioner is not so much preparing the witness but preparing *for* the witness—that is, preparing to learn the relevant facts and to capture the arc of the story during a witness interview. At a later stage of the investigation, if the company decides to disclose the results of the investigation or is otherwise preparing to report the results to a governmental body, the practitioner's role may shift to preparing the witness to tell the client's story in a cohesive and persuasive manner.

## Preparing for the Witness in the Investigatory Phase

Effective investigations are open quests for truth rather than a pursuit of a preconceived narrative. Only once all of the facts are gathered and the complete story is strung together can counsel begin to effectively craft a narrative to explain specific conduct that must be disclosed to regulators.

Once a client decides to conduct an internal investigation, the lawyer must quickly identify key individuals possessing the most salient facts about the matter at hand. Identifying key witnesses is just as important as preparing for the witness interviews themselves. This section provides a roadmap for the entire investigatory process, from selecting whom to interview, sequencing interviews, and preparing for each individual witness interview.

### Know the Law

It is imperative that a lawyer know the laws and regulations that govern the many facets of corporate conduct, particularly the ones implicated by the internal investigation. What is less clear, however, is that the application of those laws and regulations can vary by jurisdiction. Similarly written, or even identical, laws and regulations can be interpreted, applied, and enforced differently depending on the political, regulatory, and legal environment in which they are deployed. A lawyer should have a basic understanding of the legal landscape prior to launching an internal investigation to ensure he or she conducts the investigation in a manner best designed to protect the client's interests.

Furthermore, it is important for the lawyer to understand not only the technical requirements of the law, but also the potential consequences of a particular violation. Furthermore, the lawyer should understand whether the regulatory body charged with enforcement of the law would expend resources investigating and prosecuting a particular violation.

### Identify Key Documents

At their core, most internal investigations involve a company policy and an examination of how the policy was followed or violated. Before identifying whom to interview, it helps to have the relevant policy in hand. This document can be used as the starting point for identifying key witnesses. For example, rather than asking in the abstract which company employee is responsible for a particular function, the lawyer can identify initial witnesses by determining the individuals responsible for drafting or updating the policy, ensuring compliance with the policy, and the like. If feasible, relevant e-mails and other documents should be searched before conducting interviews to ensure critical information can be elicited during interviews. Witnesses are more likely able to provide key details the practitioner is looking for if they are provided with a memory refresher in the form of documents, particularly their own e-mails. More importantly, e-mail communications may reveal the relationships between employees, which can assist in sequencing the interviews, as discussed further in the following subsection.

## Develop an Interview Plan

Equally important to the way counsel approaches a particular witness interview is the order in which the interviews proceed. The sequencing of witness interviews should not be overlooked as an element of the investigation strategy. Neglecting to strategize about the order of the interviews may result in wasted effort and lost opportunities for factual development. Counsel can approach the ordering of interviews from multiple angles; the manner selected will depend on the objectives of the investigation. One way to proceed is a pyramid approach, which begins with the employees in lower-level positions and elicits testimony from those employees about their reporting lines within the organization. Counsel then proceeds up the reporting chain pyramid until reaching the peak or the final decision maker. In the authors' experience, this is likely how the government will conduct interviews should it choose to investigate. In a case where documents or preliminary client discussions reveal that the nucleus of facts concerns the behavior of higher-level employees, or where there is a danger that certain employees may leave the company, counsel may want to proceed in a reverse pyramid order or use a fan approach, beginning with the individuals at the center of the known nucleus of facts and working outwards from there.

Whereas the practitioner should think critically about the goals of an investigation and develop an interview plan tailored to achieve those goals, the smart practitioner knows when to deviate from the plan as needed. As investigations progress, new facts may come to light that justify revising the original roadmap.

## Know Your Audience

In the trial context, a reference to knowing one's audience typically refers to knowing the background and practices of the judge, as well as the demographics and inclinations of the jury. In the investigatory phase of an investigation, knowing the audience refers to understanding the company's culture and hierarchy, the tone that has been set with employees, whether employees are aware of the existence of the investigation or not, the economic climate of the company, and the like. Counsel should gather as many facts as possible from internal counsel, the Internet, and other sources before beginning a single interview. For example, if a client retains a lawyer to investigate allegations of fraud and embezzlement inside the company and the company's shares have recently experienced a dramatic drop in the market, the lawyer is likely to encounter witnesses who are fearful and apprehensive about their jobs. That fear and anxiety will impact the tone and delivery, and perhaps the order of the lawyer's questions. For example, the lawyer may want to save certain difficult questions for the end of the interview, to ensure the witness remains calm and focused throughout.

In internal investigations, the company often appoints key personnel to assist lawyers directly in fact-gathering, identifying relevant employees, and obtaining documents. Often, these employees become so much a part of the fabric of the investigation, or become so well acquainted with counsel, that it does not occur to counsel that they also should be subject to a formal interview. Be vigilant about this phenomenon and take an expansive view when selecting witnesses for interviews. No matter how awkward it might be, it is important the universe of employees interviewed does not reflect an omission that is likely to raise questions about the investigation's integrity.

Finally, realize that there is no guarantee that a particular witness can be re-interviewed, so plan accordingly. Whereas in many investigations witnesses are called for follow-up interviews without incident, the ability to interview the witness is linked to the individual's employment with the client. Be efficient and do not squander the interview opportunity on the assumption that the witness will be available for subsequent interviews.

## Master the Substance

That preparation is key in every context is hardly a revelation to the practitioner. However, lawyers often struggle with witness interviews in the investigation context because it is sometimes deceptively open-ended. The relatively structured environment of a deposition or trial is absent; no formal discovery has taken place, and it is sometimes unclear what, if any, role the witness may have played in the scenario being investigated. As such, effective preparation for a witness interview in this context may differ in some material ways from deposition or trial preparation. One paradox lawyers often face is the desire for the interview to proceed in a natural, relaxed manner pitted against the specific information that must be elicited. Ironically, the greater the factual preparation, the easier it will be for the lawyer to conduct the interview with an almost conversational ease. Some key elements of preparation include reviewing, where available: (1) the witness's e-mails; (2) the witness's CV and background (much of this biographical information can now be gathered through social media); (3) the company policies that the witness drafted, enforces, consults, or otherwise uses in his daily tasks; (4) organizational charts showing the witness's place in the reporting hierarchy; and (5) prior interview notes or statements where applicable.

Of course, counsel should consider where the use of documents could hinder or help the fact-finding process and how they should best be used. There are two basic ways to use documents during the witness interview. Either the lawyer can have the witness tell his or her story and show the witness the relevant documents afterward, or the lawyer can present the witness with documents prior to the witness providing the story. The order in which the lawyer elicits testimony and presents documents can materially affect the outcome of the interview.

For example, in a case where it is important to understand the reporting chain and who is responsible for particular functions, having an organizational chart handy will allow the witness to walk through the reporting chain with relative ease. On the other hand, if counsel has already learned through e-mails or other documents of a witness's misconduct, counsel may wish to conduct an open-ended interview without alerting the witness to counsel's knowledge in this regard, instead waiting until the end of the interview to question the witness about certain documents.

## Understand the Attorney-Client Privilege

The attorney-client privilege applies to and protects against forced disclosure certain communications between an attorney and a client. In order to be privileged, a communication must have been made for the purpose of seeking legal advice. In internal investigations, the corporation is typically considered the "client" for purposes of the privilege. In the context of witness interviews, it is important to understand both the relative breadth of the privilege as applied to investigations and the restriction that applies only to communications themselves.

The U.S. Court of Appeals for the District of Columbia recently clarified the scope of the attorney-client privilege as it applies to internal investigations. In *In re Kellogg Brown & Root, Inc.*, (KBR), [2] the court found that, as long as providing or obtaining legal advice is *one* of the significant purposes of an investigation, the attorney-client privilege protects the documents related to the investigation, regardless of whether the investigation was required by statute, regulation, or company policy.

In addition, *KBR* emphasized the breadth of the privilege as applied to internal investigations. The privilege exists to protect not only the attorney giving legal advice, but also the information given by the client to enable his lawyer to give legal advice. As such, the attorney-client privilege covers a factual investigation by an attorney in connection with the provision of legal services to a client. The *KBR* decision also suggests that *all* documents related to the subject internal investigation are protected by the attorney-client privilege.

Though the decision is well reasoned and the authors believe the decision reached in *KBR* is sound, other decisions have taken different views on the scope of the attorney-client privilege. Lawyers should be aware of the particular jurisprudence of the jurisdiction in which the investigation takes place and in which any disclosure would ultimately be made.

It should be noted, however, that the privilege protects only the contents of a *communication itself* from compelled disclosure and does not protect the underlying facts communicated therein. It is imperative that practitioners, and the clients they represent, remain vigilant about protecting the attorney-client privilege and avoid inadvertent waiver of the privilege throughout the course of an investigation.

---

2. *In re* Kellogg Brown & Root, Inc., 756 F.3d 754, 757 (D.C. Cir. 2014).

To protect the attorney-client privilege, as well as the integrity of the investigation, the lawyer should instruct each witness not to discuss the fact that there is an ongoing investigation or the contents of the interview itself. Lawyers should recognize that confidentiality in this context is not necessarily a natural reaction. It is likely an unusual occurrence to have a cadre of outside lawyers descend upon the client's offices and interview employees in a conference room. The witness is likely to be asked by co-workers why and about what they were interviewed. Some witnesses might also want to tell their co-workers about the investigation. Thus, it is important for the lawyer to affirmatively explain why confidentiality is necessary and instruct the witness not to discuss the interview with anyone else. The lawyer should recognize, however, that although some witnesses will take that instruction seriously and remain close-lipped, others will ignore it entirely.

## *Issue* Upjohn *Warnings*

At the start of the witness interview, the lawyer must advise the witness of his relationship to the witness and the company. That is, the lawyer must make clear that he represents the company and not the particular witness. Known as an *Upjohn* warning (or a "corporate *Miranda* warning") and derived from the U.S. Supreme Court's decision in *Upjohn v. United States*,[3] this prefatory language is critical not only for the witness's understanding, but also to ensure that the company is able to claim privilege with respect to the interviews and other fact-finding conducted as part of the internal investigation. Though the basic content of an *Upjohn* warning is well established, each lawyer will have his own style of rendering the warning, which can depend on the witness's position within the company, the witness's or lawyer's demeanor, and the nature of the interview. The practitioner should seek to strike a balance between what is necessarily an awkward moment between the interviewer and the interviewee by being candid and straightforward while at the same time not minimizing the importance of the message. In some cases, the lawyer may want to document the rendering of *Upjohn* warnings in writing by having the witness sign a statement that the warning was given. In most cases, asking: "Do you understand these instructions?" or "Do you understand?" may be sufficient to ensure the witness understands the relationship between the interviewer, himself, and his employer. Some lawyers choose to explain to the witness that the warning is not personal and must be given to every witness, thus effectively creating a distance between the message ("I am not your lawyer") and the bearer of the message (the lawyer).

The lawyer should consider how a particular witness might respond to the warning and anticipate the questions he may ask. Employees who have never been interviewed in connection with an investigation may be preoccupied with their own job security. Seasoned or high-level corporate employees, on the other hand,

---

3. Upjohn v. United States, 449 U.S. 383 (1981).

may have been involved in investigations in the past and may be un-phased by the warning itself. Instead, they may ask about the nature of disclosure to regulatory bodies. Taking the time to anticipate witness reactions will ensure that the interview proceeds as seamlessly as possible and that the lawyer builds trust with the witness early in the interview.

## Anticipate Witness Questions

It is only natural for some witnesses to become nervous after receiving an *Upjohn* warning and being questioned about what they may or may not have done in connection with their professional duties. Though a lawyer cannot and should not reassure the witness one way or the other about the ultimate outcome of the investigation or the witness's role in it, the lawyer is well served by anticipating questions and being able to answer them in a calm, unruffled manner. The lawyer's preparation on this front can mean the difference between moving forward in an interview and stopping or stalling the interview to untangle the witness's various concerns.

Some common questions a witness may ask in the context of an internal investigation interview include: (1) Do I need my own lawyer? (2) Am I going to jail? (3) Are you going to report this to the authorities? (4) Am I going to get fired? and (5) Do I have to talk to you? As stated earlier, it is best to communicate calmly and clearly that you cannot give legal advice to the employee and that you do not know what the outcome of the investigation will be. In some cases, the client may agree to appoint a pool of counsel for employees so that they may have these questions answered substantively. The lawyer also may want to have available for himself a question and answer sheet to reference during the interview that contains precleared answers to these questions. What is vital at this stage is to plan to answer the questions as honestly as possible with minimal disruption to the flow of the interview.

## Proceed with an Eye Toward Disclosure

At the time of witness interviews, counsel is unlikely to know whether the results of the investigation will be disclosed to a regulator. Accordingly, the practitioner should be mindful of the possibility of disclosure throughout the witness interview process and act accordingly. This process involves proactively considering who should participate in the disclosure and how to protect the attorney-client privilege during the disclosure.

As with any witness, a seasoned lawyer will listen to what the witness has to say and assess that witness's demeanor and credibility while the individual is testifying. The myriad ways to determine whether and why a witness is lying are beyond the scope of this chapter. However, counsel in internal investigations should be keenly aware of the difference between a truthful witness and a forthcoming witness.

Internal investigations, depending on the severity of the potential wrongdoing at issue, are shrouded in fear; the fear of heavy civil penalties, the fear of criminal penalties, or the fear of retaliation for blowing the whistle on the company. It is in this context that lawyers encounter witnesses who either purposefully misrepresent information to cover up their wrongdoing or omit information, not because they want to hide information, but because they are afraid to divulge information or become embroiled in a contentious investigation.

Fundamental to any deposition or trial preparation is instructing the witness to answer only the question that is asked and nothing more. Most practitioners have prepared a witness from over-answering, but fewer have extensive experience dealing with witnesses who under-answer questions. This is perhaps the biggest challenge in an internal investigation, which at its heart is an attempt to turn over every stone and piece together the puzzle of events that may or may not reveal wrongdoing. Practitioners should be mindful of the purpose of the investigation and continue probing less-than-forthcoming witnesses until they have satisfactorily answered all necessary questions.

While extracting the entire version of the facts from witnesses, counsel should not forget the ever-important attorney-client privilege. Aside from rendering *Upjohn* warnings, which explain the possibility of disclosure (discussed in more detail earlier), counsel should be mindful of the written product generated from the interviews. To minimize the risk of disclosure of privileged information, counsel should ensure that such written product (1) contains all necessary headers ("attorney-client privilege" and "attorney-work product"); (2) contains prefatory language explicitly stating that it is not a verbatim transcript of the interview and that it contains the lawyer's *impressions* and *opinions* of what the witness would say if he testified on certain matters; and (3) that the statements are not given to the interviewees or others inside the company for review or any other purpose. In short, the lawyer should minimize dissemination of any notes from witness interviews and all work product synthesizing or incorporating impressions from the interviews should be handled to minimize inadvertent waiver of the privilege.

## Be Mindful of Cultural Elements and Data Privacy Rules in International Internal Investigations

Many of the issues discussed previously may have to be considered differently in an international context. Though a full discussion of the distinction between domestic and international investigations is beyond the scope of this chapter, the following are key issues that a practitioner should examine when interviewing witnesses in an international investigation:

- **Data Privacy Rules.** In many countries, data privacy and secrecy rules limit what an employee may be asked and which documents counsel may examine. For example, a lawyer may not be able to legally inquire about an employee's past employment or what his function was at a prior job without violating data privacy rules. Or, counsel may be prohibited from showing a witness particular documents. Counsel should review these restrictions with local counsel prior to beginning any witness interviews in an international context.

- **Employer-Employee Relationship.** In some instances, a particular country's law may prohibit an employer from interviewing a witness. Some countries may limit the extent to which the *Upjohn* warning can be given, or prohibit an employer from reviewing an employee's e-mails. Counsel may have to customize the *Upjohn* warnings and review employment contracts with the aid of local counsel before approaching particular witnesses for interviews.
- **Attorney-Client Privilege.** Most importantly, the attorney-client privilege may be narrower in certain countries, and may not be applicable to the company and the interviewer as U.S. counsel understands it. For example, the EU does not extend the attorney-client privilege to in-house counsel. Therefore, having in-house counsel lead an investigation could waive the attorney-client privilege pertaining to the critical components of an internal investigation.

In all cases, a lawyer should conduct witness interviews in coordination with and upon advice of local counsel to avoid running afoul of any foreign laws.

### Follow Up with Witness

In depositions or trials, following up with a witness requires some level of formality: serving a supplemental document request, keeping the deposition open, or seeking the court's permission to recall a witness. Such formality is largely absent in the context of an internal investigation interview, and the lawyer should use this flexibility to his advantage. For example, the lawyer should methodically note other individuals and documents the witness mentions during an interview and arrange prompt follow-up. A witness may mention particular logs or reports that he keeps relating to the policies or procedures at issue. With no obligation to prepare a formal document request or seek the ruling of a judge, the lawyer should prepare a list of documents for the witness to produce and request them at the end of the interview or the next day.

## Preparing the Witness for Self-Disclosure or Proffer

Sometimes internal investigations reveal that no wrongdoing occurred. In those situations, the investigation concludes, and the client leaves with a reassurance that it has complied with the law or regulation at issue. In other investigations, there may be a technical violation of the law, but one that had minimal, if any, repercussions and involves an issue unlikely to be investigated or prosecuted by a regulatory body. This is perhaps the most nuanced outcome because a client is faced with the decision between self-reporting, which risks exposure to an investigation and/or fines that otherwise would not have been imposed, and remedying the issue but remaining silent. Absent any affirmative duty to self-report, many clients, depending on the severity of the violation, will elect not to report given the remote chance of prosecution otherwise. However, lawyers should carefully consider the ramifications of non-disclosure with their clients. Consider, for instance, a case where a disgruntled employee discloses the company's previous violations to regulators. Although the company will have an opportunity to explain how minor the violation was and how it has since been cured, in this scenario the client is forced to try and "un-ring the bell" and is disadvantaged from the inception of the interview. When faced with this outcome, the lawyer should be very careful about memorializing interviews and discussing options, if any, with the client.

Of course, some investigations uncover that some regulation or law was violated in a significant way. It has become a recent trend among corporate clients to self-disclose wrongdoing in the hope that it will soften the blow with regulators and spur a collaborative remediation as opposed to a contentious and bitter prosecution. Even absent a voluntary disclosure, regulators can launch a compelled investigation as a precursor to, or a part of, an enforcement action.

In many cases, the disclosure and subsequent discussions will occur between regulators and counsel for the corporation. There is a chance, however, that the regulator will want to speak directly to witnesses to further ascertain the underlying facts and the extent of the wrongdoing. Selecting the right witnesses and maintaining attorney-client privilege are two of the most important considerations for counsel during the course of self-disclosure to regulators.

## Select the Right Witnesses to Testify

After the decision is made to proffer a witness for a voluntary disclosure to regulators, the most important decision to be made is who should serve as the corporation's witness. Counsel should review the documentation of the investigation meticulously and determine which witness's story makes the most sense in light of the desired narrative and the core questions being asked by regulators.

In addition to *which* story the witness tells, counsel should be particularly mindful of *how* the witness tells it. Witnesses provide the facts and bring a story to life, but that story is only as compelling and credible as the person delivering it. The witness who is selected to disclose potential wrongdoing on behalf of the corporation should be able to deliver a believable version of events to regulators and withstand the inevitable scrutiny of regulators trying to determine whether and to what extent the portrayed narrative is a self-serving cover-up of more egregious behavior.

## Protect the Attorney-Client Privilege

Counsel should strategize in advance of a disclosure about whether and how to negotiate a selective waiver of the attorney-client privilege to maximize cooperation with regulators. Only certain courts recognize the doctrine of selective waiver.

Under this doctrine, when a company takes affirmative steps to protect documents provided to the government—such as pursuant to a confidentiality agreement—the production of the documents waives privilege only with respect to the government and not as to any other party. Even assuming counsel successfully negotiates a selective waiver, he should be aware that such a waiver may not protect his client from being forced to turn over all privileged documents in the context of a subsequent private lawsuit focused on the same issues.

In assessing privilege issues, counsel also should be aware of the recent memorandum issued by the Department of Justice in September 2015 which should guide any decision making with respect to privilege in the disclosure context. The memorandum, colloquially known as the Yates memo,[4] indicates that, in order for corporations to get the full benefit of disclosure, regulators expect them to assist in identifying culpable individuals and prosecuting the claims. In light of this, it is unclear to what degree privileged information can still be withheld in this context.

# Administrative Hearings

Agency rulemaking has proliferated in recent years. As a direct result, agencies are increasingly flexing their enforcement muscles and cracking down on alleged wrongdoers. For example, a recent study found that the U.S. Securities and Exchange Commission (SEC) filed 807 enforcement proceedings in 2015, a record-breaking number for the agency.[5] The vast majority of these proceedings represent substantive enforcement actions as opposed to routine filings (i.e., delinquent filings). What is most striking about the study was the stark increase in the use of administrative proceedings, as opposed to civil court actions, as an enforcement vehicle. In 2015, 76 percent of the SEC's enforcement proceedings against public companies were brought as administrative hearings. Just a few years prior, the converse was true, with 65 percent of enforcement proceedings pursued through civil litigation. The abrupt about-face in the SEC's forum selection was brought about by the passage of Dodd-Frank, which enabled the SEC to obtain the same monetary penalties available in civil litigation. Similar legislation has been passed

---

4. Full memorandum entitled *Individual Accountability for Corporate Wrongdoing* (Sept. 9, 2015), *available at* https://www.justice.gov/dag/file/769036/download (last visited Nov. 28, 2016). In addition to the guidance afforded by the Yates memo, see also U.S. Department of Justice, U.S. Attorneys' Manual § 9-28.710 (2008), *available at* http://www.justice.gov/usao/eousa/foia_reading_room/usam/ (last visited Nov. 28, 2016). The recently issued Foreign Corrupt Practices Act (FCPA) Guidance specifically references this provision of the U.S. Attorneys' Manual in noting that in assessing a corporation's cooperation in an FCPA enforcement action, prosecutors are generally prohibited from requesting attorney-client privileged materials. *A Resource Guide to the U.S. Foreign Corrupt Practices Act*, U.S. Dep't of Justice & U.S. Sec. & Exch. Comm'n, 53 (Nov. 14, 2012), *available at* http://www.sec.gov/spotlight/fcpa/fcpa-resource-guide.pdf (last visited Nov. 28, 2016).

5. *SEC Enforcement Activity Against Public Company Defendants: Fiscal Years 2010–2015*, N.Y. Univ. Pollack Ctr. for Law & Business, *available at* http://www.law.nyu.edu/sites/default/files/SEC-Enforcement-Activity-FY2010-FY2015.pdf (last visited Nov. 28, 2016).

to expand the administrative enforcement powers of other agencies as well.[6] It is clear that Congress is evincing a preference for delegating enforcement of federal laws to agencies, empowering those agencies with alternatives to civil litigation. In this active regulatory environment, practitioners must understand the nuances of defending clients in the administrative context and preparing witnesses to present the most effective narrative.

The principal purpose of an administrative hearing is fact-finding with one, or multiple, finders of fact, where a specific ruling or outcome is sought. In that sense, an administrative hearing bears the strongest resemblance to a courtroom trial.

There are, however, critical distinctions between a trial and an administrative hearing; principally, the limited scope of inquiry and the level of formality. Administrative hearings tend to be more conversational than the traditional direct and cross-examination styles employed in a courtroom trial. The rules of evidence may not apply as stringently. The proceeding itself typically takes place in a less formal environment than a courtroom. In many instances, an administrative hearing will take place over the telephone or in a conference room of a federal or state agency. Though the practitioner should be cognizant of the varying degrees of formality and adjust the focus of his preparation accordingly, this relative informality should not affect the robustness of his preparation.

## Understand the Enabling Statute

Congress or state and local legislatures vest authority in administrative agencies through enabling statutes. These statutes create the agency and specify the agency's powers. Agencies are limited to the powers delegated to them from the legislature. If an agency exceeds the power conferred on it by the legislature, its actions will be considered void.

It is important to understand the scope of an agency's jurisdiction. Administrative hearings are not open fact-finding missions like depositions or internal investigations. There are certain actions that agencies can and cannot take due to the limitations of the agency's enabling statute. Enabling statutes can contain both procedural and substantive requirements. Once armed with a thorough understanding of why the agency exists and what it is empowered to do, the practitioner can determine which of the client's objectives can be accomplished through an administrative hearing.

## Know the Regulations

Just as the enabling statute defines the outer bounds of an agency's rulemaking authority, the regulation itself determines the scope of a client's potential liability.

---

6. *See* Emily M. Lanza, *Food Recalls and Other FDA Administrative Enforcement Actions* (2014), *available at* https://www.fas.org/sgp/crs/misc/R43794.pdf.

Agencies propound regulations pursuant to their authority to enforce a particular statute. Often these regulations are obscure, lengthy, and narrowly prescriptive in terms of what is permissible or impermissible under the statute. It is important for counsel to understand exactly what the regulations require to understand how the client allegedly deviated from those requirements.

## Utilize Public Records Requests

Administrative complaints or charges may contain veiled references to a regulation or municipal code that has been allegedly violated. Federal courts and most state courts have certain pleading requirements designed to put defendants on notice of the allegations or charges against them. Such pleading requirements generally do not exist in the administrative context. Clients can be a bit behind the eight ball when defending themselves against an administrative enforcement action. To further compound the problem, administrative hearings, unlike traditional litigation, rarely provide for traditional discovery.

To hedge against this informational asymmetry, practitioners can utilize so-called freedom of information or sunshine laws to request documents or other information pertinent to the administrative action. Lawyers can request records pertaining to the complaint against their clients, evidence contemplated to be used in an administrative hearing, and records from prior administrative hearings involving the same subject matter or decision maker. In enforcement proceedings convened pursuant to federal law, requests can be made under the Freedom of Information Act. Most, if not all, states have similar statutes allowing citizens to request certain records in the possession of state and local agencies.

Open records laws vary among jurisdictions. They vary in scope, and each contains exemptions for certain categories of documents. The procedures for requesting records also vary. Counsel should take care in ascertaining the scope of records that can be requested, the prerequisites to making an official records request, and the time frame by which agencies are obligated to respond to requests. The window for receiving documents can be statutorily defined. If there are any disputes about the sufficiency of the production or the invocation of certain privileges against production, the deadline for receiving documents can be extended. Public records requests are only effective to the extent the information can be obtained prior to the administrative hearing. The lawyer should be cognizant of the relevant time frames and request continuances, where appropriate, to ensure that he has adequate time to receive and analyze the documents well in advance of the hearing.

The practitioner should maximize every opportunity to gather evidence and glean not only the facts upon which agencies base their enforcement proceedings, but also how the agency and the decision maker have approached similar enforcement proceedings in the past.

## Identify the Setting and Level of Formality

As previously noted, administrative hearings tend to be less formal and occur in a more relaxed environment. Lawyers should familiarize their witnesses with the anticipated setting for the proceeding. Unless the witness routinely attends such proceedings, his expectation may be a scene closer to what is portrayed in courtroom television dramas. Therefore, witnesses can be taken aback if they attend a relaxed and informal administrative proceeding when they are expecting a more traditional courtroom setting.

There is no single template for how administrative proceedings are conducted. The hearings are heavily influenced by a particular agency's regulations, and the disposition and proclivities of the individual administrative law judge or officer presiding over the hearing.

Lawyers should consult other practitioners who regularly appear in these types of hearings to gain an understanding of how the hearing will be conducted. Details, such as where attendees sit, what style is utilized by administrative officers, whether opening and closing statements are favored or permitted, and how long hearings typically last, are both easy and critical for both the lawyer and the witness to understand in advance.

In this respect, preparing for an administrative hearing is quite similar to preparing for a trial. Determining the customs of the tribunal and the decision maker's preferences are important regardless of which forum is being used. However, these variables tend to be far more predictable in a formal courtroom setting where the public is generally welcome and a judge's rulings are easily accessible.

## Understand the Role of the Rules of Evidence

In most administrative proceedings, the traditional rules of evidence, either federal or state, are applied in a relaxed manner. At the federal level, the Administrative Procedure Act (APA) provides for the blanket admission of any oral or documentary evidence, but requires that the individual agencies promulgate rules that exclude irrelevant, immaterial, or unduly repetitive evidence. Many agencies have supplemented the APA's evidentiary rules. Some agencies expressly preclude application of the Federal Rules of Evidence, others adopt some or all of the Federal Rules of Evidence, and still others develop their own admissibility rules.

Thoroughly understanding the evidentiary rules applicable to a particular agency's hearing is critical in preparing and presenting a case. Knowing which evidence can be used at the hearing and how it must be admitted determines which witnesses are needed and how they must be prepared. For example, in some contexts, the admissibility of certain documents can be stipulated in advance. If that is the case, it is unnecessary to select or prepare witnesses who can authenticate or lay the foundation for particular documents; the documents can simply be read into the record.

These procedures can alleviate the burden on witnesses, particularly during the administrative proceeding itself. Counsel can present a well-crafted narrative without detracting from the story arc by having the witnesses testify about certain documents. This method can be particularly efficient and powerful when the documentary evidence is voluminous or overly technical.

Counsel should be cautious about the leniency of admissibility rules of certain agencies. Documents remain a critical component in preparing for administrative hearings, because they can educate the witnesses and lay the foundation for the rest of the narrative. The difference between trials and administrative hearings is that preparation for an administrative hearing does not have to focus on *how* documents get into evidence, but rather on what benefit those documents provide to the substance of the proceeding.

## Prepare for Examination by ALJ or Presiding Officer

Unlike a trial, where the judge cannot serve as a vehicle to admit evidence, an administrative law judge (ALJ) or hearing officer may ask questions of the witnesses who develop the evidentiary record. It is important for counsel to inform their witnesses of this possibility in advance. Counsel should advise their clients to answer the ALJ's questions as if it were a direct or a cross-examination by opposing counsel. Counsel should be prepared to take the lead on direct or cross-examination. However, if the hearing officer is a more engaged participant, counsel should defer to the hearing officer to conduct the initial questioning in the proceeding. If critical information is not elicited by the ALJ, the onus is on the lawyer to ensure the full narrative is presented for consideration.

The circumstances in which an ALJ will be more engaged will vary by agency, whether the proceeding is at the state or federal level, and what issue is being decided. Administrative proceedings span the spectrum from a seemingly open-ended question and answer session around a conference room table to something more akin to a civil trial with opening and closing statements and the examination of witnesses. Intelligence gathering from fellow practitioners will provide some insight into what the lawyer and witnesses can expect. The practitioner should prepare the witness for all possibilities and should not shirk on preparation based on the assumption that an administrative proceeding will be less formal than a trial.

# CONGRESSIONAL HEARINGS

From the standpoint of witness preparation, congressional hearings are perhaps the most distinct setting from a trial. There is no arbiter of fact and law and no specific relief sought from a particular party. Congressional testimony generally arises in one of three contexts: (1) legislative hearings—a witness is invited by a congressional committee to testify as a subject matter expert on a policy issue that may or may not be addressed through legislation; (2) oversight hearings—a witness is asked to testify on the quality of federal programs and whether the executive branch's execution of laws comports with legislative intent; and (3) investigative hearings—a witness is called or subpoenaed to testify when Congress suspects wrongdoing by public officials or private citizens that can be remedied or ameliorated by legislation.

Of the three, investigative hearings are most similar to the traditional courtroom adversary proceeding, in that someone who has been accused of wrongdoing must defend or justify his actions. Advice on witness preparation in this context will draw heavily upon the guidance articulated previously, as well as general witness preparation principles described elsewhere in this book. On the other hand, special care should be taken to prepare for legislative and oversight hearings because they do not carry the indicia of adversarial proceedings.

Legislation can either advance or hinder a client's goals. The purpose of a congressional hearing, be it legislative, oversight, or investigatory, is to determine whether legislation should be enacted, repealed, or modified. Unlike trials or administrative hearings, congressional inquiries cannot result in the direct levying or imposition of sanctions or penalties. But, the hearings can form the basis of new legislation that is drafted and potentially passed. This legislation can directly impact a client's behavior or a corporation's business. It can also spur executive agencies or private individuals to pursue adversarial legal actions to enforce new congressional mandates.

Congress is the ultimate source of most federal laws. Effective advocacy at the legislative level could mean the difference between legislative protections or legislative handcuffs. And this advocacy begins with effective preparation of testifying witnesses.

## Understand the Scope of the Inquiry

Congressional power to investigate and elicit testimony is not expressly authorized by the Constitution. Nonetheless, the power has been frequently exercised and sanctioned by the U.S. Supreme Court. Justice Earl Warren described congressional authority to conduct investigations as a broad and inherent part of the legislative process.[7] However broad that power may be, it is not unlimited. Congress does not have general authority to probe into the private affairs of individual citizens. The power to inquire is bounded by the power to legislate, and congressional inquiry must not only be related to, but also must further, a legitimate task of Congress.

Practitioners should be mindful of the purpose of a congressional inquiry, particularly in the context of investigative hearings. If the focus of Congress lies beyond its legitimate legislative abilities, clients may be able to avoid being compelled to

---

7. Watkins v. United States, 354 U.S. 178 (1957).

testify. Given the expansive interpretation of the Commerce Clause, prohibited areas of congressional inquiry will be few and far between for most clients. But, considering the burden and potential impact that congressional testimony will have for most clients, a lawyer should strictly vet investigatory requests and nip a congressional hearing in the bud if there is little upside to a client testifying. This is particularly true if there are any Fifth Amendment concerns for the client. If there is a risk of self-incrimination, the lawyer should pay careful attention to whether, and how much, a client participates in the congressional hearing. Recent developments in this area suggest that objections based on Fifth Amendment privileges should be exercised unequivocally and early in the hearing process.

Even beyond the potential ability to quash congressional testimony, it is critical to understand the scope of the inquiry and the witness's role within the proceeding. What is the driving force behind the congressional inquiry? What role does the witness play in educating Congress about that topic? Once counsel understands these foundational elements, he can more effectively mold the testimony strategy and prepare his witness accordingly.

## Consult Agency Guidance

Federal agencies publish formal manuals on congressional testimony. Unless counsel represents a federal agency, the guidelines in these manuals will not necessarily restrict how counsel prepares his witness. The guidelines can, however, provide insight into how an agency representative would testify if called. This can be useful information that guides the practitioner's preparation of the witness. For example, if the witness is testifying on the agency's failure to enforce legislation in accordance with congressional intent or the agency's overreach in enforcement, the manuals will provide some clues about what the agency representative can or cannot say. Counsel should be aware of any weakness or pressure point indicated in these manuals, and counsel should prepare the witness to testify in a way that exploits those pressure points. Alternatively, the witness may find himself aligned with a particular agency's position. Knowing where the government counterparty is unable to fully testify allows counsel to prepare the witness to supplement the record in a way that leads the committee to view the joint positions favorably.

## Submit a Written Statement

The written statement is the springboard for the entire hearing. It informs the witness's oral statement, the committees' questions, and any follow-up requests after the hearing. It also functions as the official public record of the witness's testimony before the committee. The statement is critically important to the hearing itself, but is also widely disseminated outside the context of the hearing. Therefore, it should be crafted carefully and deliberately, with significant attention to the content, format, and style of the statement.

Initially, counsel and the witness must determine the objectives of the testimony. From there, counsel and the witness can identify the thesis of the statement and the themes for presenting the narrative. Besides being absolutely accurate from a typographical, grammatical, spelling, and syntax perspective, the statement must be impeccably written, tailored to the target audience, and reflect an understanding of competing viewpoints and opposition.

During the testimony, the written statement should serve as a guide for the witness. Oral testimony should be a summary or synthesis of the written statement. The statement should establish all of the facts necessary to make the record for the hearing. Each committee may have its own rules for the format and content of the written statement. Counsel should consult the committee's rules prior to drafting the statement to ensure that all of the requirements are met.

## Know the Time Limitations

Many congressional hearings impose strict time limits on oral testimony. The amount of time may vary by committee or the subject matter of the testimony. Practitioners should consult committee rules or congressional aides to fully understand the time limitations on the witness. Though implicit time limits exist in other contexts (i.e., trial witnesses may not be afforded several days to present evidence on a discrete issue), time limitations in congressional hearings may be shorter, more clearly defined, and strictly enforced.

Once counsel is aware of the time limitations, he can help the witness decide how much time should be devoted to each topic of testimony, how much detail should be provided, and how much time should be spent responding to certain questions from committee members.

## Keep It Simple

This may seem like advice that goes without saying, but it is often forgotten and bears repeating, particularly in the context of congressional hearings. Committee members are politicians by trade, and they generally do not have subject matter expertise in many of the topics that are the subject of congressional hearings. A lawyer should prepare his witness to understand the inevitable knowledge gaps and coach him on the best ways to bridge that gap.

Consider the following hypothetical: A major pharmaceutical company develops a new drug to combat cancer. Though generally effective, there are some known instances of the drug causing death. Despite knowledge of the deaths, the pharmaceutical company continues to market and sell the drug. Congress launches an investigation into the pharmaceutical company's practices and whether it has committed any wrongdoing in continuing to market the drug. The pharmaceutical company's primary witness is an expert in pharmacology who was instrumental in the research and development of the drug. Now, assume that the committee members who are conducting the hearing are not experts in pharmacology and do not have an understanding of how certain drugs interact in cancer patients.

In this scenario, counsel should prepare the witness to deliver credible testimony that is backed by hard science. However, the primary focus of the written and oral testimony should not rely on jargon-laden descriptions of the underlying chemistry of the drug compounds, how the body metabolizes the compounds, and how those compounds interact with certain cancer cells. Rather, the takeaway should be enough explanation of the pharmacological effects of the drug to lend credence to the witness's testimony.

This may sound familiar to litigators who have prepared expert witnesses for a deposition or trial. Indeed, preparing experts, or any witness for that matter, to give accessible and digestible testimony applies regardless of the context in which the witness testifies. Congressional hearings, however, are different in that, unlike a trial, Congress is not constrained to only consider the evidence presented to it in a hearing. Congress is free to look beyond the hearing and solicit other witnesses to testify or to accumulate information from any other source. Therefore, it is imperative that a witness present reliable, timely, and digestible information that would convince a committee member that it had all of the information needed to inform his legislation-making.

## Be Cognizant of Body Language and Make Eye Contact

In congressional testimony, the lawyer's role is behind the scenes whereas the witness takes center stage. Not only must the witness possess a fulsome understanding and comprehension of the subject matter, his delivery style and demeanor will be vital to telling his story, particularly if the topic of the testimony is controversial.

Like the words used to tell a story, body language is a matter of personal style. Though the manner of delivery will largely depend on this personal style, certain body language can be universally unappealing to an audience. In particular, the lawyer can advise the witness to avoid body language that makes him appear overly closed, disinterested, or apathetic, such as crossed arms, downcast eyes, or a monotone voice. Watching the witness practice his delivery and/or producing a recording of this practice session will help identify if the witness exhibits any of these behaviors.

Beyond addressing these behaviors, the lawyer can closely assess the witness's communication style. Does he speak loudly or in softer tones? Does he gesture frequently with his hands or are they mostly at his sides? Does he move in close or lean back in his chair? Does he often speak too slowly or too fast? Once he has a sense of the witness's style range, counsel is in a position to meaningfully advise the witness on how to vary his style for a more effective delivery. Resist the urge, however, to dramatically change the way the witness carries himself. Instead, exploit his personal style in a way that will suit the narrative. If he is naturally soft-spoken and mild-mannered, his soothing demeanor can soften the delivery of damaging facts.

If his style is animated and makes use of frequent hand gestures, have the witness use this tendency to keep the audience engaged during the more mundane parts of the story.

As any successful public speaker will advise, eye contact is critical to conveying confidence, authority, and credibility. Making eye contact with the audience engages the listener and leads him to believe the message that is being conveyed. Eye contact also slows down the witness's speech, making it easier for the audience to follow along. It also prevents the witness's gaze from wandering and getting distracted or sidetracked from the testimony at hand.

A witness can only be coached so much on these behavioral components, particularly when preparation time is limited. Counsel should teach the witness these basic public speaking skills as much as possible, but also recognize when the effectiveness of the testimony may be impinged by the witness's delivery. Are there ways to restore the witness's credibility or otherwise supplement the record to offset any diminished credibility to the overall narrative?

## Comprehend the Question and Answer Element of the Hearing

In many contexts, there are two parts of congressional testimony. First is the oral testimony, which can consist of reading a prepared script or summarizing previously submitted written testimony. Second, is a question and answer session where members of the committee ask questions of the witness.

This portion of the testimony can vary in the degree of formality, which generally depends on the committee members' disposition, the subject matter of the testimony, and the type of congressional hearing (i.e., oversight versus investigatory). Often this session can be conversational, but counsel should prepare witnesses to deliver technical responses even in a more relaxed environment. For example, if, during a congressional investigation into an airplane manufacturer's widespread recall of airplanes for faulty landing gear, a committee member inquires when the manufacturer became aware of the problem and what steps were taken at that time, the witness should be able to accurately crystallize the specifics of when the company found out, what specifically the issues were with the landing gear, who knew what and when they knew it, and what was done to remedy the situation. In many instances, the question and answer session by the committee members are more open-ended fact-finding exercises, rather than narrowly tailored cross-examination questions. It is important that counsel prepare witnesses on how to respond to certain questions accurately, but also in a way that paints the most favorable narrative. Practicing responses to key questions will benefit the witness at the hearing, but be careful to avoid making the witness's response appear too rehearsed. Finally, it may be possible to negotiate some of these elements beforehand (at least with respect to those affiliated with the witness's position), and counsel should investigate this possibility at the outset.

## Prepare a Briefing Book

Counsel should also consider whether to prepare a briefing book for the witness. A briefing book acts as a reference guide for all of the materials relied on by the witness and the materials previously submitted to the committee. It can serve as a quick reference guide during the question and answer session. In addition to the documents previously submitted to the committee, the briefing book can contain prepared answers to questions counsel anticipates that the committee might ask. Not every witness needs a reference book. It depends on the level of preparedness of the witness, whether the witness is well versed in the facts, and whether counsel believes the briefing book will be an effective tool for the witness. If the substance of the hearing is not overly technical and references to voluminous data or statistics is not required, then a briefing book may be more of a distraction than an aid. Also, if the witness has a tendency to overly rely on the briefing book as a crutch during testimony, the witness's credibility can be called into question. Counsel should consult with the client about what content to include in the briefing book and how it should be utilized during the testimony prior to the hearing.

## Follow-up to Committee Member Requests

It is not uncommon for committee members, during the question and answer session, to ask questions that the witness will not be able to readily answer. Counsel should prepare witnesses on how to handle questions when they do not have answers available. In that same vein, it is important for counsel to understand the obligations for follow-up on committee member requests and the mechanism that exists to allow follow-up. The rules may not be the same in all instances, so be sure to understand how the committee wishes to receive follow-up information. Key elements to consider are deadlines, procedures for submitting supplemental information, and the format of such a submission.

# CONCLUSION

> He who is best prepared can best serve his moment of inspiration.
>
> —*Samuel Taylor Coleridge*

Whether inside the courtroom or not, lawyers are charged with a particular brand of storytelling. The lawyer who fully understands the backdrop against which the story will be told will be best prepared to focus fully on the artistry of advocacy, with minimal disruption from unanticipated ministerial details.

Although many of the foundational witness preparation concepts can be applied to any witness in any setting, the distinction between the traditional courtroom setting and alternative forums may impact how the narrative, and the facts underpinning the case, are received by the fact finder. Though this chapter is intended to be neither exhaustive nor prescriptive, it provides an issue-spotting guide for the practitioner who finds himself in new territory, showcasing the distinctions between how facts are presented, viewed, and weighed in various non-trial contexts. The lawyer's awareness of these elements ensures that the client's narrative is best crafted to achieve the desired outcome—inside or outside the courtroom.

# FURTHER READING

William N. LaForge, *Testifying Before Congress*. Alexandria VA: The Capitol Net, 2010.

Barry F. McNeil, *Internal Corporate Investigations*. 3rd ed., ed. Barry F. McNeill and Brad Brian. Chicago: Section of Litigation, ABA, 2007.

V. Hale Starr, *Witness Preparation* (with contributions from Paul D. Beechen). New York: Aspen Law and Business,1998.

# INDEX